HOW LOCAL POLITICS **SHAPE FEDERAL POLICY**

 THE LUTHER H. HODGES JR. AND LUTHER H. HODGES SR.
SERIES ON BUSINESS, SOCIETY, AND THE STATE

WILLIAM H. BECKER, *editor*

HOW LOCAL POLITICS
SHAPE FEDERAL POLICY

*Business, Power, and the Environment
in Twentieth-Century Los Angeles*

SARAH S. ELKIND

The University of North Carolina Press
CHAPEL HILL

© 2011 The University of North Carolina Press
All rights reserved

Designed and set in Arno Pro with Scala Sans display by Rebecca Evans. Manufactured in the United States of America. The paper in this book meets the guidelines for permanence and durability of the Committee on Production Guidelines for Book Longevity of the Council on Library Resources. The University of North Carolina Press has been a member of the Green Press Initiative since 2003.

Library of Congress Cataloging-in-Publication Data
Elkind, Sarah S., 1963–
How local politics shape federal policy : business, power, and the environment in twentieth-century Los Angeles / Sarah S. Elkind.—1st ed.
p. cm.—(The Luther H. Hodges Jr. and Luther H. Hodges Sr. series on business, society, and the state)
Includes bibliographical references and index.
ISBN 978-0-8078-3489-3 (cloth : alk. paper)
ISBN 978-1-4696-1897-5 (paper : alk. paper)
ISBN 978-0-8078-6911-6 (ebook)
1. California—Economic policy—20th century. 2. California—Politics and government—20th century. 3. Environmental policy—California. I. Title.
HC107.C2E45 2011   333.91009794—dc22   2010052561

Portions of this work were previously published, in somewhat different form, in "Black Gold and the Beach: Offshore Oil, Beaches and Federal Power in Southern California," *Journal of the West* 44:1 (2005): 8–17, © 2005, reprinted with permission of ABC-CLIO; and "Public Oil, Private Oil: The Tidelands Oil Controversy, World War II and the Control of the Environment," in *The Way We Really Were: The Golden State in the Second Great War*, ed. Roger Lotchin (Champaign: University of Illinois Press, 2000) 120–42, © 2000 by the University of Illinois Press, reprinted with permission.

FOR BETH HOLMBERG

CONTENTS

Acknowledgments xi
Abbreviations xiii

1 INTRODUCTION
BUSINESS INTERESTS, SPECIAL INTERESTS, AND THE PUBLIC INTEREST

17 CHAPTER ONE
OIL AND WATER
The Public and the Private on Southern California Beaches, 1920–1950

52 CHAPTER TWO
INFLUENCE THROUGH COOPERATION
The Los Angeles Chamber of Commerce and Air Pollution Control in Los Angeles, 1943–1954

83 CHAPTER THREE
FLOOD CONTROL AND POLITICAL EXCLUSION AT WHITTIER NARROWS, 1938–1948

117 CHAPTER FOUR
PRIVATE POWER AT HOOVER DAM
Utilities, Government Power, and Political Realism, 1920–1928

148 CHAPTER FIVE
THE TRIUMPH OF LOCALISM
The Rejection of National Water Planning in 1950

178 CONCLUSION
SMALL GOVERNMENT AND BIG BUSINESS IN
THE MID-TWENTIETH CENTURY

Notes 185
Bibliography 239
Index 251

ILLUSTRATIONS AND MAPS

ILLUSTRATIONS
The Los Angeles Chamber of Commerce's vision of the area's sixty-year progress 3
Gushing oil well 23
"The March of the Derrick" 27
"Another Beach Club" 31
"Dog Days Doggerel" 36
Smog in downtown Los Angeles, 1948 66
Anti-smog campaigners picketing the Los Angeles County Supervisors, 1955 79
Los Angeles River flooding in Glendale, 1927 89
The Los Angeles River overflows its banks in Burbank, 1938 95
Store closed as a result of Whittier Narrows flood control basin displacement 112
Hoover Dam, 1940 119
"Hydro(electric)phobia" 126
"Boulder Dam" 131

MAPS
Public beaches and oil fields in Greater Los Angeles 18
Communities active in Los Angeles air pollution debates, 1943–1950 53
Flood control on the Los Angeles and San Gabriel rivers 84
Colorado River basin and the All-American Canal 118
Boundaries of the major river basins in the United States 149

ACKNOWLEDGMENTS

This project began with the World War II and California Conference at the Huntington Library organized by Roger Lotchin in 1995, in which I was honored to participate. It was nurtured by the Los Angeles History Group; I cannot imagine a more welcoming and intellectually engaging group of people assembled anywhere. Clark Davis did much to set that tone and is sorely missed.

Special thanks to Peter Blodgett, Dan Lewis, and all the readers' services staff at the Huntington; Dace Taube and the Regional History Center at the University of Southern California; Paul Wormser and the regrettably relocated Laguna Niguel branch of the National Archives; Charles Basham, who so kindly allowed me access to Southern California Edison's archives; the Los Angeles City Archives staff; and the Special Collections department of the Claremont Colleges Libraries. Also special thanks to Christopher P. Konrad for his insights into flood control and hydrology and to Brit Storey and Larry Nuss at the Bureau of Reclamation for their thoughts on Hoover Dam.

My research was supported in part by the National Science Foundation, the Huntington Library, and San Diego State University. Clay McShane and his colleagues in the History Department at Northeastern University and Rachel Brant and the Department of Urban and Environmental Policy and Planning at Tufts University kindly provided me with quiet places to work. I am indebted to David Nye, to Chuck Grench at the University of North Carolina Press, and to William Becker and the other readers for the press; this work is much stronger for their suggestions and critique.

Martin Melosi continues to be a mentor and friend. Thanks also to Bruce Seely, Jeffrey Stine, and Marty Reuss for their support and suggestions. Jared Orsi has been a wonderful flood control coconspirator. Jennifer Martinez generously helped me with countless research questions. Joel Tarr, Harold Platt, Kathy Kolnick, Cheryl Koos, Tom Sitton, Laura Watt, Art Verge, Mark Wild, William Myers, Matt Kuefler, and the students in my political history and Los Angeles history seminars all helped with this project, providing assistance, encouragement, friendship, or all three. My spouse, Beth Holmberg, prepared the index, sacrificed much so I could finish this project and pursue my career, and has shared my delight in figuring out how things work. And, finally, I would like to thank my parents for nurturing that delight in the first place.

ABBREVIATIONS

AFL	American Federation of Labor
APCD	Los Angeles County Air Pollution Control District
APOL	Altadena Property Owners League
CIO	Congress of Industrial Organizations
LAACC	Los Angeles Area Chamber of Commerce
LACFCD	Los Angeles County Flood Control District
LACSFC	Los Angeles County Smoke and Fumes Commission
PWA	Public Works Administration
PWRPC	President's Water Resources Policy Commission
SPA	Shoreline Planning Association

HOW LOCAL POLITICS **SHAPE FEDERAL POLICY**

INTRODUCTION

BUSINESS INTERESTS, SPECIAL INTERESTS, AND THE PUBLIC INTEREST

When Americans imagine their democracy, they envision government institutions that protect and nurture the public interest. So far, so good. But this vision quickly gets complicated and contradictory: Americans vilify equally the influence of uninformed public opinion and that of so-called special interests. And yet interest groups have played a role in American politics from the very beginning. In the earliest years of the Republic, merchants and consumers pressured congressional representatives for lower tariffs, while manufacturers advocated higher import duties. Farmers took up arms against taxes on whiskey because they enriched urban merchants at the farmers' expense. The Fugitive Slave Law, recognition of squatters rights in western lands, and dozens of other nineteenth-century policies reflected the desires and needs of specific economic, regional, or political factions in American politics. Although leaders from James Madison and John Adams in the eighteenth century to Barack Obama in the twenty-first have excoriated special interests as threats to American democracy, interest groups remain entrenched in American politics.

Of all the interest groups active in American cities, the local business organizations have enjoyed the greatest legitimacy and influence. Chambers of commerce, merchants and manufacturers organizations, realty boards, and a myriad of smaller organizations made up of prominent business leaders have enjoyed political influence out of proportion to their numbers or economic importance. In fact, these groups enjoyed such political legitimacy during the mid-twentieth century that they were rarely described as special interests at all. The central question of this book is how this type of organization secured its special status in local politics and how that status was transcribed into national politics in the second quarter of the twentieth century. To answer that question, I have examined local environmental policy in Los Angeles and the interactions of Los Angeles municipal and county officials with federal agencies and federal politics between the 1920s and 1950s.

Business groups earned their legitimacy by supporting city and county officials with a wide range of political services that these elected officials desperately needed. Los Angeles's experience with this is representative: the Los Angeles Chamber of Commerce[1] identified which emerging problems merited public action, studied policy options, drafted legislation, and framed public debate about emerging issues. City and county officials enacted ordinances drafted by the Los Angeles Chamber of Commerce and routinely forwarded chamber recommendations to Sacramento and Washington for state and federal action. The city council also looked to the business alliance to provide "public" reactions on the very policies that the chamber had initially proposed. Federal agencies undertaking major public works for cities and counties looked to these same groups when they needed public input. In essence, public officials at all levels of government treated chambers of commerce and similar organizations as the voice of the people. The business groups themselves believed they represented the public interest, and they actively defended their status when challenged.

The Los Angeles Chamber of Commerce's influence never quite rose to the level of hegemony. Frequently, other community members organized to oppose specific chamber of commerce proposals. These challengers usually began their campaigns by asserting that they represented the public and that the chamber of commerce was merely a special interest. They offered alternative values for public policy that weighed home, community, and public services and recreation more highly than what they dismissed as "mere profits." Their arguments echoed common American critiques of industrial growth and corporate consolidation and were clearly inspired by the stunningly rapid pace at which oil rigs and heavy industry displaced Los Angeles's orange groves and rural suburbs in the twentieth century. However, those who challenged the Los Angeles Chamber of Commerce usually mobilized after local government, with the assistance of favored business organizations, had already established the framework for understanding and

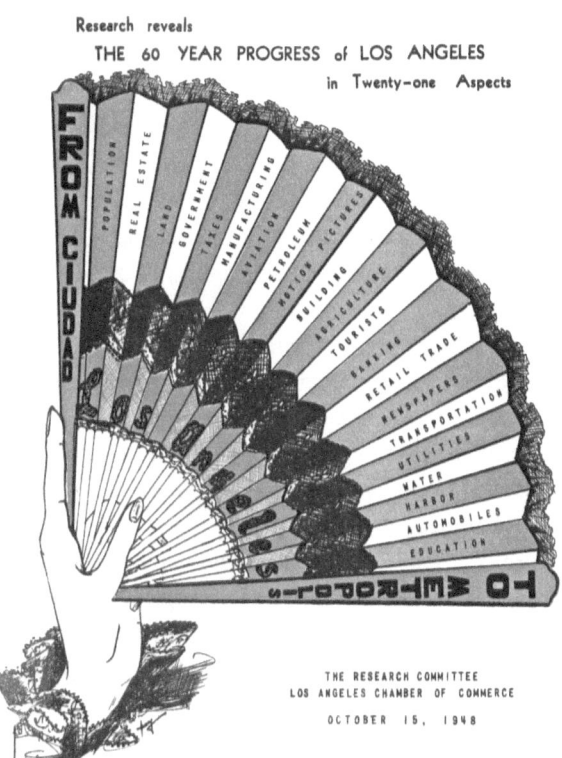

From the 1920s through the 1940s, the Los Angeles Chamber of Commerce's vision for this region emphasized a diverse economy that seamlessly combined heavy industry, real estate, and tourism, as well as the cooperation of business and government. Reproduced by permission of The Huntington Library, San Marino, California.

solving environmental problems; as a result, they were excluded from the conversations most critical to formulating policy. Moreover, both before and after World War II, new industrial jobs attracted hundreds of thousands of new residents to Los Angeles who endorsed probusiness policies. Even the longtime residents struggled to balance the appeal of industrial prosperity with their desire to protect their communities from the changes that accompanied industrial growth. In the end, the economic importance of industry, the rise in the numbers of voters dependent on industrial jobs, and the close relationship between the chamber of commerce and local officials combined to deprive critics of the Los Angeles Chamber of Commerce of political traction. Even when these critics did speak for a larger public, they could not displace the Los Angeles Chamber of Commerce as the recognized representative of public opinion. The status of the Los Angeles Chamber of Commerce excluded other groups from the policy-making process. In other words, the power of the chamber of commerce meant that the general public in Los Angeles had surprisingly little voice in its own governance.

The influence of the Los Angeles Chamber of Commerce did not end at the borders of Los Angeles County. During the Great Depression the federal government implemented numerous programs for and with American cities and towns. To carry out these initiatives, key federal agencies looked to city and county governments and to local powerbrokers like chambers of commerce for project recommendations. This, in turn, transposed business groups' influence in local politics onto federal policy. The status of the Los Angeles Chamber of Commerce and similar organizations was further enhanced between 1930 and 1950 as Americans grew increasingly frustrated with and suspicious of the power of the federal government and as local control and private enterprise emerged as counterweights to Washington's power. The central argument of this book, then, is that the institutional structures and practices of American municipal government gave business groups political legitimacy at the local level and unanticipated influence over federal policies. With this new power, American business groups recast private enterprise, localism, and fragmented government authority as the best guarantors of American democracy.

It is important not to overstate the policy realignment that took place in the second quarter of the twentieth century. As scholars of the nineteenth century and of the Progressive Era have shown, private enterprise has always been an important force in American politics and society. In the mid-nineteenth century, as Robin Einhorn explained, cities built public works to promote economic growth and meet the needs of property owners. The use of special assessments to fund public works was responsible for an astonishing, but inequitable, array of public improvements in the middle decades of the nineteenth century.

A broader understanding of the public interest, one that included taxing property owners to pay for sanitation and basic services for the poor, began to emerge in the 1860s.[2] However, large corporations profited from many Progressive Era regulations, and even the creation of national parks benefited the urban elite at the expense of the rural poor, so much so that it can be tempting to dismiss Progressives' critiques of business as insincere or, at least, ineffective.[3] Nevertheless, Progressives did believe that government authority could and should be used to counter the power of business in American politics and society; the cases explored here reveal very real movement away from this ideology in the transitional period that followed the Progressive Era.

Many other scholars have explored the growth of business influence in public policy after World War II. Historians have described Progressive Era politics as driven by the contrast between national or general interests and "the demands of special interests."[4] As early as the 1950s, they noted the eclipse of Progressive ideology by the more business-oriented ideas outlined here and traced this realignment to the deprivations of the Great Depression, the production shortages and crisis mentality of World War II, and the anticommunism of the Cold War. Clayton Koppes termed this transition the replacement of "commonwealth liberalism" by "corporate liberalism."[5] Alan Brinkley, Louis Galambos, and many others have explained the postwar rejection of Progressive-style business regulation as a result of evolving economic theory and of business influence in government.[6] Most of these studies have focused on federal policy and on changes wrought from within federal agencies themselves. They have not considered the local manifestations of postwar retrenchment, the way federal collaboration with local governments increased business-oriented groups' influence, or the institutional roots of business influence in local politics.[7]

Questions of political influence and federalism have not been a major focus for historians of Los Angeles either. A series of excellent books on Los Angeles history, many of them nurtured by the Huntington Library's Los Angeles History Group, have focused on the social construction of race and on the politics of place and the efforts of minority and working-class Angelenos to shape their communities.[8] Becky Nicolaides and H. Mark Wild discuss the Los Angeles Chamber of Commerce's opposition to unions and its role in the creation of Los Angeles's industrial suburbs and the racially segregated bedroom communities. But the main emphasis in these works is community development, race relations, and working-class life and politics in Los Angeles, not the political influence of Los Angeles's powerful business elite itself.[9] In other important recent works, Douglas Flamming, Josh Sides, and William Deverell examine the complex racial politics of the Los Angeles region.[10] By placing minority and working-class Angelenos at the center of their analyses, these scholars have reinvigorated social and urban history and complicated the history of race and class in America in felicitous ways. Meanwhile, scholars of Los Angeles's geography and politics, such as Greg Hise and Robert Fogelson, have explained the origins of Los Angeles's decentralized, sprawling geography and equally fragmented governance.[11] In all these works, the Los Angeles Chamber of Commerce and the editors of the *Los Angeles Times* appear as powerful political actors whose decisions determined the shape of Southern California's landscape, environment, and communities. While the works that focus on Los Angeles's racial politics do suggest that the Los Angeles Chamber of Commerce did not always speak for the public, none of this excellent literature on Los Angeles has sought to explain how business elites came by their influence or how they extended their reach from local to federal politics.

As it turns out, Los Angeles is a particularly good city in which to begin to answer these questions. The Los Angeles Chamber of Commerce left excellent records of internal discussions and political activism, as did several city and county officials. Southern California is widely considered prototypical of twentieth-century American urban politics and development. Take sprawl, for example: Los Angeles's pattern of residential and industrial suburbs, linked by highways to each other and to shopping malls, has come to dominate the American urban landscape. Electoral politics, too, are distinctly twentieth-century, with nonpartisan elections and governing authority fragmented by municipal, county, and special authority boundaries. Finally, the region's industrial economy and urban infrastructure exist largely because of federal spending. The Army Corps of Engineers built the port that made the city a center of Pacific trade and the flood control channels that have made sprawling development possible. The Bureau of Reclamation's Hoover Dam eliminated the looming energy shortage that threatened to halt industrial growth in the 1920s; the U.S. Navy bought the region's oil; federal investment jumpstarted Los Angeles's aerospace industry; and war mobilization reinvigorated automobile, rubber, and chemical manufacturing, the core heavy industries in the region.[12]

If Los Angeles embodies twentieth-century American urbanization, it is unusual in two respects that make it particularly useful for understanding just how business groups secured their political influence: the range of environmental problems besetting the city, and the nature of the Los Angeles business community's political influence there. So much of the business of city government involves managing the urban environment that it is fair to say that urban history is a story of the relationship between people and nature. Most American cities have struggled with some combination of nuisance industries, air pollution, flooding, and water and energy shortages. Very few, however, have had to manage all these at roughly the same time. Similarly, chambers of commerce or merchants and manufacturers organizations have long enjoyed a great deal of power in American cities. But Los Angeles's business organizations encountered little viable opposition. Labor unions were unusually weak. Progressives such as John R. Haynes worked tirelessly to inject other priorities into Los Angeles's civic and political life, but he and his allies never enjoyed the kind of influence that they would have had in, say, San Francisco.[13] Meanwhile, the probusiness, antiunion *Los Angeles Times* dominated the newsstands, enhancing business influence even when the *Times* and the chamber of commerce disagreed on policy details. The Los Angeles Chamber of Commerce did not, for all its influence, entirely live up to the stereotypes of business organizations. As the main booster for Los Angeles, the chamber grappled more aggressively than its counterparts elsewhere with industrial pollution and oil drilling that threatened agriculture, real estate, and tourism. The exaggerated quality of Los Angeles's environment and politics makes this city a distillation of national urban trends and thus an ideal jumping-off point for understanding environmental politics and the power of business interests during the transition from the guarded confidence in centralized government that marked the Progressive Era and New Deal to the localism and guarded confidence in the private sector and the antigovernment politics that have evolved from World War II to the present.

Los Angeles's myriad environmental problems, its dependence on federal aid, and to a lesser extent its political conflicts, as well, derived from geography and growth. The Los Angeles basin is an extensive sloping plain surrounded by steep mountains. The city was founded on the banks of the Los Angeles River, one of several flood-prone streams that course through the basin. Compared with the gold rush towns of northern California, during the nineteenth century Los Angeles grew slowly. Residents came to the region looking for respite from sooty, industrial cities; for decades boosters promoted the region as a natural sanitarium for those suffering from tuberculosis and other respiratory diseases. The Los Angeles River and rain-fed aquifers supported the region's largely agricultural economy. In the early twentieth century, rail links and the federally constructed harbor at San Pedro sparked rapid growth and real estate speculation. Then an oil rush of the first order transformed the region. Boosters energetically promoted Los Angeles throughout the Great Depression and World War II, attracting hundreds of thousands of new residents with depictions of a healthy, idyllic life and an economy that seamlessly combined petroleum, industry, and agriculture. The Los Angeles County population more than doubled between 1920 and 1930 (from 936,455 to 2,208,492 residents) and then doubled again to 4,151,687 in 1950.[14] New residents built homes, businesses, and factories that narrowed river channels, increased runoff, and thus multiplied the danger of and damage from the floods that regularly swept down from the mountains.[15] Newcomers competed for space along Los Angeles beaches with each other, with private developers, and with the oil industry. Automobiles, wartime manufacturing, and oil refining combined with climate and topography to raise air pollution to critical levels in the early 1940s.[16] Growth overtaxed the city's water and power networks, forcing public and private utilities alike to seek resources farther afield.[17]

Each of these problems—the pollution and chaos of oil drilling, air pollution, the danger of flooding, hydroelectric power shortages, competition for water resources, and conflicts over access to and use of Los Angeles area beaches—precipitated city, county, or federal action during the second quarter of the twentieth century. In fact, many other urban environmental problems emerged during this same period that illustrated similar political patterns. Traffic congestion, urban planning, the creation of the Los Angeles Department of Water and Power, solid waste disposal, the regulation of oil drilling in Los Angeles's residential neighborhoods, and a host of other public policies all grew out of the interactions of local officials and favored interest groups. The five case studies presented here were each selected to explore a single aspect of the relationship between business groups and local or federal government; linked together, they form a composite picture of the way political influence transformed American cities and the way American democracy worked in the second quarter of the twentieth century.

Each of the five chapters in this book explores a single environmental controversy. They are not arranged in a strict chronological order, in part because so many of these stories overlap with one another. Instead, they are arranged to emphasize how the daily functioning of municipal politics privileged groups like the Los Angeles Chamber of Commerce and then how these patterns of political influence shaped national politics. There are some disadvantages of this thematic organization. In particular, moving back and forth through time can obscure the differences between the Los Angeles of the 1920s and the city of the 1940s or 1950s. World War II changed Los Angeles in many ways. After the war, the city was larger and more industrial and had stronger unions. Moreover, the industrial workers who arrived during World War II did not share the same vision of Los Angeles as residents who had arrived earlier.

The book begins on Los Angeles's beaches, the origin of some of most indelible images and profound resource conflicts of Southern California. This chapter shows how contentious and malleable the concept of "public interest" was and how business-focused public policy developed in the second quarter of the twentieth century. Oil companies began drilling for offshore oil from piers built over the ocean in the 1920s.[18] Some homeowners along the shore leased their property to oil companies, eager to cash in on oil royalties. Some desperately wanted to keep oil out of their neighborhoods to protect their homes and property values from oil spills, fires, and the devastating explosions that accompanied early oil development. Other Angelenos protested the appropriation of recreational beaches for industrial development. Meanwhile, starting in 1938, Secretary of the Interior Harold Ickes tried to assert federal control over undersea oil deposits hitherto managed by the states. Out of this welter of conflicting claims the public beach movement emerged, spearheaded by a self-appointed group of Realty Board and chamber of commerce members. They pressed for public ownership of the recreational shoreline, the better to protect the businesses, real estate values, and tourism in coastal Los Angeles County. They succeeded in setting aside more than thirty miles of beachfront for public use and institutionalizing their own influence over the land use planning process. Because of racial segregation, their successes also reduced beach recreation opportunities for Los Angeles's black community.

The second chapter explores more specifically how the Los Angeles Chamber of Commerce secured its influence and thus limited the political influence of opposition groups and the general public. In the summer of 1943 clouds of car exhaust and industrial smoke blinded drivers in downtown Los Angeles and introduced Los Angeles and the nation to the modern scourge of smog. The Los Angeles Chamber of Commerce responded immediately, studying the causes of air pollution, enforcing voluntary smoke reductions among its members, and writing reports and ordinances for the Los Angeles City Council. These actions ensured that industries complied with new regulations, prompted the creation of a regional air pollution control board to coordinate antismog measures across the whole county, and blunted the demands of smaller clean air advocacy groups to limit industrial growth in greater Los Angeles. Moreover, its assistance with air quality control made the chamber of commerce the only public voice that mattered in air pollution policy. Scattered opposition groups across the county objected to official policies and to the Los Angeles Chamber of Commerce's role in developing them; considerable public protests surfaced again and again because so many Angelenos believed that officials ignored industrial pollution and failed to examine the public health implications of smog. However, these critiques had little impact on policy debates. The conflicts over air pollution control revealed great differences in opinion about the causes of air pollution, policy priorities, and who spoke for the public.

The debate over who represented the public interest continues in the story of San Gabriel River flood control in chapter 3. In the late 1930s, the Army Corps of Engineers planned comprehensive flood control for Los Angeles County, based largely on the recommendations of Los Angeles County's own flood control board. One major component of the Army Corps' plan for the San Gabriel River, a dam at Whittier Narrows, divided the business communities above and below the dam. One group, based in Long Beach and in the industrial and agricultural communities downstream from the proposed dam, argued that the dam offered cost-effective flood control and water conservation. Representatives of downstream businesses met regularly with the Army Corps of Engineers and participated fully in early policy debates. The upstream group opposed the dam because it displaced more than a thousand people, threatened a brand-new public school, and sacrificed residents' prosperity for the benefit of larger agricultural and industrial interests downstream. The opposition, however, enjoyed little contact with the Army Corps and had almost no ability to alter flood control policy. The relationships between the Army Corps and San Gabriel River valley residents and business organizations reinforced the local distribution of power within Los Angeles County. Moreover, because Whittier Narrows Dam grew out of local power structures, federal involvement in local public works transposed Los Angeles's local power structure onto federal policy.

The final two chapters focus on national policy debates of great interest to Los Angeles. Chapter 4 relates the political compromise that allowed private, for-profit utility corporations to develop hydroelectric power at Boulder Dam.[19] Early proposals for Boulder Dam on the Colorado River specified that the Bureau of Reclamation would control floods, irrigate the Imperial Valley of Southern California, supply Los Angeles with drinking water, and generate electricity for Arizona, Nevada, and Southern California. Planners expected and Congress required hydroelectricity revenues to subsidize construction of the dam and irrigation networks. The Water Power Act of 1920 required that the

Bureau of Reclamation sell electricity from the dam to nonprofit utilities owned by cities or rural electrical cooperatives. The dam proved so controversial, however, that Congress dropped restrictions on who could generate and sell electricity from Boulder Dam and allowed Southern California Edison, a private corporation, into the dam. The battle over Boulder Dam was a bitter one, but the compromise on who would operate the generators in the dam, and the resulting cooperation between the public and private sectors in dam operations, were trumpeted as the epitome of good governance. Ultimately, this depiction of Hoover Dam weakened the public power movement and, more important, helped recast the private sector as the moderator of government excess.

The challenges of federal leadership in natural resources development became still clearer after World War II. As part of postwar reconstruction, Congress approved dozens of major dams, many of which seemed ill considered or uneconomical. President Harry Truman, under pressure both to approve these dams and to cut federal spending, appointed the President's Water Resources Policy Commission to draft a new water policy to resolve these contradictory pressures. Chapter 5 examines the commission's work and the wholesale rejection of it by a nation grown leery of federal power. The commission, made up largely of former New Dealers, recommended that the federal government establish agencies to coordinate public and private water resources development for entire river basins. Its plan never even came before Congress, stillborn by red-baiting, localism, and the status that the private sector had achieved over the previous decades. By the time the President's Water Resources Policy Commission completed its work, many Americans believed that only private enterprise and home rule could protect their interests from excessive, tyrannical federal power.

Los Angeles's efforts to manage oil development and public access to beaches, air pollution, and flood control and national debates over water resources and hydroelectricity development reveal huge disparities in power, influence, and the ability to participate in policy debates. They demonstrate who had a voice in local politics, who did not, and how local politics shaped national policy. In each case, the Los Angeles

Chamber of Commerce or another business coalition claimed to speak for the general public, and local elected officials accepted them as the legitimate voice of the public. Because the federal government relied heavily on local leaders, both within and outside government, to articulate goals for federal programs in urban areas, the entry of the Army Corps of Engineers, the Bureau of Reclamation, and other agencies into the field of urban public works did not substantially reorganize political influence in local government. When Americans rejected "big government" after World War II and began the long process of dismantling the New Deal and wartime programs, they did so partly with the conviction that centralized government power posed a greater threat to their interests and to democracy than even the largest corporations in the private sector. This further reinforced the power of local elites.

A number of individuals and groups did try to challenge the legitimacy of the Los Angeles business groups, from the Altadena Property Owners League and the Citizens Anti-Smog Action Committee, which disputed the Los Angeles Chamber of Commerce's authority to shape air pollution control policies, to the El Monte Citizens Flood Control Committee, which questioned flood control strategies on the San Gabriel River. Because these opposition groups always emerged in reaction to specific policies, they always entered the political debate after city and county officials had established policy strategies and working relationships with the groups they considered representatives of the general public. The opposition, therefore, entered the policy debate late, too late to effectively introduce new values into policy discussions or to establish itself as the real voice of the people.

Over the course of the twentieth century and into the twenty-first, new groups have achieved more success in challenging the status quo and securing seats at the policy-making table. After decades of activism, ethnic, racial, and social minorities have come to enjoy greater visibility, influence, and political representation than they had before World War II. Local and federal regulations, including particularly environmental regulations, expanded the representation of nonindustry groups on agency advisory panels, required greater reporting of policy objectives and consequences, and made public comment periods and public hearings a more common part of the policy-making process than they were in the 1950s.[20] Some of these changes grew out of broad shifts in public priorities, signaled by rising environmental concern in the 1960s and 1970s.[21] Some of them were the result of deliberate campaigns on the part of environmental groups to challenge business as the voice of the people.

When national environmental groups entered local policy debates, they brought with them a political weight sufficient to balance local business elites and to redefine business groups as special interests. However, the role of national groups in local policy debates was not a simple victory for the public interest. National groups did win significant environmental battles and transform land use and pollution regulations. But they did not necessarily represent public opinion or encourage public participation any more than the business organizations they challenged. Moreover, these groups routinely shifted the venue of key policy debates—addressing local issues through state or federal legislation or, more recently, asserting state authority when the federal executive scaled back regulatory enforcement—which could also reduce local participation in policy debates. Clear signs of the resulting paradox emerged in the late twentieth century as urban environmental justice groups began to accuse national environmental powerhouses of elitism, racism, and the sacrificing of cities and people for trees and birds.

One of the central attributes of late twentieth- and early twenty-first-century politics in the United States has been the rise of the New Right, and with it the rejection of regulations as unnecessary barriers to enterprise and progress, and decades of campaign promises to eliminate waste in government and reduce public spending. These trends have complex origins in American political culture. But a number of phenomena from the second quarter of the twentieth century played a crucial role in this political transformation. First, the business community protected its legitimacy as the voice of the public in city government. Next, close cooperation between business and government, brought on by political conflict and the exigencies of environmental crisis, was celebrated as necessary for good government. This helped to undermine public support for adversarial regulations like those promoted by some

Progressives. Finally, Americans embraced local control and the private sector as the best bulwarks against excessive federal authority, which, in the end, brought American politics full circle. This transitional period in American environmental and political history gives new meaning to Tip O'Neill's famous assertion that "all politics is local."

CHAPTER ONE

OIL AND WATER

*The Public and the Private on Southern California Beaches,
1920–1950*

Los Angeles beaches have changed since the 1920s. Old photographs reveal people lounging in the sand, playing in the waves, and fishing from piers. They show lifeguard towers and crowds of umbrellas. But these crowds play in the shadow of oil rigs and ornate beach clubs that have mostly disappeared from Los Angeles's shoreline. It took nearly thirty years, but miles of Los Angeles area beaches were eventually acquired by state, county, and city governments. The campaign was spearheaded by prominent individuals in the Los Angeles Chamber of Commerce and the Los Angeles Realty Board with support from the outspoken superintendent of the Los Angeles City Department of Playgrounds and Recreation. Efforts to secure public rights to the beach were not unique to Los Angeles; on the contrary, groups like the American Shore and Beach Preservation Association supported public access movements nationwide. These movements thrived on the widely held conviction that beaches were a distinctly public and recreational resource.

In the 1920s, most of Los Angeles's beaches and adjacent lands were in private hands; some private holdings dated from eighteenth-century Spanish land grants. Much of this private land lay undeveloped and open for recreational use by local residents and visitors alike. The real estate and oil booms of the second and third decades of the twentieth century accelerated the development along the shoreline and constrained recreational access with a suddenness that surprised and alarmed Angelenos. Oil companies began drilling near the shore, then on the sand, and finally from piers that stretched out into shallow waters. Real estate developers erected fences and houses that blocked customary public access. These booms, of course, also brought more people to the region who wanted to use the beach.[1] Unsurprisingly, the

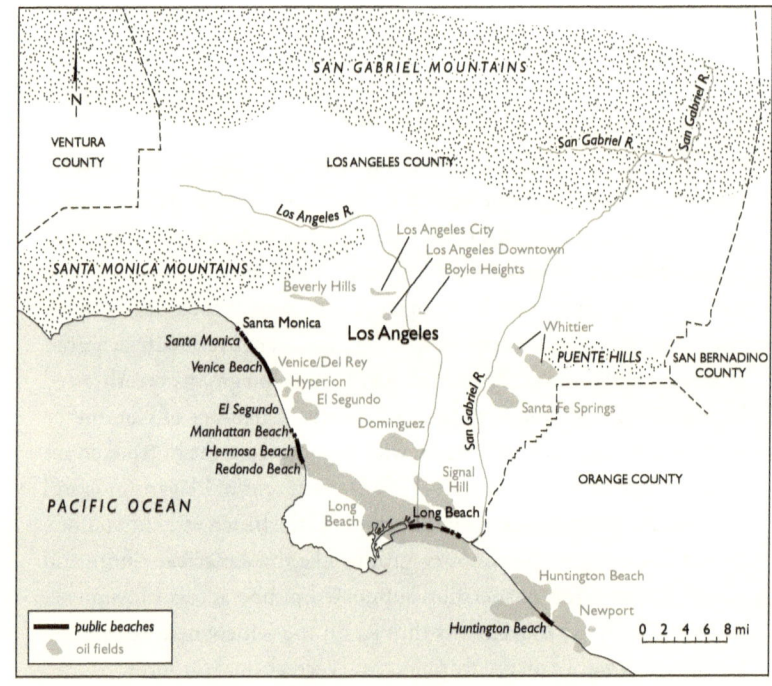

Public beaches and oil fields in greater Los Angeles

conflict between these incompatible uses of the shoreline resources quickly coalesced into campaigns to ban oil drilling on the beaches and then to move drilling farther and farther from the coast. These campaigns rested on assertions that the beaches were uniquely public, noncommercial, nonindustrial spaces.

During the New Deal and World War II, visitors continued to swarm to the beaches in large numbers. Neither the coastal erosion that narrowed beaches nor sewage pollution so severe that the state board of health quarantined most of the Santa Monica Bay shoreline deterred them. New construction along the shore slowed; landowners up and down the coast abandoned property because of bankruptcy or when erosion damaged their homes beyond repair. Meanwhile, a national movement emerged to preserve public access to the recreational shoreline. In Los Angeles, this movement inspired civic leaders in coastal communities to organize the Shoreline Planning Association to promote public ownership first in Los Angeles County and then in the rest of the state. They saw abandoned and depreciated coastal properties as an unprecedented opportunity to acquire beaches for the public. They also feared that Los Angeles's best chance at preserving its recreational shoreline would vanish as soon as peace reenergized Los Angeles's real estate market.

The Shoreline Planning Association largely succeeded. By 1950, city, county, and state governments coordinated their efforts to buy beach lands, install facilities, and operate the beaches. Widely promoted by Los Angeles boosters and seen by local residents as integral to the return to a peacetime lifestyle, the beaches in Los Angeles were a uniquely noncommercial space. Residents and the SPA explicitly rejected public-private collaboration at the beach. They eschewed leasing space at the beach for privately owned concessions even when those concessions would underwrite lifeguards, maintenance, and popular facilities. In fact, Angelenos rejected private ventures on the beach with nearly identical language and vehemence regardless of their scale, from major construction projects by restaurants or beach clubs to petty commerce.

Two ironies emerged from the successful public beach campaign. First, because of Los Angeles's racial segregation practices, public beaches excluded African Americans from the shore in the name of ensuring public access for all Angelenos. Second, even as the SPA proceeded to protect Southern California beaches from all types of development, the debates over shoreline oil development shifted from their initial focus on public rights versus private exploitation to a new emphasis on maximizing oil production. Because of the success of the public beach campaign and because of these apparent inconsistencies, the story of Los Angeles beaches is important for understanding both the evolution of business influence in American politics and the eclipse of Progressive Era faith in government by the Cold War confidence in private enterprise.

Like the other cases examined here, the public beach movement was propelled by business leaders with an economic stake in the policy outcome. In this case, the leadership of the Shoreline Planning Association, the organization that came to exercise more influence than any other in Southern California beach policy, brought together real estate, tourism, and commercial interests whose fortunes rose or fell on the tourism appeal of Southern California. In other words, the story of Los Angeles's public beaches illustrates the exclusiveness of city politics much as air pollution and flood control debates do. In addition, the debate over oil drilling on the beaches reveals a larger shift in public policy during the second quarter of the twentieth century toward economic productivity to the exclusion of other concerns. Nevertheless, Angelenos rejected industrial and commercial development on the beaches, which suggests that alternative values persisted in American cities in spite of this policy realignment. Many urban residents, the beach debates suggest, continued to value public services and recreation above growth. These values resurfaced perennially in critiques of industrial growth in the twentieth century, and although they may have triumphed in the beach debates, they had little traction outside recreational policy after 1940.

Oil and Water: A Brief History of Oil on Los Angeles Beaches

The first major conflict over the beaches of Southern California defined those beaches as a recreational rather than an industrial resource. By the 1920s, Californians had discovered huge deposits of oil in and around Los Angeles. Some of the most productive pools lay underneath land already subdivided for residential development. Several particularly rich deposits extended under the beaches and into the shallow waters off Venice Beach, Playa del Rey, and Long Beach in Los Angeles County and Huntington Beach in northern Orange County. In the course of developing these oil deposits, oil companies raised derricks and installed pumps, pipes, and oil tanks next to houses, on beaches, and looming over cemeteries. Oil drilling did not just bring the sights and sounds of industry, including fires, gushing wells, and gas explosions, to these distinctly nonindustrial locales. In reaction, the Los Angeles City Council imposed zoning and other restrictions to protect residential and commercial property values and to spare residents the destruction that accompanied oil drilling.[2] This same impulse, strengthened by the conviction that the shore should be recreational and scenic rather than industrial, drove Angelenos to seek to limit oil drilling in and near Los Angeles's beaches in the 1920s.

California's oil industry began in the 1870s in the southern reaches of the San Joaquin Valley.[3] The early years set the tone for California's oil industry: wildcatters treated oil exploration as an excuse to embark on a wide variety of speculative ventures. Early company charters outlined the companies' intentions "to locate, acquire . . . and sell water rights and water"[4] and "in any and every way [to] deal in real estate," in addition to "buy[ing] . . . and develop[ing] oil lands."[5] Even Standard Oil, which by 1880 controlled some 90 percent of all the oil refined in the United States, planned to "acquire [and] build . . . pipelines for conveying . . . water" in addition to oil and intended to "improve, develop and cultivate lands whether for mineral or agricultural" purposes.[6] In the 1890s, prospectors found more oil deposits in Santa Barbara, Ventura, and Los Angeles counties.

Drilling in Los Angeles began in 1892 with one shallow well located about a mile from Los Angeles's city hall. Within a decade, more than a thousand wells had sprouted up around downtown in what became known as the Los Angeles City Field.[7] On the Santa Barbara coast north of Los Angeles, oil companies built derricks on the ends of piers to recover oil from underwater pools.[8] By 1909, California led the nation in oil production, but the Los Angeles basin contributed less than 15 percent of this total.[9] This would soon change. Between 1917 and

1926, a half dozen astoundingly rich oil fields were discovered in the Los Angeles basin. Just three of these, the Huntington Beach, Signal Hill, and Santa Fe Springs, soon produced almost 80 percent of the state's total oil output. Oil production from Los Angeles swamped the market, causing oil prices to drop by two-thirds in eighteen months.[10]

The oil boom of the 1920s was one of the major engines of Los Angeles's growth, but the costs of that growth were high. Volatile oil prices and rapidly rising oil consumption spurred oil companies to claim new leases and drill and pump oil as fast as they could. Much of the land in the newly discovered oil fields had previously been developed or subdivided as small house lots. This created unique opportunities and problems for both oil companies and property owners. On the one hand, because so many different individuals owned property in the oil fields, more landowners could negotiate leases with oil companies and thus profit from the oil under their land. In addition, oil companies of all sizes could lease and drill, so no single landowner or oil firm could establish a monopoly in these fragmented fields. On the other hand, this pattern of land ownership encouraged oil companies to erect oil wells very close together and to drill and pump oil as fast as they could to maximize their yields. As Daniel Yergin described the Signal Hill field, "The discovery created a stampede. . . . Money flew all over the hill as oil companies, promoters, and amateurs scrambled to get leases. The parcels were so small and the forest of tall wooden derricks so thick that the legs of many of them actually interlaced." People even received royalties for oil pumped out from under a Signal Hill cemetery.[11] The rapid pace of oil production exacerbated price fluctuations and oversupply. It also threatened the long-term production from each oil field by depleting the gas pressure that made it possible to pump oil out of the ground.

Oil development in Los Angeles's residential areas caused a myriad of problems. Natural-gas explosions, runaway wells, noise, odor, and sprayed or spilled oil befouled these communities.[12] Fires raged out of control among tightly packed wooden derricks, open oil tanks, and spilled crude. One resident who stayed in Huntington Beach despite the bedlam there complained: "These oil men have taken everything except the food in the icebox. . . . My back yard is an oil well, a sump

The gushers, explosions, and fires that accompanied oil drilling in Los Angeles contributed to public support for many campaigns to protect recreational beaches and residential areas from the oil industry. Hearst-Examiner Photograph Collection. Courtesy of Doheny Memorial Library, University of Southern California, Los Angeles, California.

hole. My fence is gone and the inside of my house is a mess."[13] Given the destruction that followed in the wake of each new strike, it is unsurprising that Angelenos did not view the oil companies as good corporate citizens. Meanwhile, ongoing revelations of corruption and market manipulation by the oil industry—exposed by a Federal Trade Commission report in 1915, a Senate investigation led by Robert M. La Follette in 1922, and the Teapot Dome scandal from 1923 to 1928—fed public antipathy toward oil companies.[14] The industry's reputation as a corrupt special interest added to public outrage and to local efforts to regulate the industry. From Huntington Beach to Ventura, communities reacted to the chaos by trying to impose regulations on where and how oil companies could operate. When the oil companies thought regulations would reduce competition and risk, they cooperated; when regulations curtailed their access to the oil fields, they resisted.[15]

As oil drilling spread from dry land onto Los Angeles beaches in the 1920s, derricks, drilling piers, fences, pipes, and equipment proliferated along the shore. Competition for oil leases was, if anything, even more fierce on the beach than inland because pier drilling proceeded in a legal vacuum; the property laws that regulated oil leases on dry land did not apply to navigable and coastal waters. As on dry land, oil companies rushed to erect wells and pump as much oil as fast as they could, but on the beaches and tidelands, as nearshore areas were known, oil companies also tried to impede competitors' access to their leases, sometimes buying long, narrow strips of land to block other companies' leases and piers.[16] Oil drilling interfered with recreation, too. Fences and equipment blocked access; crude spills fouled the beaches. Simply walking along the beach through this maze of equipment became increasingly difficult. Derricks, piers, and other unsightly machinery threatened to reduce tourism and prosperity in shoreline communities. Spilled oil, derrick fires, noise, and fumes from the oil-drilling operations transformed the beaches from recreational to industrial landscapes. Although one defender of pier drilling dismissed complaints by comparing Los Angeles's oil rigs to "New England's rotting fish-wharves, which painters... sketch and tourists admire," local opposition to the oil piers mounted.[17]

The California legislature reacted to the chaos along the shore first by passing the Submerged Land Leasing Act in 1921 and then by banning oil piers in 1927. The Submerged Land Leasing Act finally established state authority over offshore leasing and property rights in California. This brought some legal order to the chaotic tidelands oil fields, but the legislation brought few improvements for recreation.[18] Oil wells and unsightly machinery still cluttered the shore and walled off large sections of beach from public recreational use. Spills, fires, and blowouts still threatened the beaches. These ongoing problems fostered support for the pier-drilling ban in 1928. This measure was portrayed by supporters explicitly as protecting the public interest. When Governor C. C. Young signed the pier-drilling ban in January 1928, he heralded the measure as a victory for the public in a long battle to protect the priceless California coast from the private exploitation and ruin.[19]

The oil companies' reactions to these bills undermined the characterization of these measures as victories for the public's rights to the beach. The biggest participants in the oil industry—the Majors—supported both bills. In fact, the Majors helped develop oil-drilling regulations to bring order to the oil industry. They sought to reduce market fluctuations and reduce oil waste by slowing and stabilizing production and by reducing competition in the oil fields. The Majors emphasized slower production in particular because rapid oil extraction contributed to crippling boom-bust price-and-supply cycles and depleted the all-important underground natural-gas pressure that pushed oil into pipes and allowed companies to pump it to the surface. Rapid depletion of gas pressure stranded oil under ground. The smaller firms, known as the Independents, opposed these rules vehemently because their profits depended on maximum production in the short term. The conflict between the Majors and Independents grew quite bitter, with the Independents accusing the Majors of monopoly and the Majors calling the Independents wasteful and irresponsible.[20]

The Majors endorsed the Submerged Land Leasing Act of 1921 because it gave them stronger and clearer state leasing laws, which made it easier for them to operate. Public discussion of the legislation did not engage the importance of clear drilling rights. Instead, newspaper coverage of the Submerged Land Leasing Act focused almost exclusively on the way drilling on the beaches interfered with public recreation.

This made the Submerged Land Leasing Act seem like an effort by the oil industry to increase its rights to the shore at the expense of the public. The Majors also supported the 1928 pier-drilling ban because they believed that moving wells off the beach would reduce public opposition to drilling in the Huntington Beach, Venice Beach, Playa del Rey, and other nearshore oil fields.[21] Because of technological innovations, well-financed firms no longer needed piers to exploit tidelands oil. They could drill diagonally from dry land into the tidelands; called whipstocking or slant drilling, this technology promised to open vast territories to new oil exploitation.

The pier-drilling ban did not completely protect the oil companies from criticism of their impact on the beaches. Although oil companies did not erect any new oil piers after 1928, they continued to operate existing wells. In addition, they built new rigs that loomed over miles of beach as they whipstocked into offshore deposits. In 1930, a private social club that owned facilities on the beach urged the city council to "take every measure within their power to prevent the drilling of oil wells along or adjacent to the sea coast" in Santa Monica Bay on the grounds that such development impaired beach recreation "to the great detriment of the community as a whole."[22] By the mid-1930s, communities all along Santa Monica Bay, from Malibu to Palos Verdes, demanded a ban on all drilling within half a mile of the water.[23] The Los Angeles City Council passed an ordinance in 1935 to do just this but never enforced it.

Pressure for an extended drilling ban persisted, and slant drilling became an issue on land, too. In 1936, the Los Angeles City Council contemplated leasing the right to drill for oil underneath the city's Hyperion Point sewage treatment plant. If the council had approved the idea, oil companies would have whipstocked from private land adjacent to the plant and paid the city royalties on the oil they extracted.[24] Although this could have yielded considerable revenue for the city, it raised the specter of a new boom and the spread of derricks throughout the city to exploit oil reserves unavailable to the oil companies because of hard-won regulations protecting beaches and neighborhoods.

In response to mounting pressure to move oil drilling farther and farther from the lucrative shoreline deposits, and in reaction to public

THE MARCH OF THE DERRICK.

Have we any guarantee that it will stop at Sunset Park?

The above is the record of the City Council in the matter of oil encroachment. With each modification of the limit the public has been solemnly assured that it would be the last.
The "Smooth" Councilman to the Private Oil Speculator: "Come on; you can't do me any harm; never mind the public protest."

This cartoon suggests that the speculators were the main force behind the extension of oil drilling into residential neighborhoods, but homeowners also pressed city officials to permit them to realize oil profits from their lands. "The March of the Derrick," *Los Angeles Times*, 24 May 1900.

fears about whipstocking, in 1936 Standard Oil sponsored a state ballot initiative to explicitly legalize whipstocking into offshore oil deposits.[25] Protest erupted immediately. The West Los Angeles Chamber of Commerce and the *Venice Evening Vanguard* newspaper repeatedly demanded the creation of new setback rules to prevent "commercial development along the beach."[26] Newspapers in Venice and Playa del Rey opposed both the Hyperion Point drilling proposal and Standard Oil's 1936 referendum because they feared that legalizing slant drilling would increase drilling operations near beaches and in residential neighborhoods.[27] Opponents called Standard Oil's ballot proposal "vicious" and "impudent"; they demanded legislation to "clearly define the public's right to full enjoyment of the beach, without regard to the plans or desires of private interests."[28] Chambers of commerce from West Los Angeles, Santa Monica, Venice, Manhattan Beach, Palos Verdes, Redondo Beach, Hermosa Beach and Playa del Rey joined the campaign.[29] Drilling restrictions gained considerable support from inland residents who visited the beach and who had their own experiences with the hazards and nuisances of petroleum exploitation.[30]

Los Angeles County supervisor John Anson Ford criticized slant drilling as "detrimental to [the] beaches."[31] The secretary of the Hermosa Beach Chamber of Commerce decried the ballot measure as "a medium for satisfying the private greed of certain large oil interests ... [and] a vehicle through which ruin and destruction will be carried to our beaches."[32] Independent oil producers charged Standard Oil with drafting the bill to monopolize the oil fields.[33] But the slant-drilling initiative earmarked half of the oil royalty payments for the state to acquire and maintain public beaches and parks statewide. This windfall for public recreation enticed the California State Park Commission and the majority of California voters to support Standard Oil's slant-drilling ballot proposition.[34]

Tension over the place of drilling in Los Angeles erupted periodically for decades after the slant-drilling proposition passed as first World War II and then postwar economic growth fed demands for ever more oil and thus challenged the wisdom of prohibiting oil extraction in residential and shoreline areas. In the late 1930s, however, Los Angeles's efforts to control oil production on the beaches were eclipsed by federal claims to tidelands oil. In August 1937, Senator Gerald P. Nye of North Dakota proposed that Congress recognize the "tidelands" in California, Louisiana, and Texas as part of the public domain. Harold Ickes supported this idea; it was entirely consistent with his vision of federal management of vital natural resources. Nye, Ickes, and their allies believed that federal management of offshore oil reserves would ensure that the whole nation, rather than just a few lucky states, shared the benefits of oil royalties. The idea of federal management of the tidelands actually originated with the Independents, which had been effectively excluded from California's lucrative nearshore oil fields by the regulations sponsored by the Majors.[35] The Majors and the state governments of California, Texas, and Louisiana protested federal ownership as a violation of states' rights and a threat to prosperity and energy production. Although the urgency of oil production during World War II overshadowed proposals for federal ownership for a time, the issue of federal claims remained unresolved until President Dwight D. Eisenhower issued an executive order recognizing California's ownership of all oil deposits within three miles of the coast. Texas and Louisiana were given control of all deposits within three leagues of their shores.[36]

The conflicts over nearshore oil drilling in the 1920s and 1930s originated with Angelenos' desire to keep and use the beaches for recreation. They saw the coast as a scenic rather than an industrial resource. Oil industry activities—from erecting wells, piers, and fences that interfered with public recreation to price-fixing and other monopolistic and aggressive corporate practices—fueled public opposition to tidelands drilling. These activities also made the oil industry an easy target for those who did not want an intrusive industry to dominate the beach. Criticisms of the oil companies muted over time, but the campaign to remove oil rigs from the shore remained vibrant through the Depression and World War II. The organization formed to spearhead this campaign drew its leadership from the groups that dominated political debate in Los Angeles: chambers of commerce and real estate organizations. Some of Los Angeles's most elite, exclusive social clubs joined in, as did both the *Los Angeles Times* and the smaller newspapers that usually disagreed with the *Times*. This coalition of business leaders and newspapers encountered no organized opposition to its campaigns against oil drilling and for public ownership of the beaches. Still more significant, with the exception of one brief debate over a highway in Santa Monica, the coalition's right to speak for the public on this issue went unchallenged.

The 1936 proposition legalizing whipstocking passed, in spite of strong opposition by the chambers of commerce, elite social clubs, and elected officials in Los Angeles and in spite of a campaign to paint the initiative as a giveaway of public resources. Significantly, the three major laws regulating tideland and nearshore oil development in California were all sponsored by major oil companies. Clearly the Majors exercised considerable political influence on oil policy during this period. Particularly in the case of the pier-drilling ban, the Majors used public outrage over the beaches to secure the regulations they wanted.

The rhetoric used in the pier-drilling and whipstocking campaigns and, later, in the drive for public ownership of the beaches shared vehement assertions about the uniquely public nature of the shore. But consider the key advocates of public rights: elite social clubs that owned beachfront property, and newspaper editors and chambers of commerce from Los Angeles beachfront or oil-producing communities. These groups portrayed oil companies as monopolistic outsiders without legitimate claims to the beach and insisted that any oil industry presence on the beach illegitimately transferred public resources into greedy private hands. In thus juxtaposing the private interests in oil development and the public's interest in the recreational beach, this coalition of the real estate promoters, boosters, social elites, and entrepreneurs echoed Progressive Era criticisms of big business. This is ironic, given how public beaches served this coalition's economic interests and how few members of the general public actually had a hand in shaping beach policies during the second quarter of the twentieth century in Los Angeles.

Private Beach Clubs, Cafés, Mansions, and Other Threats

Starting in the 1920s, just as Los Angeles's oil production ramped up, social clubs like the exclusive Los Angeles Athletic Club built clubhouses

Another Beach Club

In the 1920s, Angelenos feared oil spills, beach clubs, and many other threats to recreational use of the local shoreline. In 1925, the Los Angeles port traffic manager blamed tankers and ships for befouling the beaches by discharging bilge oils near the shore. Of course, oil also ran into the ocean from sumps and spills in the oil fields. "Another Beach Club," by Edmund Gale, 13 Aug. 1925. Copyright © 1925, *Los Angeles Times*. Reprinted with permission.

on Los Angeles beaches. These clubs drew their memberships from the social registers and business elites of Orange and Los Angeles counties; their rolls included state senators, state highway commissioners, city councilors, writers, actors, and members of chambers of commerce, realty boards, and the Hollywood Bowl Association.[37] By 1930, eight private clubhouses offered members swimming pools, dining rooms, bars, and comfortable guest rooms for overnight stays in Santa Monica, Long Beach, Hermosa Beach, Venice Beach, Torrance, and Huntington Beach. They featured ornate furnishings and whimsical architecture; one even emulated a medieval castle complete with turrets and tapestries.³⁸ Similar developments peppered prime recreational lands in many other cities during this period. The Chicago Yacht Club built exclusive facilities in Chicago's Grant and Lincoln parks. The venerable Appalachian Mountain Club erected private cabins in Boston's Emerald Necklace. San Diego's Balboa Park is still home to at least a dozen semi-private facilities for bridge, horseshoes, lawn bowling, model railroading, and other activities.

Through the 1920s, and with few exceptions, American cities welcomed this sort of private development. Clubs brought facilities and visitors to beaches and parks at no cost to the public treasury, while the proliferation of beachside homes increased the local population, business, and tax base. Not all private development was equally welcome, of course, as protests against oil drilling in Los Angeles and against railroad monopolies of the Oakland and Chicago waterfronts suggest. Nevertheless, Americans have long credited private initiative rather than government activities for economic growth and prosperity. This was particularly true in Los Angeles, a city with few public parks for its size and population. In Los Angeles and Orange County, private ownership of much beachfront land dated from Spanish and Mexican land grants. In the nineteenth and twentieth centuries, real estate developers and railroad magnates made fortunes buying up and subdividing the old ranchos.³⁹ Elsewhere in the region, municipal, county, and state governments sold or leased public land for a wide range of private purposes, including residential and industrial development. Particularly in smaller Southern California cities, no real mechanism or motivation existed for extensive public ownership of the shoreline.

By 1930, sixty-four of Los Angeles County's seventy-one miles of beach were closed to the public.⁴⁰ With so much beach in private hands, private development no longer seemed such a universal boon. As one Cassandra put it, "Mile after mile of matchless ocean frontage has been blocked off with public clubs and private residences which range all the way from motion-picture magnates' homes to sordid shacks, while other miles have been fenced around and plastered with 'For Sale' or 'No Trespassing' signs until the general public might well paraphrase the Scriptures and cry, 'Beach, beach, but there is no beach.'"⁴¹ Newspaper editors lamented a gauntlet of food shacks and cheap entertainments that threatened to crowd Angelenos off the remaining public strands. Elected officials worried that developers were subdividing beachfront lots so quickly that little would be left for public recreation. Eventually, protests about private beach use grew so strident that public beach advocates stopped distinguishing between large-scale projects like oil drilling or real estate subdivisions and the relatively trivial commerce of umbrella and food peddlers.

Efforts to limit private exploitation of the beaches were never wholly divorced from self-interest because the coastal communities recognized the beaches as some of their greatest economic assets.[42] The civic and elected leaders of Los Angeles–area beach cities balanced the needs of new and established enterprises against each other and against their understanding of what attracted visitors to the strand. But the impetus for some of the campaigns against "commercial exploitation" on the beach grew from direct economic self-interest; curtailing new business on the shore protected older, more established ventures located farther inland. For its part, the Los Angeles Chamber of Commerce supported private exploitation as much as it did public beach development only as long as it felt that private beach clubs, food vendors, and shoreline businesses attracted money and visitors to Southern California.[43]

In 1928, the Westport Beach Club proposed building a groin to reduce erosion in front of its Venice Beach clubhouse. A groin is a small seawall extending across the beach and into the water perpendicular to the shore. Because the Westport Beach Club's groin would have functioned like a stone wall across the beach, critics of the plan accused the beach club of trying to close off the beach in front of the club to keep people from walking along the shore. A member of the Los Angeles Playgrounds and Recreation Commission who saw himself as "fighting single-handed to save the beaches for the public," protested that the Westport Beach Club's project and others like it would "giv[e] the beach fronts to the clubs."[44] Others objected because the groin damaged the "city's interests" by "constitut[ing] a menace to bathers along the beach."[45]

Battles over beach club facilities continued into the 1930s in reaction to the Pacific Coast Club's proposal to build a small pleasure-boat harbor near its Long Beach facilities and to the Surf and Sand Club's scheme to fence off part of the public strand in Hermosa Beach for the exclusive use of its members. The *Long Beach Post Telegram* protested the Pacific Coast Club's yacht harbor project as a "question of private or public beach rights."[46] The business community in Hermosa Beach had long celebrated the Surf and Sand Club, but the fence changed that. In 1935, the Hermosa Beach Junior Chamber of Commerce declared that "they could not possibly support any plan that would place a section of the publicly owned beach under private control."[47] The Hermosa City Council blocked the fence at every turn, even when the club proposed giving the city other beach lands in exchange for approval of the fence.[48] The Surf and Sand Club renewed its efforts to build a fence in 1936, warning that it would close if it did not acquire a private beach.[49] Hermosa Beach officials again refused. Chambers of commerce, municipal officials, and newspapers that had once embraced private recreational development now vehemently rejected beach club projects as appropriations of public resources for private use.

The beach clubs, of course, were not the only private interests exploiting the beach. Private homes blocked access to much more of the shore. In 1924, for example, the owners of a large beach tract at the mouth of Santa Monica Canyon suddenly subdivided and sold their land. This particular land deal created great consternation among public beach advocates because the Santa Monica Canyon tract was at that time under consideration for the creation of a state beach. Worse still, the new landowners immediately closed the Santa Monica tract to all visitors and began charging tourists a quarter just to look at the view. Such profiteering, the Los Angeles Chamber of Commerce protested, was "intolerable" and "should not be allowed."[50] Some years later, in 1933, the state of California purchased and established a state park there. Even this did not eliminate fears of private exploitation because the state park commission leased out a small plot on the beach for a privately owned café.[51] Instead of accepting this café as a welcome amenity, the LAACC called the enterprise an "encroachment of business upon the state beach ... detrimental to the public interest" and a dangerous precedent for commercial development of beaches throughout the county.[52] In a similar dispute over an amusement pier in Venice, opponents argued that private development would undermine efforts to expand the public beach.[53] The chamber of commerce's vehement rejection of business development is striking but becomes less surprising when seen in light of its connections to tourism and its commitments to established businesses and high property values in beach communities.

The LAACC was joined by the Los Angeles Playgrounds and Recreation Commission and the venerable landscape architects of the Olmsted firm in criticizing businesses as threats to the unique pleasures of the shore. In 1930, an LAACC committee commissioned the Olmsted Brothers and Bartholomew and Associates to prepare a comprehensive park plan for the city. They found "commercial exploitation ... [had] gradually put the beach ... wholly out of existence ... and ... corralled the crowd into indoor commercialized enterprises which might just as well have been elsewhere and which are on the whole distinctly deleterious in character."[54] The landscape architects so opposed private enterprise on the strand that they urged Los Angeles city leaders to control the expansion of even those private businesses that provided useful services to beach visitors.[55] In 1946, this aversion to commerce on the beach, in part, prompted the West Los Angeles Police Commission to request a citywide ban on peddling and begging on the beaches.[56] In the same year and on a much grander scale, county supervisors considered an elaborate public-private partnership inspired by newly opened facilities at Jones State Beach in New York. They proposed spending more than $8 million in county bond funds to build a "complete recreational plant, with modern public bathhouses, parking spaces, well-equipped picnic grounds, game areas, food stand, cafeterias and restaurants."[57] As at Jones State Beach, income from concessions such as snack bars, parking, and umbrella rentals was to underwrite facility maintenance and operations.[58] The Los Angeles County supervisors quickly decided that this much private enterprise was inconsistent with public recreation and abandoned the ambitious scheme. In rejecting the Jones State Beach model, they turned their back on the strategy of public-private cooperation that dominated many other areas of postwar public policy.

The Los Angeles Chamber of Commerce and others rejected the beach clubs and beachside businesses when these enterprises no longer seemed like an economic boon. Their opposition to commercial

Private development along the shore alarmed Angelenos during each of Los Angeles's major real estate booms. "Dog Days Doggerel," by Edmund Gale, 2 Sept. 1925. Copyright © 1925, *Los Angeles Times*. Reprinted with permission.

exploitation also reveals their growing desire to create accessible, public beaches as a refuge from commerce and urban life similar to grand city and national parks.[59] This image of the wild beach was widely disseminated in magazines from *Architectural Digest* to *Life* and *Home and Garden*.[60] However, the undeveloped beach rarely appeared in the professional journals directed at municipal officials such as *American City* and *Playground and Recreation*; instead, these publications promoted well-appointed public beaches with all the amenities that urban visitors might expect.[61] Although some Angelenos saw the beach primarily in economic terms and others as a respite from the world of commerce, Los Angeles's public beaches served both of these goals. The many ways beaches served public recreation suggest why campaigns against private development of the beaches were not as contentious as, say, policy debates over air pollution or flood control. The perceptions of the beach established during the 1920s and 1930s, moreover, greatly facilitated the postwar movement to expand public ownership of the shoreline.

Postwar Planning on the Public Beach

By World War II, Los Angeles could boast a record of reducing oil development on the beaches and protecting access to some beach lands. The community as a whole, including business and real estate interests, had defined the beaches as a distinctly public resource. But a surprising percentage of the beaches that Angelenos used for recreation remained in private hands and thus vulnerable to postwar development. Other threats to public recreation loomed during the war years, too. Overdevelopment of the shoreline, long-term neglect, and population growth had left miles of public and private beaches eroded, polluted, and cluttered with abandoned industrial and commercial structures. These problems threatened to turn the beaches from a tourist attraction and vast public park into unusable, even dangerous territory. In reaction, the same groups that had fought shoreline oil drilling and commercial development before the war organized to protect the beaches as public recreational resources.

Dire reports on the physical decline of Los Angeles's beaches multiplied as World War II came to a close. The national publication of the Municipal League, *American City*, reported in 1944 that severe erosion along the Los Angeles coast had undermined beachfront facilities and reduced beaches to narrow, rocky, inhospitable strips.[62] The *Los Angeles Times* fretted in 1946 that sewage had turned Santa Monica Bay into a "common cesspool" where "sands intended for quiet sunbathing [were] smeared with the scum of human filth."[63] A Venice neighborhood improvement association complained to the Los Angeles City Council in 1947 that debris from neglected piers posed a "menace to life, limb and property."[64] These conditions had eroded property values along the shore almost as fast as the beaches themselves seemed to melt away. Those behind the public beach movement recognized that these lower property values created a fleeting opportunity for local and state governments to purchase large tracts of shoreline for parks. To the casual observer, it may have seemed at the time that Los Angeles's beaches had abruptly descended into crisis. But these environmental problems had developed gradually over several decades.

Beaches are dynamic places. Sand moves constantly along the shore in a process known as littoral drift; seasonally sand moves on and off the beach, too. Wind also plays a role, carrying sand inland to form dunes or sending the sand cascading back onto the beach from those dunes. Any structure can change this equilibrium of water, wind, and sand, tipping the balance and trapping sand in one place or washing it offshore in another. As engineers were just discovering in the 1920s, structures that crossed the surf line were especially disruptive of these geological processes.[65] From the first breakwaters built to protect shipping channels to the oil drilling and recreational piers erected in the first decades of the twentieth century, structures that interfered with littoral drift multiplied in Los Angeles County, with devastating consequences. Flood control projects exacerbated shoreline erosion problems because debris and flood control basins, and the concrete channels built to contain Los Angeles's unruly rivers, all drastically reduced the amount of gravel, sand, and other sediment that washed down from the mountains to replenish the beaches.

Erosion burst into public consciousness following a particularly ferocious storm in December 1940. High tides and powerful waves forced evacuation and then undermined and damaged beachfront property from Venice to Redondo.[66] In response, the group that was to become the premier advocate of public beaches across the state, the Shoreline Planning Association, launched a series of studies that blamed flood control for reducing sand deliveries to the beaches and "unwisely planned yacht harbor developments" and amusement piers for interrupting the natural movement of sand along the shore.[67] Tight municipal budgets prevented Los Angeles from acting to halt coastal erosion even in the wake of this report. At another time, the city might have turned to the Army Corps of Engineers for assistance, but by 1942 that agency had halted all civil works for the duration. So erosion continued, damaging property and narrowing recreational beaches throughout the war and feeding dire predictions in the immediate postwar years that Angelenos would soon lose access to their coast.

Like erosion, the pollution of Santa Monica Bay developed gradually but suddenly attracted public attention immediately after World War II. The city of Los Angeles began dumping its sewage into Santa Monica Bay with the completion of its first sewage outfall at Hyperion Point in 1894.[68] Beach cities began to complain about waste and odors from the Hyperion Point outfall in 1912. Los Angeles did nothing to address these problems for more than a decade. Finally, in 1925 the city added a screening plant and a longer outfall pipe to the Hyperion Point facility. Screening was intended to reduce the amount of solid waste pouring into Santa Monica Bay. The mile-long "submarine outfall," city officials hoped, would reduce pollution by increasing dilution and removing sewage farther out to sea.

The 1925 additions did little to improve water quality in Santa Monica Bay. Almost immediately after the screening plant opened, cracks appeared in the outfall pipe, and the state board of health reported serious odor problems at the plant.[69] An earthquake opened yet more leaks in 1933, but the Los Angeles Department of Public Works quickly exhausted funds for repairs.[70] Between 1920 and 1940, the population of Los Angeles grew from 576,673 to more than 1.5 million residents.[71] So even as the city struggled with its inadequate, leaky sewage disposal plant, this population explosion overwhelmed the sewer system and any environmental gains that the longer outfall pipe might otherwise have yielded. At the best of times, city officials would have been hard pressed to build infrastructure to serve all these new residents. But the 1930s and 1940s were not the best of times.

When lack of funds forced the Department of Public Works to abandon outfall repairs, the city of Los Angeles applied for federal assistance under the New Deal. But in contrast to generous federal support for flood control described in chapter 3, the New Deal agencies rejected Los Angeles's sewage applications. Then, the war further hindered the city's ability to fix the outfall. By 1942, conditions were so bad in Santa Monica Bay that the state board of health canceled the Hyperion Point operating permit and sued the city. But because wartime production codes now prevented city action, the state board of health could do little more than excoriate the city for "procrastination and inadequate planning and financing of sewage disposal" and close the beaches to protect public health.[72] Ten miles of beach along Santa Monica Bay remained closed from 1943 to 1947. This did not keep Angelenos from the shore; in spite of dire warnings that swimming in polluted water might lead to typhoid fever, twenty million people visited the quarantined beaches in the summer of 1943 alone.[73]

The abrupt emergence of the beach crisis after 1944, therefore, did not reflect a surge in pollution, decay, and erosion. Rather, peace returned public attention to problems that had seemed unimportant or unsolvable while the United States was fighting the Axis powers. At the end of the war, however, these same problems—erosion, abandoned property, and sewage contamination—seemed to create an opportunity to establish extensive public beaches. Meanwhile, peace and the easing of wartime regulations also promised to bring to Los Angeles an unprecedented real estate boom that could drive up land prices and put public ownership forever out of reach. The Shoreline Planning Association used the opportunities created by the war to expand public beach ownership in Los Angeles and to cement its political influence up and down the state.

The Shoreline Planning Association formed in Los Angeles in the mid-1930s, an outgrowth of a national movement to increase public beach access. It grew quickly; by 1945 it all but directed the Los Angeles County beach planning and development program. Affiliated organizations dominated coastal planning statewide through the 1960s. In the 1930s, several other organizations also advocated for public beaches, but nearly all of them shared the SPA's priorities. R. Carman Ryles, for one, organized a group in 1935 to oppose a new beachside highway between Ocean Park and Venice that the SPA advocated. The Shoreline Planning Association, Los Angeles Chamber of Commerce, Santa Monica Chamber of Commerce, and the Los Angeles City Department of Playgrounds and Recreation all favored the highway because it would increase access to the shore. Ryles, whose family had given the city much of the beachfront land affected by the proposed highway, argued that the road would narrow the beach and destroy public recreational lands.[74] But this conflict was resolved within a matter of months and revealed little real disagreement over priorities or values; all the groups involved wanted to expand public beach access and saw a road as essential to doing so. Most other Los Angeles beach organizations did not even differ from the Shoreline Planning Association as much as Ryles's group had. In 1931, for example, representatives of six Southern California counties convened as the Save the Beach League to combat oil pollution on beaches, pollution they blamed on ships dumping oil at sea. Beach improvement and conservation organizations from all over the state formed the California Beaches Association in 1936 to coordinate their efforts to mitigate beach erosion and pollution, halt oil drilling in the tidelands, and develop beaches as tourist attractions.[75] Of all the public beach advocacy groups, the SPA worked most closely with local and state officials and by doing so became an institutionalized fixture in California coastal policy making.

The Shoreline Planning Association rose to such prominence because of its membership and its political tactics. Six of the SPA's 1940 board of directors, Glanton Reah, Morton H. Anderson, Edgar L. Etter, George P. Larsen, A. A. Newton, and Otto Fehling, also served as officers of the Venice, Santa Monica, Redondo Beach, Hermosa Beach, West Los Angeles, and Los Angeles chambers of commerce. Three of the SPA directors not affiliated with chambers of commerce were involved in real estate. Their number included G. Brooks Snelgrove, the manager and one of the original planners of Palos Verdes Estates, and George H. Lindey, the founding chair of the South Bay Realty Board. Geoffrey Morgan, who later became president of the Shoreline Planning Association, also served as president of the Santa Monica Community Chest and represented Santa Monica in the California State Assembly.[76] The SPA secured its influence over beach policy because of the personal power of these individuals but also because it prepared careful studies of beach problems when local officials needed them and drafted local and state legislation for local officials. This ensured that state legislation reflected the Shoreline Planning Association's priorities and guaranteed its continued role in the acquisition and development of public beaches. The Los Angeles Chamber of Commerce used similar tactics to great effect in the battle against air pollution, as chapter 2 illustrates.

From its founding, the Shoreline Planning Association pressed Los Angeles officials to curb sewage pollution and beach erosion and to expand public ownership. George Hjelte, the superintendent of the Los Angeles City Department of Playgrounds and Recreation, was a powerful ally. From 1940 on, he repeatedly urged the Los Angeles County supervisors to purchase private beachfront land for a vast public playground before prices rose or owners built on undeveloped parcels.[77] Some land came into public hands with little effort on the part of the SPA or anyone else. Beach clubs, dependent on membership dues for operating and mortgage expenses, fell into debt even before the Great Depression. Financial straits forced most of the beach clubs in Los Angeles to consolidate with the Los Angeles Athletic Club in the 1920s. The Los Angeles Athletic Club scraped through the Great Depression by accepting food staples and home furnishings in lieu of club dues. By 1942, however, gasoline rationing and war mobilization decreased membership so much that the Los Angeles Athletic Club had to sell off the Surf and Sand Club in Hermosa Beach, Deauville Club in Santa Monica, and the Pacific Coast Club in Long Beach. The Deauville Club remained in private hands. The Coast Guard used the Pacific Coast Club's yacht harbor, and the National Youth Administration operated the Surf and Sand Club during the war; the federal agencies declared these properties surplus after the war ended.[78] A number of private landowners facing the same economic pressures that undid the private beach clubs also disposed of their property during this period. In 1945, for example, Louis B. Mayer, Mary Pickford, and some of their neighbors offered to sell their Venice Beach homes to the city of Los Angeles for a dollar. This donation was a public-spirited way of dealing with the erosion and pollution that had so damaged their property.[79]

Elsewhere along the coast similar events led to the creation of public beaches. In 1930, for example, a group of Carpinteria residents bought the heavily mortgaged Cerca Del Mar Club and turned it over to Santa Barbara County for public use.[80] In 1936, Los Angeles city and county governments purchased more than a mile of beach property north of Santa Monica because the owners of the land could pay neither mortgages nor back taxes.[81] In 1937, the Playgrounds and Recreation Commission urged the Los Angeles City Council acquire a thousand feet of beach frontage in Venice from bankrupt owners.[82] In 1942, the Los Angeles Municipal League proposed the gradual transformation of private country clubs into public facilities by allowing cash-strapped members to transfer their interest in a club to the city or county.[83] The California State Senate considered appropriating funds for state purchase of tax-delinquent forest lands in 1943.[84] All over the state, proponents of public ownership viewed bankruptcy and tax delinquency as opportunities to increase public ownership.

The Shoreline Planning Association applauded land donations and beach purchases in the 1930s and 1940s, but it was not satisfied. Buying properties in foreclosure or taking tax-delinquent land increased public ownership, but only in the most haphazard way. The SPA wanted a comprehensive plan to ensure that city, county, and state agencies would work together to buy enough land in the right places to meet the regional needs. The SPA also wanted state aid for beach purchases; after all, oil royalties accumulated unspent in the earmarked fund for beach and park acquisition throughout the Depression and the war. Local officials were more than willing to go along with the Shoreline Planning Association on both state aid and planning. The Los Angeles City Council even passed a resolution urging state legislators to appropriate the funds to purchase "all privately-owned shoreline property" in California.[85] In December 1944, the county supervisors submitted a beach acquisition bill to the state legislature. The Shoreline Planning Association, the Los Angeles County Regional Planning Commission, and the state park commission wrote the bill together. The legislation appropriated $10 million in state funds to assist counties in buying beach lands; to get this aid, counties had to write an acceptable comprehensive plan and match state grants with either cash or beachfront acreage.[86] Because the Shoreline Planning Association was now the major author of beach master plans in the state, the comprehensive plan requirement all but codified the SPA's influence.

The legislature passed the beach bill in early 1945. By that summer, nine cities had approved a beach master plan drafted by the Shoreline Planning Association and the county regional planning commission. None of the newspapers in the county offered any objection to either the Shoreline Planning Association's influence or the master plan itself.

The plan called for significant crossing of jurisdictional boundaries; the county would use state funds to purchase private property inside the municipal borders of the city of Los Angeles.[87] Even this did not either spawn criticism or alarm defenders of local autonomy. Instead, the media cheered the ambitious beach acquisition and development program as a route to a postwar normalcy of prosperity, recreation, and public access in place of military installations and gasoline-rationing-induced travel restrictions: "There'll be parking spaces, picnic grounds, recreational areas and the public will be back into the swim of good living again."[88]

Before Angelenos could get "back into the swim of good living," however, the county still had to match state beach funds. So the Shoreline Planning Association campaigned to increase local spending for the public strands. In press releases, interviews, and reports, the association reiterated the same arguments it had used in the 1930s, calling beaches the state's "greatest natural recreational resource" and insisting that the shore ought to be "owned, protected and developed by the State for the enjoyment of the people."[89] It also appealed to patriotism and fresh memories of the war. Recalling both the war and the military training exercises held on Los Angeles beaches, it argued, "Our armed forces used the 'beaches' to beat enemy forces. They should now be able to enjoy publicly owned beaches in peace."[90] The association's Women's Division publicized the idea of a "'Living War Memorials' plan" through which donors giving money for public acquisition could name the strands after friends or relations they had lost.[91] The Haynes Foundation likewise suggested developing the Palos Verdes Peninsula shore as a war memorial park.[92] In 1946, the Shoreline Planning Association continued to urge state and local governments to buy all available beach property quickly before "public clubs and private residences" completely dominated the shore.[93] Beach acquisition plans proceeded apace over the next five or six years. In 1952, the Los Angeles City Planning Commission began revising the master plan because city, county, and state agencies had already acquired nearly all the "first priority" property identified in the 1945 plan.[94]

Although the initial postwar rush of beach purchases encountered little opposition, this changed dramatically in the 1950s. In 1948, a few individuals did protest government purchases of beach land. For example, property owners in Manhattan Beach went to court to keep their land.[95] In Ventura County, some property owners protested, too. The *Los Angeles Times* sharply criticized these opponents of public beach ownership, which suggests the political power of the public beach movement. When Orange County drafted its master plan in 1950, the city of Newport Beach opted out. There, the Central Newport Beach Community Association and the Ocean Front and Beach Protective Association fought public beaches because, they explained, the state government manipulated property taxes and property value assessments to force landowners to sell at unfair prices. These two organizations also tried to cast the issue as one of local control, criticizing state management of the beaches and arguing that the creation of state beaches threatened the character of their community.[96] The *Los Angeles Times* was silent on the Newport civic groups' rejection of the Orange County master plan. The newspaper clearly still supported public beaches. When opponents to Ventura County's 1955 beach master plan called it "'a vicious power grab' and a 'socialistic scheme'" that threatened property rights throughout the county, the *Los Angeles Times* dismissed the opponents as self-interested oil companies and real estate developers.[97] The growing opposition to the beach master plans, and the media's inconsistent critiques of them suggest that the consensus that had undergirded public beach development since the 1920s had begun to fracture. As it did so, critics increasingly portrayed the state government as a threat to democracy and community rather than their protector.[98]

By 1961, the public beach movement had completely fallen apart. When the Los Angeles County supervisors and Regional Planning Commission held public hearings on the new master plan, city officials from Hermosa Beach, Palos Verdes, and Manhattan Beach, "'alarmed at the authority of the RPC [Los Angeles Regional Planning Commission],'" demanded that the county exempt their communities from the master plan and return beaches to local control.[99] Although they had once welcomed beachgoers as a boon to the local economy, officials in these three cities now saw visitors as invading outsiders who increased traffic, burdened local services, and threatened the character of their neighborhoods.[100] Before World War II, Los Angeles area civic and elected leaders saw beaches as so important to economic growth and public recreation that such a response to a beach acquisition plan would have been unthinkable. But by 1960 these communities felt like victims of their own success, overwhelmed by ever growing crowds at public beaches, and by the associated costs of providing services to those visitors. The rejection of the 1961 master plan signaled a more substantial change in the way communities regarded their beaches. Residents now saw their beaches as a local rather than national or regional asset and viewed state-sponsored beach acquisition planning as a threat to home rule. Similar concerns about local control appeared in many other policy disputes of the postwar years, with profound implications for a host of other regional and national environmental decisions.

Segregation on Public Beaches

Using local and state resources, by 1961 Los Angeles County had set aside miles of public beaches. These beaches are still the region's primary recreational space and integral to the region's image. But this only partly explains the broad appeal of an accessible public shoreline. Public ownership protected Los Angeles County residents' recreational opportunities and attracted tourists to the region. Public strands served equally beach cities that built their economies on beachgoers and the larger aspirations of the Los Angeles Chamber of Commerce and other boosters who saw tourism as an engine for population growth, business investment, and regional prosperity. In the beaches, it appears, Los Angeles found the intersection of public and private interests, where the public good was defined in terms of public access instead of private exploitation. However, in spite of all that public beach advocates claimed, public ownership did not always guarantee all Angelenos equal access to the sea. On the contrary, most of Los Angeles's public beaches were racially segregated until the 1920s; some beaches remained so into the 1960s. African Americans and, to a lesser extent, Mexican and Asian Americans needed private beaches to have access to the shore.

Like so many other American cities, Los Angeles adopted Jim Crow segregation in the 1920s. The city parks department suddenly segregated swimming pools; real estate agents refused to show African Americans houses in white areas, and some communities adopted restrictive covenants that prohibited the sale of homes to African American buyers.[101] Even before Los Angeles fully embraced Jim Crow, the public beaches were off limits to blacks. African Americans could swim and picnic only on a half-mile stretch in southern Santa Monica called the Inkwell and on Bruce's Beach, an even smaller enclave in Manhattan Beach. These were not public beaches. Rather, private individuals had purchased beach frontage to create recreational space for Los Angeles's black community.[102] When African Americans tried to cross the color line and use other beaches, they were met with violence and often arrested for disorderly conduct or inciting riots.[103]

On several occasions, African Americans tried to improve their beach access by purchasing more frontage or building their own beach clubs. These efforts rarely succeeded. White segregationists, arguing that all private beach development hurt the public interest, pressured local officials to condemn lands that blacks had purchased. When public beaches were established on these condemned strands, segregation excluded African Americans.[104] In 1921, for example, a group of investors arranged to purchase a large beachfront lot in Santa Monica to build a "first class resort with beach access" for blacks. The proposal infuriated chamber of commerce director and Santa Monica resident Sylvester Weaver. During one chamber of commerce meeting, he blurted out, "I was born pretty far south to have that in front of my house."[105] The Santa Monica Bay Protective League blocked the project, first by persuading city officials to deny the group a building permit, then by pressuring the owners of the land to withdraw from their agreement to sell, and finally by convincing large landholders in Santa Monica to adopt restrictive covenants to prohibit home sales to blacks.[106] In 1924, this story repeated itself. In this case, Titus Alexander, a onetime city council candidate who was later recognized by the Los Angeles Chamber of Commerce for hosting black athletes during the 1932 Olympics, tried to lease beach frontage near the Hyperion Point sewage outfall. He hoped to build an "amusement resort" for African Americans but instead he got a court injunction that blocked the lease and a citywide ballot initiative to ban any leases of public beach for private development.[107] More than seven thousand voters signed the ballot petition.[108] Arthur W. Eckman, the leader of the campaign to block Alexander's lease, insisted that his was "simply a movement to keep the municipally owned beaches open, free to all the public, white and colored, and prevent them from being leased to private parties for gain," but of course he knew that public beaches were segregated in Los Angeles.[109] Most news coverage associated with this petition drive reinforced the racial elements of this conflict by describing Alexander's plans for Hyperion Point as "a recreation beach for colored people."[110] Regardless of Eckman's claims, race factored into the public response to the proposed ordinance.

An African American beach club and resort in Orange County met an even more devastating fate. In 1925, Hal R. Clark, a white attorney working with black partners, purchased seven acres of land, including a thousand feet of beach frontage, just outside Huntington Beach. He planned to build the Pacific Beach Club for African Americans there, with a dance hall, a bath house, and two hundred beach cottages. From the beginning, the project encountered fierce opposition from the Huntington Beach and Newport Beach chambers of commerce and from other Orange County civic groups.[111] In April 1925, the *Los Angeles Times* reported that "various organizations in Orange County" had persuaded the Pacific Electric and Southern Pacific railroads to prohibit the club from building an entrance road across the railroad tracks.[112] The California Railroad Commission ordered the railroads to permit the club to access its property.[113] Contractors refused to take on the project or abandoned it after beginning work.[114] Once Clark finally found a builder, he received warnings that the club would never open; carpenters at the site reported ill-concealed threats of arson.[115] On 21 January 1926, an arsonist destroyed the nearly completed clubhouse and dance hall. That night, opponents of the club petitioned the Orange County supervisors to condemn the club's land for a public park and beach. The supervisors did not act, but the *Los Angeles Times* reported that "it was said at Huntington Beach ... that the condemnation campaign now will be launched with new vigor" because arson had decreased the value of the Pacific Beach Club's land.[116]

As the club tried to recover from the fire, an effort that included a national appeal to African Americans for funds,[117] a Huntington Beach organization formed specifically to block the establishment of an African American enclave on the property. In 1927, Clark gave up and sold the land. Demands for a public beach at the site died out immediately, and there was nothing but fanfare when the whites-only South Coast Club purchased the land and opened its doors.[118] In Los Angeles County, segregation of the beaches slowly declined after an NAACP swim-in and massive arrests on Manhattan Beach in 1927. But in the 1920s, supporters of segregation, including white landowners with expensive shorefront property, used the expansion of public ownership as a tool of exclusion rather than access.

Conclusion: Business as the Voice of the Public

Public ownership and access to the beaches seem, on the face of it, a triumph of the public interest, in spite of the way that public beaches were used to halt development by and for African Americans. The public beach campaign was in part fueled by a broad, diffuse reaction against industrialization; development of city, county, and state beaches was guided by an image of the shore as a unique respite from the world of commerce. Elected officials, major newspapers, the Shoreline Planning Association, and voters not only targeted oil development as incompatible with recreation but also curbed more benign forms of privatism—beach clubs, some residential and commercial development, peddling—at the shore. Moreover, Los Angeles County refused the kinds of public-private partnerships at the beach that it celebrated in other aspects of postwar governance. The perception of the beach as uniquely public persisted through the 1950s; Los Angeles city and county planners received praise for advocating and coordinating public purchases of private beach property in years when other proposed expansions of public authority were loudly decried as dangerous, socialistic, and un-American.

Although justified as protecting public prerogatives, the public beaches did not result from an inclusive political process. The members of the Shoreline Planning Association took it upon themselves to craft a public beach acquisition program for Los Angeles County. They had no real expertise or official status but were well organized, astute, and reliable political allies. Goaded by public outcry against pier and shoreline drilling, local officials looked to the Shoreline Planning Association for policy recommendations. The SPA had proposals ready when public officials needed them. Its ability to respond proactively encouraged public officials to depend on the association. By 1945, this dependence permitted the SPA to write its influence into state legislation. This same combination of cooperation and support earned other business organizations comparable influence over a huge variety of local policy questions from air pollution and flood control to water resources planning and development.

The Shoreline Planning Association ultimately became the recognized authority on beach development and, in policy debates, the voice of the public. Broad public support for public, recreational beach development reinforced this status. But the relative lack of controversy reflected the special category of beaches rather than something unique about the relationship between the SPA and the larger Los Angeles public. The SPA, like other business groups, pursued its self-interests and protected its influence. The Shoreline Planning Association's board of directors included directors of the Los Angeles and suburban chambers of commerce and real estate organizations. The ties between the SPA and the real estate business make the group's self-interest obvious. The connections between these organizations made city, county, and state officials—already familiar with chambers of commerce and realty boards—predisposed to trust the Shoreline Planning Association. Close institutional affiliations also explain why the SPA's political strategies closely mimicked those of the Los Angeles Chamber of Commerce.[119] The relationship between the public and the SPA is more difficult to assess. The *Los Angeles Times* and other area newspapers focused their reporting on criticizing private ownership that barred Angelenos from the beaches; the media did not report negative reactions to the Shoreline Planning Association or its proposals. Angelenos did use beaches regularly, in huge numbers. They visited even filthy quarantined beaches by the millions in the 1940s. These numbers alone lend some credibility to the Shoreline Planning Association's allegation that people living throughout Los Angeles County supported the association's goals, or at the very least, welcomed whatever public beaches the SPA and city, county, or state governments created.

The biggest difference, then, between the public beach campaign and the policy issues to be discussed in the remainder of this book is not who proposed or influenced public policy but the fact that neither the Shoreline Planning Association's designation as a representative of the public interest nor the organization's goal of expanded public ownership seemed to have given rise to public acrimony or to have prompted other groups to challenge the SPA's political legitimacy between the 1920s and the 1950s. The story of Los Angeles's public beaches demonstrates who shaped Los Angeles politics and who did not: business and industry retained considerable clout in the city, even as Los Angeles struggled with the consequences of industrial growth and even as industry served as an easy rhetorical target for discontent. In more contentious policy debates, such as air pollution or flood control, it became harder to determine who could really claim to speak for the people as a whole. Nevertheless, business interests generally enjoyed unfettered access to policy debates and won contests over political legitimacy. In the case of the beaches, the business interests secured their status by selecting easy targets—oil rigs and private development on the shoreline—and then institutionalizing their own status in the shoreline planning process. The next chapters examine how the business community secured its influence in more contentious arenas.

CHAPTER TWO

INFLUENCE THROUGH COOPERATION

The Los Angeles Chamber of Commerce and Air Pollution Control in Los Angeles, 1943–1954

In the summer of 1943, an acrid cloud settled over downtown Los Angeles. On the streets below, cars collided as "lacrimous fumes" blinded drivers.¹ City officials received letter after letter complaining that the smoke destroyed the community, "depressed . . . [the] spirits," interfered with the pursuit of happiness, and threatened the public health.² Thus began a decades-long battle to control both air pollution and policy in Los Angeles. Within a few months of the "gas attacks," as newspapers called the 1943 smog events, city and county officials began to treat the Los Angeles Chamber of Commerce as the representative of the Los Angeles public and to dismiss other groups that tried to redirect air pollution control policies. The very controversy over smog reinforced the business community's political influence; in their struggle to clean Los Angeles's skies, beleaguered public officials needed all the political support and practical assistance that the chamber of commerce could give them.

The Los Angeles Chamber of Commerce enjoyed enormous influence over air pollution policy in Los Angeles County. For decades, city and then county officials treated the LAACC as the representative of the public interest. The business organization achieved this status by assisting and supporting public officials as they tackled what became a chronic urban problem. The LAACC anticipated public policy needs and endorsed early proposals for uniform, countywide regulation. The group secured further legitimacy by enforcing voluntary smoke reductions by its members and sponsoring air pollution research and state legislation. Its proactive responses to air pollution were something of an anomaly; in other cities, business and manufacturing organizations had fought soot and smoke reduction on the grounds that reducing

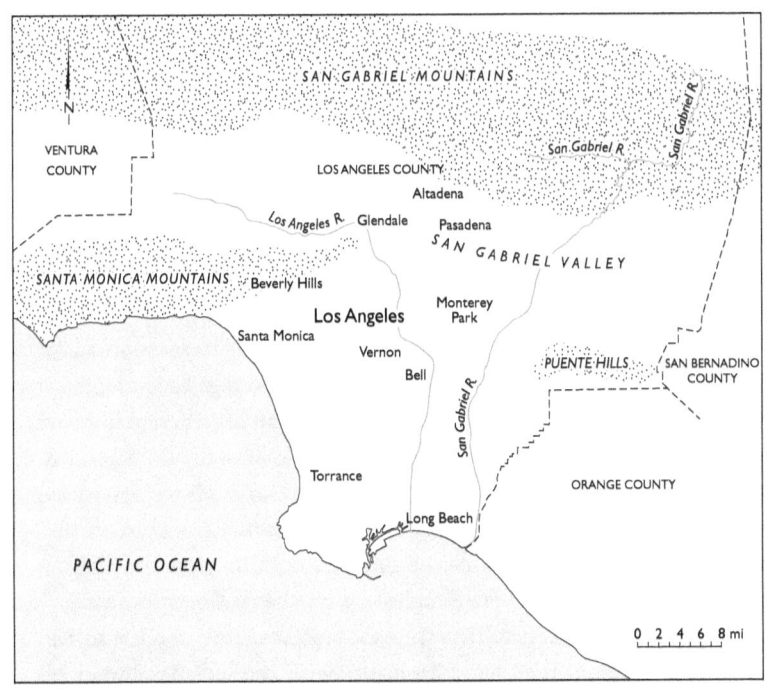

Communities active in Los Angeles air pollution debates, 1943–1950

smoke would hinder profits and productivity.³ The LAACC's cooperation contributed to Los Angeles's progress against air pollution while firmly establishing the group's influence on local policy.

The Los Angeles Chamber of Commerce was just as important to air pollution controls as the Shoreline Planning Association was to the establishment of Los Angeles's public beaches. In contrast to the activities of the Shoreline Planning Association, however, the Los Angeles Chamber of Commerce's air pollution activities excited significant criticism. A number of different organizations arose during the first decades of the battle against smog. These critics complained that public officials did too little to reduce the industrial pollution that everyone knew really caused Los Angeles's problems. They protested the lack of attention to public health research and complained that air pollution regulations focused too narrowly on economics. Their criticisms grew out of several convictions, including general antipathy toward large corporations and the suspicion that official policy harmed Los Angeles residents but protected industrial interests. This was the same suspicion of industry that was manifest in the campaign to remove oil wells from Los Angeles's beaches in the 1920s and, as chapter 3 shows, drove opposition to Whittier Narrows Dam in the 1930s and 1940s. Through all of this, these organizations disputed the LAACC's right to speak for the general public but still failed to establish the crucial relationships that gave the LAACC its influence. They were too small, fleeting, and late to gain political traction. Their opposition, moreover, pushed air pollution officials and the LAACC closer together.

Los Angeles was not the first industrial city to address air quality. Cincinnati and Pittsburgh instituted regulations to reduce smoke in the 1860s and 1870s; efforts to control coal smoke through regulation and industrial zoning spread to many other cities in succeeding decades. By 1912 all but five American cities of two hundred thousand or more residents had some sort of smoke abatement program in place.[4] These antismoke campaigns pitted urban reformers concerned with urban sanitation against defenders of industrial prosperity; reformers did not gain political traction until they successfully defined smoke as a sign of industrial inefficiency. Antismoke regulations in Pittsburgh, Chicago, and Saint Louis improved air quality by reducing the soot and sulfur compounds associated with incomplete combustion in coal fires. Saint Louis achieved great success by forcing residents and industry to switch from soft bituminous coal to harder, cleaner-burning anthracite. Some industries opted to install scrubbers and other technology to capture soot in their smoke stacks. Other regulations changed fire-building and fueling practices in industrial boilers or tightly controlled railroad engine operations.[5] But the smoke control techniques that helped coal-burning cities offered little to hydroelectric-and oil-powered Southern California. The small gains that these older smoke control strategies did bring to Los Angeles were quickly overwhelmed by the city's explosive wartime growth.

Los Angeles did not defeat smog until the Clean Air Act of 1970 mandated installation of catalytic converters on all vehicles. In the first decade of the twenty-first century, even these gains were overwhelmed by the huge numbers of low-mileage vehicles on the road. Nevertheless, cooperation between the LAACC and public officials in the 1940s yielded policies that reduced visible smoke and many industrial pollutants in Los Angeles's skies. These regulations could not eliminate smog entirely because local authorities could not reduce emissions from automobiles. The persistence of smog spawned opposition to both official air pollution policy and the LAACC's role in creating that policy, but critics of the official antismog policies, and there were many of them, had an extremely difficult time getting the official smoke control agencies to listen to them. This chapter examines how the chamber of commerce acquired and defended its special status and how the relationship between the business community and elected officials affected policy making in Los Angeles. The LAACC did not, as the Shoreline Planning Association had, write its influence into legislation. Instead, the LAACC cemented its influence by making itself indispensable to public officials and by defending its status as the voice of the public.

Smog Arrives

Newspapers treated the clouds of smoke and fumes that descended on downtown Los Angeles as unprecedented and unnatural. There had been signs of growing air quality problems for several years before the crisis hit. In 1939, for example, aviation authorities called haze in downtown Los Angeles, Pasadena, and Altadena "a serious menace to safe flying."[6] In July 1940, complaints about eye-stinging fumes at the Civic Center and Hall of Records prompted the city health department to investigate.[7] In this first study of Los Angeles air pollution, the Los Angeles City Health Department attributed the discomfort reported by visitors to the Civic Center to "industrial waste, smoke, gases and fumes" including formaldehyde, ammonia, sulfuric acid, and other chemicals from "foundries, oil refineries, chemical manufacturing plants, fish canneries, smelters, electroplating plants, fertilizer plants, packing plants, soap factories and waste disposal plants" trapped in "an air pocket."[8] This report received little attention from local newspapers. In fact, haze, fumes, and other forms of air pollution went almost unreported until the "daylight dimouts" hit the region in 1943.[9] Significantly, in 1940 the health department drew the same conclusions about air pollution that the general public did; this perception of air pollution as an industrial problem would persist well into the 1950s.

From July to October 1943, newspapers ran reports on the downtown fumes almost daily. Most of them identified a single industrial plant, a Southern California Gas Company facility on Aliso Street, as the source of the city's misery. For four months, the city council and mayor's office were besieged with complaints about this downtown plant. The Jewelers Union Local 33, for example, begged the city council for relief from eye-stinging fumes that caused "untold hardship and suffering" and "loss of working time and wages."[10] A stenographer in the U.S. Engineers Office compared "that screwy synthetic plant" to a piggery that "nice people ... can't be around" and demanded, "Why can't *you* do something about it? Aren't you important at all?"[11] Physicians at Los Angeles General Hospital complained, too,[12] and a judge blamed fumes from the butadiene plant for making the courtroom so unpleasant that he had to suspend hearings for a day.[13]

Southern California Gas produced butadiene at the Aliso Street plant for the Rubber Reserve Corporation's synthetic rubber program. City and county officials, therefore, could not regulate this facility without federal approval.[14] Even so, in August, Los Angeles mayor Fletcher Bowron began pressuring Southern California Gas to abate the nuisance by shutting down the butadiene plant, or failing that, by curbing operations during the temperature inversions that trapped noxious fumes downtown. Southern California Gas initially resisted these proposals, citing the importance of butadiene to synthetic rubber production and the war effort. In mid-September, when Bowron threatened legal action, Southern California Gas agreed to curb production during adverse weather and to install cooling equipment designed to reduce fume output.[15] The "gas attacks" persisted into October; Bowron persuaded the city council to seek an injunction to halt butadiene production entirely.[16] This finally brought the Rubber Reserve Corporation into the air pollution fray. Bradley Dewey, the director of that agency, traveled to Los Angeles in October 1943 to defend the Aliso Street plant. He accused Bowron of interfering with the war effort and insisted that butadiene production continue unless fumes from the plant began to hinder other war work. Southern California Gas echoed Dewey's arguments in a massive public relations campaign that may have eased political pressure on the plant in the short term but did nothing to alter public perceptions of fumes as an industrial problem.[17]

In the midst of the city's efforts to curb pollution from the butadiene plant, on 4 October 1943, the Los Angeles City Council asked the Los Angeles County Board of Supervisors to pass an ordinance to control smoke from industries in unincorporated county territory. When he initiated this request, city councilmember Carl Rasmussen explained, "It appears a substantial part of the smoke and fumes throughout the city originate in county territory beyond the control of the City Council."[18] The fact that fumes persisted even when Southern California Gas closed the plant may have prompted Rasmussen to turn his attention to other polluters; however, Rasmussen and his colleagues knew as well as anyone that a great number of the region's heaviest industries were located outside Los Angeles city limits. Air pollution did not stay near these plants but moved across the basin to hang over the San Gabriel Valley and other nonindustrial communities. The city council's eager adoption of Rasmussen's resolution signaled municipal authorities' recognition that they could not manage a regional problem like air pollution. Of course, county action also protected Los Angeles municipal interests. If the city alone regulated industrial smoke, the city council risked imposing burdens on Los Angeles city industries that enterprises outside municipal limits would not face and thus either handicapping local businesses or encouraging them to relocate outside city limits. Neither would help Los Angeles improve its air quality or economy. To the city council's great disappointment, the board of supervisors did not pass a county smoke control ordinance. Instead, it appointed a county smoke and fumes commission to investigate air pollution problems in Los Angeles and in the San Gabriel Valley.[19]

The Los Angeles Chamber of Commerce's First Bid for Influence

In November 1943, rain and cooler weather dispersed smoke and fumes from downtown Los Angeles and the foothill cities, abating the air quality crisis. Angelenos and their elected officials turned their attention to rationing, war-related labor problems, and the progress of the war. Smog returned, though, in the summer of 1944. The Los Angeles County Board of Supervisors called on Joseph B. Ficklen of the U.S. Health Service to study the problem; he received more complaints about air pollution from Angelenos than his staff could hope to answer. These included a petition signed by three hundred Manhattan Beach residents begging Ficklen to do something about the fumes wafting over their homes from the Standard Oil and General Chemical facilities in El Segundo and numerous letters from passengers complaining about fumes on the Ashbury Transportation Company's buses. The county board of supervisors, Mayor Bowron, and the Los Angeles City Council also received a barrage of grievances.[20] Twenty citizens attending one meeting about smog "protested so vociferously" that the district attorney promised to prosecute the polluter he judged the "worst offender" for violating county nuisance laws.[21] The *Los Angeles Daily News* dismissed these protests as a sort of mass hysteria, but no one else did.[22]

City and county officials changed their approaches to air pollution in 1944. County officials began to take greater initiative, which left city officials to criticize, compete, and cooperate with county initiatives. Two civic organizations, the Altadena Property Owners League and the Los Angeles Chamber of Commerce, now entered the fray. The Altadena

Property Owners League was a neighborhood improvement organization based in the unincorporated foothill community of Altadena. Its membership included the publisher of the local newspaper, the *Altadenan*, and the manager of Altadena Savings and Loan Bank. The APOL took on air pollution because Altadena and its San Gabriel Valley neighbors suffered mightily from smog but had few industrial plants of their own. The APOL wanted two things: aggressive regulation of industrial pollution, and county-based enforcement of smoke rules. Its members' emphasis on county administration grew in part from their status as residents of an unincorporated community; Altadenans had no local government to turn to for relief aside from the county supervisors. The Altadena Property Owners League was later credited with introducing the idea of uniform countywide smoke regulations for the Los Angeles region.[23] County supervisors did not immediately implement the APOL's demands, but a county health department study released in early August 1944 supported the league's analysis of the problem when it blamed Altadena's smoke and fumes problem on factories and oil refineries located all over the county.[24]

When the Los Angeles Chamber of Commerce joined the air pollution control debates in 1944, it concurred with the Altadena Property Owners League that the Los Angeles region needed uniform, countywide smoke rules. The chamber of commerce feared that a patchwork of municipal rules would burden industries in some communities while leaving others virtually unregulated. Such inconsistent regulations, it felt, would fail by allowing pollution to continue unabated in under-regulated areas and handicapping firms operating in cities with strict regulations. Persistent pollution, in turn, would feed public demands for ever more stringent industrial regulations while depriving proactive cities of economic growth and industrial tax bases.[25] The LAACC had reason to fear both ineffective smoke controls and what it saw as excessive public attention to industrial effluent. Around this same time, the president of the APOL publicly threatened, "If the authorities don't do something about this, the people will."[26] The LAACC read this as a warning that failure to improve Los Angeles's air quality would inspire a massive public outcry against industry. To forestall escalating public anger and to protect the economic viability of Los Angeles industry, the chamber of commerce mobilized. Within a year it eclipsed the Altadena Property Owners League as the main citizen advocate of air pollution regulations.

In October 1944, the LAACC created a smoke and fumes committee, headed by Morris B. Pendleton. At the time, Pendleton was the president of a Los Angeles–based hand tool manufacturing company named Plomb Tool. He was also a member of the All Year Club, a group of boosters funded by the city of Los Angeles and the chamber of commerce to promote Los Angeles as a year-round tourist destination, and vice chair of the Citizens' Manpower Committee, which was appointed by Mayor Bowron to investigate housing, childcare, and labor problems created by World War II. By the time he died in 1985, Pendleton held positions on the boards of the Los Angeles Metropolitan YMCA, Goodwill Industries of Southern California, and the San Gabriel Valley Boy Scouts, among others.[27] Under Pendleton's leadership, the LAACC smoke committee sponsored studies of air pollution predicated on the assumption that air pollution in the Los Angeles region did "not originate exclusively from the operation of industrial plants" but also spewed from household incinerators, car exhaust, sewage, and boiler smoke.[28] The committee was right, of course, but that did not convince Angelenos to stop blaming industry for their troubles.

In a pointed challenge to the Altadena Property Owners League, in October 1944 the LAACC announced that Altadena and the foothill cities suffered as much because of the smoke issuing from open dumps and the small incinerators nearly everyone used in their backyards as from the factories and refineries across the county. This view of the problem cheered Fletcher Bowron, deluged as he was with complaints that Los Angeles pollution harmed the San Gabriel Valley cities.[29] Even so, Pendleton and the LAACC did not ignore industrial pollution. As Pendleton constantly reminded his LAACC colleagues, public anger could become "a source of harassment to Southern California industry of all sorts."[30] In other words, Pendleton argued that local industries could not afford to simply oppose air pollution regulations. So he urged all LAACC members to reduce their smoke, to pressure their fellows to do the same, and, failing that, to support government action to "take care of the recalcitrant members of industry who will not listen to reason."[31] Pendleton's strategy of research, policy recommendations, and voluntary smoke reductions made the Los Angeles Chamber of Commerce a useful ally for public officials tackling air quality problems and eventually convinced Bowron not only to consult with the chamber of commerce but also to demand that the county include the LAACC in its air pollution policy deliberations.

The competition for influence between the Altadena Property Owners League and the Los Angeles Chamber of Commerce revealed itself explicitly in the fall of 1944. The APOL pressed the county supervisors to regulate smoke density from industries operating in unincorporated Los Angeles County. In August, the Los Angeles County Board of Supervisors announced that it would begin drafting a county smoke ordinance. Then, in September, the Altadena Property Owners League also proposed the appointment of a "fumes czar" to oversee all air pollution control activities in the county.[32] The LAACC watched both the progress of the county smoke ordinance and the APOL's rhetoric with alarm. In their meetings, LAACC directors dismissed the APOL as part of a "hysterical movement" that was threatening lawsuits and "attempting to get up an argument with us."[33] When, in September 1944, the city of Los Angeles announced its plans to bring nuisance charges against five companies operating and polluting in the city, the LAACC warned that "precipitate action at this time could seriously hamper war production."[34] "We not believe," the business leaders cautioned, "that citizens demanding hurried action or attempting to short circuit the smoke and fumes commission or the health officers can bring about a satisfactory solution of the problem."[35] Instead, they urged city officials to take into account the fact that military production prevented industry from acquiring or making the kinds of equipment that they needed to reduce pollution.[36] Thus, the LAACC strove to counter the APOL's influence and promote a smog policy that was based on voluntary cooperation and improved efficiency in industrial operations—a policy that would be generally more amenable to Los Angeles's industrial sector.

While the LAACC, county supervisors, city officials, and the Altadena Property Owners League debated regulatory strategy, the Los Angeles County Smoke and Fumes Commission began its own investigation of air pollution.[37] The county supervisors had appointed this commission in October 1943 to study the Aliso Street butadiene plant and had originally instructed the group to report on the best means to regulate industrial pollution and the implications of regulations for the Los Angeles region's economy. Supervisors specifically directed the commission's attention to smoke from industrial processing and from the smudge pots that citrus farmers used to protect their orchards from cold weather.[38] The LACSFC met with representatives from the county engineering, planning, fire, and building and safety departments; the county counsel; the district attorney; and the county grand jury, as well as the Los Angeles City Board of Health, the Los Angeles Chamber of Commerce, and major regional newspapers.[39] The Altadena Property Owners League and similar groups were conspicuously absent from this list.

In its preliminary reports, the LACSFC largely confirmed the Los Angeles Chamber of Commerce's analysis of the smog problem. In September 1944, the commission identified burning dumps, domestic incinerators, and vehicles as major sources of fumes. But it also blamed Los Angeles's geography, which prevented smoke from Los Angeles's growing industries from blowing away.[40] A report issued the previous March had compared the butadiene fumes to tear gas and described the alarming impact of air pollution on war production when workers lost sleep due to irritation of their eyes and throat.[41] The commission now found that manufacturers in the city of Los Angeles emitted enough fumes to create a "public nuisance" but that oil refineries and industries located in other parts of the Los Angeles basin produced most of the smoke and fumes that plagued the region. Significantly the commission also warned that cities acting alone could never solve air quality problems.[42] Municipal powers were too limited. City officials could not regulate polluters located outside their boundaries. Nor could they use nuisance laws to prosecute polluters because they could not link specific plants to particular pollution problems. This same difficulty in apportioning responsibility for large-scale problems has continued to frustrate environmental regulators into the twenty-first century. But Los Angeles's air pollution problems ran still deeper. Many of the communities in the region with the greatest concentrations of polluting industries had no smoke ordinances at all. In some suburbs, industry so dominated local government that elected officials had no incentive to regulate factories and refineries. In others, local populations did not demand air quality regulations, either because they depended on polluting industries for their livelihood or because smoke and fumes did not linger where they lived and worked. The LACSFC, therefore, urged the Los Angeles County Board of Supervisors to place air pollution control in the hands of an independent smoke abatement bureau modeled after bureaus created in Chicago and other eastern cities or, failing that, to adopt uniform smoke regulations for the entire county.[43]

The Los Angeles County Smoke and Fumes Commission's 1944 reports, with their recommendations for uniform, regional smoke controls and their careful attention to nonindustrial sources of pollution, should have put the Los Angeles Chamber of Commerce at ease. But the LAACC remained worried that continued public pressure would force the county board of supervisors to adopt rigid, impractical regulations. The LAACC did not oppose measures to reduce industrial pollution, but Morris Pendleton believed that industry could do its part by taking such moderate steps as maintaining industrial boilers and capturing valuable by-products in their smokestacks. To prove his point, he cited the Riverside Portland Cement Company, which collected and sold enough arsenic to cover the costs of installing state-of-the-art electrolysis dust collectors in its smokestacks. Pendleton did not see the LACSFC as the right group to help either industry or county officials reduce smoke and fumes because he saw the commission's technical staff as "university engineers" who did not know enough about plant operations to give industry or city officials any practical advice.[44] At the same time, the LAACC reiterated that it did "not believe that citizens demanding hurried action or attempting to short circuit the [Los Angeles County Smoke and Fumes] Commission or the Health officers can bring about a satisfactory solution of the problem."[45]

To protect its interests and counter the influence of the Altadena Property Owners League, the LAACC drafted a smoke control ordinance for the county. Although the APOL offered county supervisors suggestions for what a smoke ordinance should include, it had not actually drafted sample legislation.[46] Although they revised it heavily, the supervisors did use the LAACC's text as the basis of a model ordinance in October 1944. The county's ordinance set a maximum allowable smoke density from stationary smokestacks and thus imposed regulations on industries and on open pit dumps that burned waste. But the proposed law exempted many other polluters deemed problematic by the LACSFC or the Los Angeles Chamber of Commerce, including railroads; steamships, buses, and trucks; backyard incinerators; and smoky fires that citrus farmers used to protect their orchards from frost damage.[47] This disappointed the LAACC; it had hoped for something more comprehensive. Even so, Pendleton urged his colleagues to support the county ordinance, reassuring the LAACC directors that city and county officials had deliberately written a limited ordinance in order to get some kind of legislation on the books and that city, county, and even federal officials had promised to consult with the LAACC's own smoke committee before enacting any changes to local air pollution legislation.

Its influence with the county supervisors assured, the LAACC backed the October 1944 ordinance. But the chamber of commerce was one of the few groups that did. Because county ordinances applied only to unincorporated territory, the supervisors, the LAACC, and the Altadena Property Owners League all hoped incorporated municipalities would adopt the county ordinance and thus create uniform, countywide air pollution regulations.[48] Unfortunately, the model ordinance received a chilly reception from local newspapers and municipal governments. The *Los Angeles Times* attacked the county's authority over smoke control and criticized the supervisors for drafting an ordinance that conflicted with state laws requiring, for example, beekeepers to burn diseased apiaries, and state employees to burn brush and abandoned orchards.[49] By 1946 most cities in the county still refused to adopt the model ordinance.[50]

In the face of this disappointment, the LAACC continued to strengthen its influence with local public officials. In November 1944, when the county smoke and fumes commission began planning a countywide conference on industrial pollution, the LAACC prevailed on Fletcher Bowron to lobby the LACSFC to allow Pendleton's chamber of commerce smoke committee to organize the conference. Bowron did so, arguing that LAACC leadership would broadcast a powerful message about the chamber's "willingness to seek a solution" to municipal officials and to other businesses throughout the county. In a letter to Pendleton, Bowron explicitly acknowledged the LAACC's legitimacy in smog policy debates, describing the commission as "merely some citizens that have no more authority and far less representation than your own committee."[51] This exchange also reveals how industrial pollution and regulation brought Bowron and the LAACC together. Their shared interest in preserving the city of Los Angeles's industrial economy drew them into a close working relationship that guaranteed the Los Angeles Chamber of Commerce a voice in air pollution policy debates for many years. This first round of debates over the county smoke ordinance also demonstrates how the LAACC's support for much-criticized smoke control efforts and officials gave it access and influence.

The 1944 model ordinance revealed the LAACC's growing power in air policy, but it did not live up to the chamber of commerce's expectations. It established a county smoke control agency headed by H. O. Swartout, who was also the head of the Los Angeles County Health Department. But the county's authority was so limited that effective smoke control still rested on municipal action. Few cities in the Los Angeles basin adopted either the county's model ordinance or any other air pollution regulations in 1944 or 1945. Several of the most heavily industrialized cities did not even participate in countywide conferences on smoke control in 1945.[52] Their inaction precipitated a great deal of criticism of city and county governments by the local press and by Angelenos themselves. More protests erupted because Swartout seemed unwilling to aggressively enforce smoke limits on industrial polluters. Even before he took over county smoke enforcement efforts, Swartout had publicly announced that wartime conditions prevented aggressive smoke abatement.[53] To the county supervisors, Swartout expressed great sympathy for industrial polluters, warning that an overenthusiastic effort to curb pollution would damage the region's economy and insisting that he would enforce only those rules "with benefit to the community and with profit to many smoke producers."[54] The LAACC, for its part, consistently praised the city and county for their cautious and "reasonable" approaches in the face of near universal public criticism from individuals, newspapers, and other industry groups.[55] This

An Air Pollution Control inspector and a maintenance foreman for Pacific Telephone and Telegraph survey thick clouds of smog in downtown Los Angeles. "Smog Control in Downtown Los Angeles," 7 Dec. 1948. *Los Angeles Examiner* Negatives Collection 1950-1961. Courtesy of Doheny Memorial Library, University of Southern California, Los Angeles, California.

encouraged elected officials, under siege as smog evolved into a perennial summer plague, to see the Los Angeles Chamber of Commerce as an important ally.

The Los Angeles County Air Pollution Control District under Fire

Although Swartout, the Los Angeles Chamber of Commerce, and many others made much of the way the war interfered with smoke abatement, air pollution control efforts fared little better after the war. By August 1946, only four cities had adopted the county smoke ordinance: Glendale, South Pasadena, Beverly Hills, and Bell. More municipalities joined them in the next few months, but at least two of the region's most industrial cities, Vernon and Torrance, had no intention of adopting pollution regulations. This failure of the informal regional effort fed demands for a stronger regulatory institution.[56] At the beginning of the 1947 legislative session, Pasadena's representative to the California State Assembly, A. I. Stewart, introduced a bill to authorize California counties to create air pollution control districts with authority over even those polluters located inside incorporated municipalities.[57] This measure, Assembly Bill No. 1, reflected the numerous public hearings, protests, and meetings held throughout 1946; it also bore the imprint of the Foothill Cities Smog Abatement Committee, a group that Stewart had joined as Pasadena's city director. The chambers of commerce of California, Los Angeles, and Pasadena; the Los Angeles division of League of California Cities; and the Automobile Club of Southern California all endorsed Stewart's bill.[58]

At this time, Harold W. Kennedy, counsel for Los Angeles County, accused most of Los Angeles's industrial organizations of secretly opposing strong air pollution regulations. He attributed their quiescence to the influence of a few business leaders "public spirited enough" to convince their colleagues not to oppose the bill. Two of these "public spirited" leaders were William Jeffers, the president of Union Pacific Railroad and later chair of the Los Angeles County Air Pollution Control District's Citizens Smog Advisory Committee, and William Stewart, a vice president of Union Oil Company. Ironically, the oil, railroad, and lumber industries worked the hardest to gut the bill. Even those who ignored Jeffers and Stewart tempered their public statements against the bill, however, because they recognized the "serious public relations problem" that open opposition to Assembly Bill No. 1 would create. The California legislature approved Stewart's bill almost unanimously, and Governor Earl Warren signed it into law on 10 June 1947.[59]

In October 1947, the Los Angeles County supervisors established the Los Angeles County Air Pollution Control District and hired Louis McCabe as its first director. A University of Illinois–educated geologist, McCabe began his career working for the Mississippi Coal Corporation and the Illinois Geological Survey. During World War II, he served in the Quartermaster General's Office and managed coal production and distribution in Belgium as a member of General Dwight D. Eisenhower's staff. Los Angeles hired him away from the U.S. Bureau of Mines, where he was chief of the coal division. Based on his experience with coal and coal-burning industries, McCabe understood smog, as Los Angeles's air quality problem was now widely known, as a product of sulfur dioxide and particulates in dense smoke. Sulfur dioxide attracted attention in Los Angeles as the most likely of the invisible components of industrial smoke to cause the eye and lung irritation and the other physical symptoms most often reported during smoggy days in Los Angeles. Sulfur compounds were also blamed for the air pollution deaths in the Meuse River valley, Belgium, in 1930 and in Donora, Pennsylvania, in the fall of 1948.[60]

McCabe planned to reduce particulates and sulfur in the air by imposing strict regulations on all known sources of pollution, including household incinerators as well as "oil refineries, chemical plants, oil burning industries, and rubbish dumps." His broad approach satisfied no one; rather, angry Angelenos accused him of "playing politics with smog control."[61] McCabe's proposal that Angelenos cease burning rubbish in their small backyard incinerators prompted surprisingly robust protests. Incensed residents protested that restrictions on their incinerators would increase the costs of waste disposal and would accomplish "nothing... to eliminate smog conditions in Southern California." The harshest critics of the household incinerator ban calculated that the frequent rounds by diesel garbage trucks and combustion of rubbish in municipal incinerators would produce nearly as much smoke as households had by burning their own waste at home.[62] McCabe had actually recommended that municipalities build sanitary landfills rather than incinerators, but most communities including the city of Los Angeles opted for centralized incinerators to save on the cost of land and transportation for cut-and-fill dumps.[63] Municipal incinerators operated properly at high temperatures did pollute less than burning waste in open pit dumps and household incinerators had, but they still created more air pollution than sanitary landfills would have. McCabe did not succeed in banning household incinerators outright; both the APCD's efforts to eliminate this source of pollution and vehement protests against the inconvenience and expense of an incinerator ban continued for another decade.

Industries protested nearly as much as the residents who wanted to keep using their backyard incinerators. When McCabe identified sulfur dioxide from oil refineries and chemical plants as the "chief cause of smog in Los Angeles," the Western Oil and Gas Association demanded proof and insisted that the APCD delay regulations until the district had it.[64] McCabe rejected the Western Oil and Gas Association's demand for further research as a delaying tactic. "We must get the control program started and do the research job along with it," he angrily retorted, "otherwise we may fool around for years."[65] Of course, McCabe had no plans to shut industries down. Under his direction, the APCD developed a system of operating permits that allowed manufacturers to stay in business while they worked to reduce their smoke. First, the APCD issued each plant a temporary permit regardless of the amount of smog it produced. Once a company met specific emissions standards based on "existing and economically feasible methods of control," the APCD granted it a permanent permit. If a polluter refused to cooperate, the APCD could cancel the temporary permit.[66] The permit system encouraged cooperation between the regulators in the APCD and the region's businesses, something that both the LAACC and key public officials such as Fletcher Bowron and county supervisor John Anson Ford had long advocated. But the permit system also made the APCD vulnerable to enormous criticism.[67]

In 1948, McCabe found himself in the middle of a gathering storm. The permit system prompted citizen groups and individuals to accuse the APCD, and McCabe personally, of allowing the region's filthiest factories to continue polluting and of imposing more rigid standards on some industries than others.[68] State legislators criticized McCabe for neglecting his public responsibilities because he based pollution targets on available technology rather than on public health.[69] The Western Oil and Gas Association, still critical of McCabe's particular attention to refinery emissions, hired the Stanford Research Institute to study smog, hoping this would exonerate the petroleum industry.[70] At least in the public mind, the Western Oil and Gas Association's protests were proven groundless when a major strike shut down more than fifty Los Angeles area refineries for a week in September 1948. The *Los Angeles Times* announced, "Bingo! Just like that approximately 6/7ths of the 'smog'... thinned out from the air over Los Angeles." Even this led to even more accusations that McCabe was "valiantly covering up for the darling big shot oil refineries and other 'to heck with the people, we're out to make profits' industrial producers and dispensers of poison gas."[71] Now William M. Jeffers, the chair of the Citizens Smog Advisory Committee in 1947 and initially one of the APCD's boosters, joined the chorus of criticism, declaring that county officials had "more or less obligated themselves to industry and business" and had promised business and industry "more than a square deal."[72] In November 1948, he announced that he would no longer attend Los Angeles City Council meetings on smog because city officials ignored the voices and suffering of the majority of its constituents.[73] In just two years, a disenchanted Jeffers had become one of the APCD's most vocal critics. McCabe, caught between public frustration and industry resistance, left Los Angeles under a cloud of public rancor in 1949. Some critics saw even McCabe's departure as evidence of an industrial conspiracy, insisting that McCabe lost his job because he took on the petroleum industry.[74]

The Los Angeles Chamber of Commerce had mixed success shaping air pollution policy during McCabe's short time with the APCD. McCabe had sought out the LAACC's assistance, thus increasing its influence. In 1948, the LAACC helped ease tensions between the oil industry and the APCD by endorsing the permit system and participating in a series of crucial negotiations after which the Independent Refiners Association of California, the Petroleum Industry Committee on Smoke and Fumes, and Union Oil finally withdrew their objections to APCD policies.[75] At the same time, the LAACC tried to weaken Assembly Bill No. 1 in the legislature and joined other industries in trying to delay industrial regulation, which frustrated McCabe and threatened to undermine the LAACC's reputation as a key ally of county pollution control efforts. When Robert L. Daugherty, a professor of mechanical engineering at Caltech and the chair of the APCD's Citizens Smog Advisory Committee, began to press McCabe to invest more time in research and to meet frequently with the chamber of commerce, the LAACC lost further ground. McCabe angrily reported that Daugherty "was sucked in and used by the Chamber of Commerce crowd." He complained, "The Chamber is trying to tell me what to do and I am suspicious."[76]

LAACC Support for the APCD

McCabe's departure in 1949 did little to change either public opinion or APCD smog abatement strategy. The county board of supervisors promoted McCabe's assistant director, Gordon Larson, to head the APCD. He largely continued his predecessor's policies. But in addition to the routine complaints from Angelenos and local industries, the APCD now faced criticism from the California legislature. Randall Dickey, a Republican from the San Francisco Bay Area community of Alameda and chair of the Assembly Interim Committee on Water and Air Pollution, introduced a series of proposals to transfer air pollution regulation from county to state government. According to Dickey, the APCD failed Los Angeles by basing emissions standards on existing technologies, issuing operating permits to polluting industries, and enacting other policies that did not significantly improve air quality. In November 1950, Dickey convened three days of hearings in Los Angeles to investigate the APCD and find evidence to support a transfer of air pollution control to the state government. These hearings ultimately did little to alter APCD policy. They may have reversed the tension between the LAACC and the APCD. Dickey's hearings certainly revealed the deep public frustration the APCD and the huge gap between public and official understanding of smog.[77]

Randall Dickey's smog policy recommendations were contradictory and the motivations for his attacks on the APCD unclear. His challenges to the APCD began in late 1949 when he declared voluntary smoke reductions superior to the APCD's government-imposed regulation and insisted that local officials throughout California delay smoke regulation until definitive research revealed the causes and health consequences of smog.[78] In 1955, Dickey criticized the APCD for focusing too narrowly on industrial pollution and accused the agency of forcing small industrial firms to buy ruinously expensive abatement equipment that ultimately did little to reduce smog, and he reiterated his attack on government regulation of industrial emissions.[79] During the 1950 hearings in Los Angeles, however, Dickey accused the APCD of not doing enough to reduce industrial air pollution. Not only were Dickey's many statements at odds with one another, but his most common demands, for voluntary smoke reductions and more research, echoed industry delaying tactics.

Dickey has been credited with attempting to force the APCD to replace air pollution targets based on existing technologies with new standards based on systematic public health research. This may in fact have been his intention. Los Angeles civic leaders and public officials had stubbornly delayed public health research, although for different reasons. McCabe had felt that too much emphasis on research would delay air pollution regulation. The LAACC, in contrast, seemed to fear that public health research would enflame public fears and force officials to adopt more stringent pollution controls. But Dickey's calls for public health–based regulations were so at odds with his proposals for voluntary smoke reductions that they read more as attempts to inflame public anger in Los Angeles than as sincere efforts to strengthen air pollution standards.[80]

Nine months before the Los Angeles hearings, in February 1950, Dickey introduced legislation that would have given the state of California authority to create air pollution districts that crossed county lines. In March, he proposed that the state set aside a small fund for research on the health impacts of smog. On the face of it, these proposals appeared to address both the regulatory needs of metropolises that crossed county lines, and the resistance by agencies like the APCD to public health research. However, both of these bills would also have shifted air pollution oversight from county to state officials at a time when such a change was as likely to weaken as to strengthen regulations. Los Angeles's legislative delegation vehemently opposed the changes. It managed to kill Dickey's bills before they even reached the floor of the California State Assembly by arguing that no one could evaluate Los Angeles's smog control tactics until major industrial plants brought long-awaited smog control devices online that summer.[81] The APCD, major newspapers, and the Los Angeles Chamber of Commerce portrayed Dickey as a threat to both effective smog regulations and local control.[82]

During National Smoke Abatement Week in October 1950, just a month before the hearings in Los Angeles, Dickey launched another yet attack on the APCD. He cited severe smog in both Los Angeles and San Francisco as evidence that "the present State air pollution law is ineffective" and insisted that "any improvement was due to a combination of cool weather and hot publicity."[83] He once again proposed that the California legislature replace county-based air pollution control districts like the Los Angeles County Air Pollution Control District with "regional" districts under state supervision. To Dickey's credit, the San Francisco Bay Area did need a regional air pollution district to coordinate pollution controls across six counties, much as Los Angeles had needed a district with the authority to regulate smoke in dozens of independent municipalities. But improved regulation for the Bay Area did not appear to be Dickey's main motive; even San Francisco's mayor withdrew his support for Dickey's proposals when he realized they would undermine Los Angeles's regulatory efforts.[84]

The Assembly Interim Committee on Water and Air Pollution convened in Los Angeles on 27 November 1950.[85] Randall Dickey opened the three-day-long proceedings by calling Los Angeles County's smog control "one of the most vicious and costly deceptions of all time."[86] The district had fallen victim, he asserted, to "'persons or interests' deliberately endangering public health for profit." Dickey accused Gordon Larson and the APCD of corruption, of making "consistently false statements" about the anti-smog program, and of demonstrating greater concern about their jobs than about reducing smog or protecting the public.[87] Things quickly grew heated; Dickey insisted that he had "no desire to upset anything that Los Angeles County wants to do"[88] and complained that the APCD had greeted his fact-finding mission "with boxing gloves on."[89] The Los Angeles press did not believe him. Only one newspaper, the *Los Angeles Times*, even reported Dickey's protestations that his committee had not made up its mind about Los Angeles smog control, but this statement fell at the end of an article under a headline that called Dickey the "Smog Control Attacker."[90] Meanwhile, the original author of the smog control bill, A. I. Stewart, pledged to "defend with all my energies the present State law."[91]

At the hearings, Dickey listened to testimony from factory owners angry about APCD enforcement who accused the agency of all but forcing them to purchase smoke reduction equipment from specific, favored manufacturers while giving the region's largest polluters preferential treatment. Several witnesses also complained that the APCD required them to install equipment they could not afford.[92] A former Caltech meteorologist named Irving P. Krick, hired by Dickey to conduct an independent study of Los Angeles smog, questioned the effectiveness of APCD policy; he testified that favorable weather gave a "false impression of smog improvement" in Los Angeles's air quality.[93] Dickey also spent an entire day of the hearings listening to testimony about the health dangers of smog; a half dozen physicians, including representatives from the Los Angeles Medical Association and the National Cancer Institute in Bethesda, Maryland, presented evidence that air pollution increased death rates and risk of cancer in Los Angeles.[94] Dickey responded to these witnesses by claiming to have information in his files that proved that the APCD and special interests within Los Angeles had "intentionally sacrifice[d] the public health for a mercenary gain."[95]

When Gordon Larson, director of the APCD, appeared before the committee, Dickey accused him and the APCD of mismanagement and misinformation, of neglecting public health research, and of botching air pollution control. At one point, Dickey demanded, "Isn't it true, that the cause of eye irritation has been discovered, but that the information has not been made public?"[96] A. J. Haagen-Smit, a Caltech chemist working for the APCD, had synthesized smog in his laboratory just weeks before the hearings began. Larson denied keeping Haagen-Smit's findings secret and could have pointed to a lengthy article on Haagen-Smit's research in the *Los Angeles Times* to prove it.[97] For much of the rest of his appearance, Larson attempted to defend the APCD's approach to air pollution control and its sparse public health research. Statements by factory owners present at the hearings and Dickey's questions to Gordon Larson about their complaints revealed Dickey's antipathy toward both the APCD as an institution and its strategy for reducing air pollution.

The Interim Committee on Air and Water Pollution concluded its hearings in Los Angeles on 29 November and departed for northern

California the next day. The hearings had provided a very public forum for groups and opinions that had no political traction in policy debates long dominated by organizations determined to balance smoke reduction with economic growth. Accounts of the testimony about the health dangers of smog read as though these fears and opinions had simmered for many years. Dickey did not ultimately change Los Angeles County policies, but his trip to Los Angeles stirred up a great deal of criticism and anger. County supervisor Kenneth Hahn dismissed the APCD's "pretty reports" with the angry assertion that "the people don't care about reports. *They want the air cleaned up*."[98] "'The job of getting rid of this foul menace is not being done,' thundered Councilman Ernest Debs. 'I think that Larson is not being given the tools with which to work.'"[99] The Los Angeles City Council dismissed the APCD's claims of air quality improvements as "hogwash" and "propaganda"[100] and then passed resolutions instructing city health officer George Uhl to find a "pharmaceutical to relieve eye irritation" from smog and to prosecute industrial polluters more aggressively.[101]

Thomas J. Doyle, a member of the Interim Committee on Water and Air Pollution and assembly representative from Los Angeles, added his voice to posthearing criticisms of the APCD. He suggested that "maybe the whole program should be taken over by the state" because the APCD needed to take "more drastic steps." Referring to the APCD's ongoing efforts to reduce pollution from burning garbage, and echoing Dickey's criticisms of the APCD, Doyle declared that regulating small industries and "little backyard incinerators" could not yield significant benefits.[102] Many local newspapers, the *Los Angeles Times* excepted, responded to the hearings by stepping up their negative coverage of the APCD, Gordon Larson, and Los Angeles's smog program. *People's World*, for example, accused donors to Caltech of hindering research on industrial pollution:

> Cynics claimed today to have solved the mystery of why the California Institute of Technology's famed scientists can't find the industrial source of smog.
>
> They pointed fingers to a cozy little club known as the California Institute Industrial Associates. Membership, according to

Caltech President Lee A. DuBridge, is limited to those who will pay a membership of $10,000 to $25,000.

A $115,000 kitty already has been raised from the Standard Oil Co. of California, E. I. Du Pont de Nemours Co., Union Oil Co., Socony-Vacuum Laboratories, Douglas Aircraft Co., Lockheed Aircraft Co., North American Aircraft Co., Republic Aviation Corp., Richfield Oil Co., and Shell Development Co.[103]

The *Hollywood Citizen News* reported that the Assembly Interim Committee left behind "a lot of aroused tempers and unsettled questions" about the Air Pollution Control District.[104] The *Herald Express* fumed that Los Angeles had squandered more than a million dollars in its fight against smog and that "stupid politics" kept the region from making "any real progress" against "nauseous, eye-smarting, lung-irritating, health-destroying fumes."[105] Echoing the statements made by representatives of moderately sized businesses at the hearings, the *Herald Express* asked, "Why is it that the industrial plants which are known smog offenders are not forced to close their doors? Why aren't buses and trucks forced to use equipment which will burn up their excess fumes? Why aren't air pollution laws enforced no matter who the offender may be?" Angelenos wanted answers, but Los Angeles would make no progress until it rooted out "stupidity, politics and possibly, graft" from air pollution administration.[106] In the meantime, the APCD's apparently light touch with polluting industries did "not rest well with a public which has been irritated and angered beyond all reason by the wasteful and apparently futile expenditure of public money to eliminate the nuisance."[107]

Larson, keenly aware of press criticism and declining public confidence, began a public relations campaign immediately after Dickey left Los Angeles. He arranged tours of APCD laboratories and facilities for the Los Angeles City Council, "managing editors of newspapers, directors of radio and television stations, and officials of the Los Angeles County Medical Association, PTA, League of Women Voters and other groups."[108] One hundred "representatives of public information" boarded buses on 15 December to see smog controls at oil, chemical, and steel plants and other sites throughout the Los Angeles basin. Each tour also met with a panel of district officials, scientists, and consultants who pledged to answer any and all questions.¹⁰⁹ Larson took fourteen of Los Angeles County's thirty-two state legislators on a similar tour in an attempt to forestall a legislative reaction to the crescendo of criticism that followed the hearings.¹¹⁰ In addition to these tours, Larson visited the Los Angeles Chamber of Commerce. There Larson flatly denied Dickey's charges of incompetence and corruption, defended the APCD's permit system, and presented data that showed that backyard incinerators caused more pollution than all of Los Angeles's industries.¹¹¹ The LAACC had not joined the mounting criticisms of the APCD and did not really need Larson's visits to convince it to continue to support the APCD. The business group, however critical it had been in the preceding two or three years, now strongly supported both the permit system and regulations on backyard incinerators. Larson's visits served to cement an alliance that would certainly come under fire if public grumbling yielded an effort to rewrite APCD policy.

A groundswell against the APCD could have been quite damaging to Los Angeles's air pollution control institutions because Dickey continued to introduced bills to transfer air pollution authority the state in successive sessions of the California legislature.¹¹² These measures received sporadic support from groups like the League of California Cities,¹¹³ but none of them passed. Even Dickey's second attempt to authorize state funding for health research in 1951 failed.¹¹⁴ Nevertheless, continued criticism from Sacramento convinced the county supervisors to create a new citizen "steering committee" to improve public relations and enhance public participation in policy making. It is a testament to the status of chambers of commerce in general, if not the Los Angeles Chamber of Commerce in particular, that the supervisors looked to local chambers of commerce to name representatives from unincorporated communities to this new steering committee.¹¹⁵

Throughout this period, the LAACC regarded Dickey's proposals with deep suspicion and cautioned that his bills would "kill the effectiveness" of Los Angeles's air pollution control. The LAACC directors credited their own working group, now known as the Air Pollution Control Committee, with defeating Dickey's proposals in committee.¹¹⁶ Their opposition was not, of course, simply an effort to protect

Los Angeles's local autonomy or to defend a regulatory agency they believed effective. Privately, the Los Angeles Chamber of Commerce Board of Directors fretted that any change in policy or the Air Pollution Control District administration would penalize those industries that had already invested time and money complying with APCD rules.[117] As business owners, many of whom had already invested in air pollution equipment, the members of the chamber of commerce had a considerable stake in the existing regulatory regime.

In 1955, in spite of its long defense of the APCD, the LAACC began a campaign to make the APCD a fully autonomous agency, rather than subordinate to the Los Angeles County Board of Supervisors. Its efforts to frame and promote this idea reveal the LAACC at its most effective. The Los Angeles County Board of Supervisors had many responsibilities in addition to overseeing the APCD, and, the LAACC now argued, air pollution control required more attention than the supervisors could devote to it.[118] Arnold O. Beckman, chair of the chamber's air pollution committee and member of a committee formed in 1954 to help the APCD draft a smog emergency plan, spearheaded the campaign for an independent air pollution control district. He volunteered the LAACC to study how best to create an independent air pollution agency and thus ensured that the business leaders worked closely with the county counsel on this issue.[119] Once he had laid the groundwork, the LAACC convened a hand-selected citizens committee to promote public support for changes to the APCD.[120] Beckman also claimed legitimacy for the LAACC as representative of the public by virtue of its long involvement in smog control.[121] In spite of the explosion of public anger that followed the Dickey hearings in 1950, the county board of supervisors and other public officials accepted the LAACC as a primary public voice in air pollution policy and continued to pursue the kinds of policies that had grown out of the relationship between the LAACC and public officials.

Conclusion: Cooperation and Legitimacy

Between 1943 and 1955, a series of organizations and individuals arose that challenged Los Angeles air pollution policies or the LAACC's in-

Women picketing a Los Angeles County Supervisors meeting in October 1955. These and many other Angelenos dissatisfied with air pollution policies blamed industry for polluting the skies and demanded greater attention to the public health effects of smog. "Smog Pickets," 14 Oct 1955. Hearst-Examiner Photograph Collection. Courtesy of Doheny Memorial Library, University of Southern California, Los Angeles, California.

fluence. The first of these, the Altadena Property Owners League, was widely credited with introducing the idea of countywide, uniform smoke enforcement. Even so, in 1944, the county health officer dismissed Altadena citizens' smog concerns as "largely psychological."[122] The Southern California Automobile Club took up the air pollution campaign in 1945, warning that a public aroused by continued pollution would eventually "demand removal of all industry from this area."[123] In 1948, William M. Jeffers, former president of Union Pacific Railroad, resigned very publicly from the official Citizens Smog Advisory Committee in frustration, saying that he would no longer "be a party to any 'dress rehearsals.'"[124] By 1950, the Pasadena Council of Women's Clubs had an air pollution control committee, as did the Pasadena Council of Parents and Teachers and the Los Angeles County Medical Society.[125] The city of Monterey Park formed a smog committee that advocated action against all sources of smog including automobile exhaust and invisible fumes.[126] The Pure Air Committee formed in 1952 to provide "a central organization and clearing house, independent of political bodies," and to "bring pressure where needed" on air pollution control.[127] It was succeeded by the Citizens Anti-Smog Action Committee, a Pasadena-based group that staged protests in 1954 that drew national news coverage in *Time* and *Life*,[128] and objected to the Air Pollution Control District's use of the Air Pollution Foundation's research because of links between the Air Pollution Foundation and Southern California industries.[129]

Most of these groups shared the APOL's political strategy. They criticized county supervisors and public health officials for ignoring the smog crisis, brought the smog problem to the Los Angeles County Grand Jury, and undertook vigorous and highly visible campaigns to generate public outrage.[130] They also shared a common critique of Los Angeles's smog policies: all these groups advocated more stringent industrial regulations and more attention to public health; they all scoffed at the notions that backyard incinerators or automobiles caused smog.[131] They kept the smog problem before the public and encouraged Angelenos' readiness to blame smog on industrial pollution and to criticize the Air Pollution Control District for ignoring public health or maintaining a cozy relationship with industry. Their methods did not, however, convey to any of these organizations the kind of legitimacy enjoyed by the LAACC or, for that matter, the Air Pollution Foundation. The fact that the LAACC maintained its influence in the face of public anger and this political competition says a great deal about the policy needs of local officials and about how local governance works.

The city and county officials charged with solving Los Angeles's air pollution problems in the 1940s needed information, policy ideas, and allies. The LAACC's ability to provide all three laid the foundation for the close collaboration between the business group and local officials. This relationship allowed the chamber of commerce to shape policy to its liking. The LAACC did not hesitate to oppose policies that it feared would damage Southern California commerce. For example, in 1945 the chamber opposed new restrictions on industrial and transportation emissions, and in the following year it blocked the Los Angeles City Sanitary Engineer's request that the California legislature define abatable pollution as "unreasonable and unnecessary" to manufacturing.[132] These positions did not reduce LAACC influence.

County officials could have built alliances with other supportive groups. A number of organizations supported the Air Pollution Control Bill of 1947, for example, and could have rallied Los Angeles residents to back stricter regulations. County officials judged the League of California Cities particularly critical to the passage of the bill; the Pasadena Chamber of Commerce, the 1947 Los Angeles County Grand Jury, and the California Fruit Growers Exchange also endorsed this legislation.[133] The *Los Angeles Times* also promoted the cause with extensive coverage of progress and with editorials urging more aggressive public action. In addition, Norman Chandler, the owner of the paper, organized the meetings that eventually convinced the petroleum industry to contribute to rather than fight air pollution control.[134] None of these groups attempted to lead the smog campaign, however; their support for the air quality efforts did far more to reinforce the Los Angeles Chamber of Commerce's influence than to challenge it.

The LAACC justified its influence by arguing that it represented the whole Los Angeles community, as when Arnold Beckman told the county supervisors, "We appear before you as a group of citizens interested in effective government in Los Angeles County and in the earliest possible cure of our smog problem. We have participated, individually and collectively, in previous conferences and other attempts to help in its solution. We represent no one organization or group, nor do we come from one part of the County."[135] Public anger at slow progress and unpopular policies merely encouraged public officials to lean more heavily on cooperative, noncritical groups. In other words, widespread criticism pushed elected officials into ever closer relations with the LAACC, even when that criticism singled out regulations that seemed excessively solicitous toward industry. Thus, the Los Angeles Chamber of Commerce protected the Los Angeles business and industrial community from more stringent regulations and ensured that air pollution policy met its own institutional goals.

In 1951, *Businessweek* carried a lengthy article on Los Angeles's air pollution control efforts under the headline "L.A. Kills Smog with Kindness." The article began with the admonition that "the best way to strip the clammy blanket of smog from your city is to win the cooperation of the industries that cause the trouble in the first place."[136] The article went on to describe the APCD's permit system and how it made allies of the industries that came under regulation. This emphasis on cooperation was in part the result of the LAACC's response to air pollution but was not unique to Los Angeles. This sort of cooperation between business and government was also a crucial component of federal New Deal and World War II economic projects. As the next chapters show, the LAACC's efforts to cooperate with city and county officials, together with its proactive efforts to study policy problems, draft legislation, and support officials embattled by public frustration, gave the business organization a policy reach that extended far beyond air pollution and far beyond Los Angeles County.

CHAPTER THREE

FLOOD CONTROL AND POLITICAL EXCLUSION AT WHITTIER NARROWS, 1938–1948

Interstate 605 runs north along the San Gabriel River from the coast at Seal Beach to the San Gabriel Mountains near Duarte. About halfway along, the road climbs up over a saddle in the hills that separate the San Gabriel Valley to the north from the coastal plain below. There it passes a low earthen dam that guards a basin studded with picnic tables, ball fields, a nature center, a disc golf course, and all the trappings of a major urban park. The recreational facilities obscure the real function of the dam: to slow floodwaters before they reach the crowded coastal plain below. The park also hides signs of the community of truck farmers and industrial wage workers who once battled to hold on to these lands.

The saddle, known as Whittier Narrows, marks a pinch point for waters underground as well as for the San Gabriel River and the Rio Hondo running on the surface. The same geological processes that made the ridge and saddle known as the Narrows pushed up an underground layer of rock. That rock layer, in turn, forces groundwater nearly to the surface of the broad basin above the Narrows. In the 1850s, this easily accessible groundwater attracted truck farmers to the valley above the Narrows, where they established an agricultural economy that persisted into the early twentieth century. By the 1890s, railroad links from Los Angeles to Whittier and the development of a number of small, private irrigation companies also supported successful commercial citrus and walnut below the Narrows. In the 1920s, the city of Long Beach, then a growing industrial, oil, and port city eager to compete with Los Angeles, saw in the Narrows an ideal site for a reservoir that would free it from dependence on water supplies that Los Angeles controlled. As explained in chapter 4, the promise of Hoover Dam soon made such local provisions for water supply less urgent in Los Angeles

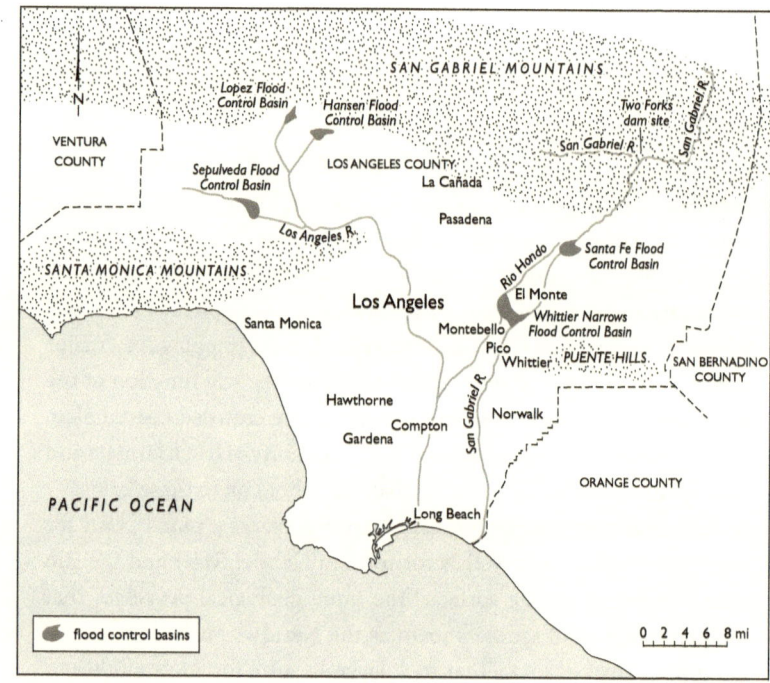

Flood control on the Los Angeles and San Gabriel rivers

County. The idea of a dam at Whittier Narrows lived on, however, in local and then federal flood control planning.

The debate over Whittier Narrows Dam does not provide as clear an example of business influence in local politics as air pollution does because chambers of commerce lined up on both sides. Moreover, the Los Angeles Chamber of Commerce itself was relatively quiet on the Whittier Narrows Dam question. This dam merits discussion here, however, because it reveals how local power structures shaped federal policy. The conflict over Whittier Narrows Dam began in the middle of a larger debate over flood control for the Los Angeles region. Following devastating floods in 1914 and 1916, Los Angeles County and the Army Corps of Engineers undertook the first of many flood control projects in Los Angeles County. The structures they built widened, deepened, and straightened sections of the Los Angeles River and Ballona Creek but also excited considerable controversy over the relative merits of dams and river channelization to control floods in the region. These discussions of flood control on the Los Angeles and San Gabriel rivers, including the conflicts over Whittier Narrows Dam, echoed a larger national debate over flood control strategy.[1]

In 1930, the Los Angeles County Flood Control District added Long Beach's proposed dam at Whittier Narrows into county flood control plans. Because of this, the dam eventually came to the attention of the Army Corps of Engineers. The communities on the coastal plain downstream from the Narrows, from Whittier to Long Beach, supported the dam because it protected their property and businesses both from floods and from the disruption of flood control construction itself. Upstream from the Narrows, however, a coalition of residents in the proposed flood control basin and business leaders in nearby El Monte protested that the Army Corps of Engineers' dam would sacrifice their homes and futures to protect their wealthier downstream neighbors.

Whittier Narrows Dam politics replicated both Los Angeles's earlier flood control debates and the politics of air pollution. As in these other episodes, key government agencies looked to a limited number of civic organizations for policy ideas and support but largely ignored the groups that opposed them. Civic groups on all sides of these issues sought to increase their influence by claiming to represent the general public. Excluded groups repeatedly complained that industries hurt Los Angeles–area homeowners and that selfish, large corporations were crushing small, independent citizens. In the communities harmed by the dam, organizations formed to demand that the government protect small farmers and homeowners from large industry, rather than the other way around. But these groups never gained sufficient political traction to shape local or federal flood policy.

The biggest differences between flood control and air pollution arose from the Army Corps of Engineers' political activities. The Army Corps' responsibility for flood control derived from a Supreme Court decision in the 1820s that confirmed federal authority over navigable rivers. Under this mandate, the Army Corps of Engineers built river channel improvements designed to reduce the damage flooding caused to Los Angeles Harbor. After the Mississippi River disaster of 1927 and the floods in the mid-1930s, Congress passed the Flood Control Act of 1936, expanding the Army Corps of Engineers' responsibility for flood control to non-navigable as well as navigable waterways.[2] Under this act, local officials, civic organizations, or "local interests" proposed projects, Congress authorized them, and then the Army Corps submitted plans to Congress for appropriations.[3] Congress would not authorize a flood control project without local endorsement; this made the Army Corps dependent on local interests, including city or county elected officials, citizen groups acting at the behest of local government, or unofficial, self-appointed spokespersons acting without a real public mandate.[4] Their special relationship with the Army Corps privileged the groups that initially sponsored a project over other parties that might have different priorities. Because, as the air pollution chapter demonstrated, only some civic organizations were in a position to propose flood control projects, federal flood control activity reinforced local patterns of political influence.

On the face of it, congressional requirements about local interests would seem to ensure that the Army Corps built projects that reflected a balance of technical expertise and local consensus. If the Army Corps' recruitment and cultivation of local interests in the Whittier Narrows Dam controversy is typical, however, federal flood policies instead reflected a tightly controlled debate that largely isolated critics. The Army

Corps kept such a tight rein on policy participation that it refused multiple requests for a public hearing.[5] This excluded opponents of the dam in much the same way as the Air Pollution Control District marginalized its detractors. In other words, the dispute over the Whittier Narrows Dam reveals how the institutional practices intended to coordinate federal with local institutions limited the very local political debate that they were intended to encourage. The decision to build Whittier Narrows Dam was not antidemocratic in the pure sense. More people supported the dam than opposed it; it protected a majority instead of catering to a small minority. It worked as designed to reduce flood danger along the San Gabriel River and cost less than any of the proposed alternatives. Whittier Narrows was a successful project by many measures. Nevertheless, the political process that yielded Whittier Narrows Dam was neither inclusive nor encouraging of public debate. As in air pollution, in flood control the key decision makers chose which groups they would include in policy debates and marginalized their opposition. This pattern calls into question the frequent complaints about federal interference in local governance heard after World War II.

From Water for Long Beach to Federal Flood Control

Los Angeles has a long history of devastating floods and acrimonious debate over what to do about them. Twenty-one major deluges hit the region between 1811 and 1954; major flood control efforts began after the flood of 1914 when the county board of supervisors hired consulting engineers to draft a comprehensive flood control plan for the county.[6] The majority of these engineers proposed controlling floods with dams in the mountains, levees along the rivers, and spreading grounds to soak up floods and recharge underground aquifers. A single dissenter advocated river channel improvements to contain floods and speed them out to sea. In 1915, the county board of supervisors created the Los Angeles County Flood Control District to manage flood control projects for the region, with the supervisors themselves as LACFCD governors, and appointed the dissenting engineer from the 1914 board, James W. Reagan, to direct the new agency.[7] From its inception to the mid-1930s, the LACFCD worked with the Army Corps of Engineers to divert and contain the Los Angeles River to protect Los Angeles Harbor. After state funding for flood control ended in 1933 and after Congress passed the Flood Control Act of 1936, the county turned over flood control construction almost entirely to the federal government.[8]

Proposals for Whittier Narrows Dam first attracted the attention of the Los Angeles County Flood Control District in the late 1920s, a period of particular disarray for the district. The oil, real estate, and industrial booms of the period rendered flood control plans badly out of date. As more people and businesses moved to the Los Angeles basin, they built flood-prone areas. New roads, factories, and homes replaced permeable open land and orange groves with impermeable surfaces that multiplied the volume and rate of storm runoff. In short, Los Angeles's explosive population growth simultaneously increased the scale and frequency of flooding along Los Angeles waterways and the number of people and value of property in harm's way. Reagan did not adjust the county flood program in response to Los Angeles's growth or changing hydrology. As a result, criticism of his apparently capricious, ineffective, and fragmented approach to flood control forced Reagan to resign in 1927. Things got still worse for the flood control district in 1929, when the wall of a canyon being prepared for a huge flood control and water supply dam in the San Gabriel Mountains collapsed. The dam, called the Two Forks or San Gabriel Dam, was to have been the cornerstone of flood control on the San Gabriel River. The county halted construction and paid a fat settlement to the contractors to compensate them for canceling the contract. Then a county grand jury investigation revealed that the contractors had known all along that Two Forks Canyon could not support a dam, had hidden this fact from county officials, and had bribed county supervisor Sidney Graves to secure their settlement.[9] Occurring just eighteen months after the deadly collapse of the Saint Francis Dam in San Fernando Valley, the construction site landslide cast doubt on the safety of impounding floods behind large mountain dams and on the LACFCD's competence.

The city of Long Beach took advantage of Reagan's resignation in 1927 to submit to the Los Angeles County Flood Control District a proposal for a municipal waterworks intake and flood control for the San Gabriel River at Whittier Narrows. Mindful of the water rights

A flood in February 1927 destroyed this bridge over the Los Angeles River in Glendale. Frequent floods in the early twentieth century increased support for county and federal flood control. At the same time, scandals and the apparent failure of expensive projects to prevent flood damage undermined this support. "Los Angeles River looking toward Glendale and Atwater Village." Feb. 1927. H. B. Miller, photographer. Courtesy of the Special Collections Room, Glendale Public Library, Glendale, California.

claimed by the small irrigation companies active at the Narrows, the new county flood control engineer, Eugene C. Eaton, forwarded Long Beach's proposal to the California Division of Water Resources.[10] His effort to sort out water rights at the Narrows became a small piece of a three-year hydrological investigation of Los Angeles County.[11] Based on this study, Easton drafted a new comprehensive flood control plan that, among other things, incorporated important aspects of Long Beach's proposal: a spreading grounds above Whittier Narrows to allow floods to percolate into the ground, and a dam at Whittier Narrows for "valley storage" of floodwaters.[12] Eaton submitted his comprehensive plan to the Los Angeles County supervisors in October 1930; they adopted it as the master plan for the county and the basis of their applications for federal loans and appropriations for nearly a decade.[13]

No sooner had county supervisors approved Eaton's master plan than the LACFCD sought permission to use bond revenues originally earmarked for the San Gabriel Dam to build two smaller mountain dams in the San Gabriel watershed. Long Beach objected, fearing that the flood control district would turn its flood control attention to the mountains and away from Whittier Narrows. So in 1932 the Long Beach Board of Water Commissioners met with the county supervisors to lobby for the Whittier Narrows Dam and spreading grounds. Long Beach argued that so much rain fell in the foothills and coastal plain that dams in the mountains could not adequately protect Long Beach. To keep the coastal plain safe, Long Beach urged the county supervisors to use the Two Forks Dam bonds for projects like Whittier Narrows Dam.[14]

Apparently Long Beach was convincing. A month after this meeting, Eaton asked the supervisors to hire Donald Baker, a geologist and consulting engineer, to review Long Beach's scheme.[15] Baker viewed mountain dams as inappropriate for Los Angeles County generally and preferred spreading grounds to conserve flood waters.[16] In May 1933, Baker reported favorably on Long Beach's proposal; like the California Division of Water Resources, Baker believed a dam and spreading grounds at the Narrows would increase percolation enough to make new water rights available at the Narrows for Long Beach.[17]

By the time Baker submitted his report, the Los Angeles County Flood Control District was hard pressed to build much of anything. The scandal over the San Gabriel Dam and the onset of the Great Depression made voters hostile toward new bonds. The state of California, which had assisted Los Angeles with flood control funding since 1919, terminated that aid in 1933.[18] Seeking alternative sources of money, the LACFCD in September 1933 applied to the California State Advisory Board of the Public Works Administration for a federal loan of $33 million for twenty-one flood and water conservation projects. The plan submitted to the PWA included a dam in the San Gabriel River mountain watershed and extensive work within the Angeles National Forest as well as Whittier Narrows Dam. County supervisors justified these projects, which they estimated would cost a total of $136 million, on the grounds that they would employ ten thousand workers over two years.[19]

The Los Angeles County Board of Supervisors hoped for rapid action from the PWA, but the board was disappointed. In October, F. E. Trask, the chief engineer for the California State Advisory Board of the PWA, forwarded Los Angeles's application to Washington because the PWA wanted to coordinate all flood projects with its "general national plan."[20] In November, the PWA returned the application to Trask for a technical review of Whittier Narrows Dam and two other proposed structures.[21] Trask appointed three engineers, T. M. Robins of the Army Corps of Engineers, F. D. Hermann, and C. H. Paul to scrutinize these projects. Their review took eight months.[22] When Los Angeles officials complained about the delay, Trask retorted that he "obey[ed] Washington," not the county board of supervisors, and he blamed the additional reviews on Los Angeles's aggressive lobbying campaign.[23]

The county supervisors' and LACFCD's frustration over delays mounted; frustration turned to desperation after New Year's Eve, 1934. Thirteen inches of rain fell on 30 and 31 December 1933. On New Year's Eve, the saturated hillsides above the La Cañada Valley let go. More than half a million cubic yards of mud and rock rumbled down the slopes, killing forty-four people and staggering Los Angeles residents and flood control engineers alike.[24] In March 1934, the Los Angeles County Flood Control District abandoned its PWA application in favor of direct federal aid. At the time, Congress was considering a Rivers and Harbors Improvement Bill to fund dams, breakwaters, river channel improvements, and harbor-dredging operations across the country. If Los Angeles could attach its flood control projects to this bill, the county supervisors reasoned, would relieve the flood control district of the responsibility of designing, constructing, and funding flood control. It was a timely idea. The Two Forks Dam fiasco still cast a shadow over county flood control efforts. Even the Los Angeles Engineering Council viewed the LACFCD as thoroughly discredited and recommended turning flood control over to federal agencies.[25] The financial advantages of the Rivers and Harbors Improvement Bill were also enticing. The PWA loaned money and could be expected to issue loans for only a fraction of the 1933 flood master plan. In contrast, if Congress added Los Angeles's flood control to the Rivers and Harbors Bill, the national treasury would underwrite Los Angeles's projects free and clear.[26]

The Los Angeles County supervisors submitted a $77 million flood package to Congress in 1934. At the end of May, Robins and his colleagues on the PWA Board of Review issued their report, concluding that river channel improvements would likely protect the lower San Gabriel River as well as the Whittier Narrows Dam.[27] By this time, Los Angeles had abandoned its PWA application, but Robins's position on river channels was significant because the subsequent debates over San Gabriel River flood control hinged on the relative merits of river channels and dams. In June, the California State Supreme Court ruled that the district could use funds from the 1924 San Gabriel Dam bonds for channel improvements and other projects on the San Gabriel River.[28] With this ruling in hand, the flood control district asked voters to approve new $26 million bonds to build twenty urgent flood projects. The list did not include Whittier Narrows Dam. Voters narrowly rejected the bonds in November, dashing hopes at the LACFCD that the district might make progress on its own. Clearly, the San Gabriel Dam fiasco and the Great Depression outweighed the urgency of flood protection for voters. Los Angeles flood control now depended on Congress.[29]

In 1934 and 1935, Whittier Narrows Dam seemed to be a dead issue even though it remained in the plans submitted to Congress. The PWA Board of Review had rejected it. Eaton, who as chief engineer of the LACFCD had great latitude in choosing flood control projects, did not consider it a priority. On his suggestion, in May 1935 the county supervisors dropped the dam from county flood control plans to help move the rest of Los Angeles's projects through Congress.[30] By this time, Long Beach had joined the Metropolitan Water District and pinned its water supply hopes on Hoover Dam rather than the San Gabriel River. Nevertheless, city leaders in Long Beach still wanted a dam at Whittier Narrows.[31] Nothing else, they believed, would provide them with the flood protection they wanted.

Army Corps of Engineers and Interested Parties

Whittier Narrows Dam did not stay off the agenda for very long. As part of its campaign for federal dollars, the Los Angeles County Flood Control District sent its 1933 master plan, including Whittier Narrows Dam, to the Army Corps of Engineers. The Army Corps used this master plan a template for its own flood control planning.[32] Moreover, many residents of the coastal plain seized on the Army Corps' new role in Los Angeles flood control to promote the dam. So even though the Flood Control Act of 1936 omitted Whittier Narrows Dam from the $70 million appropriation for Los Angeles County projects, by 1938 Whittier Narrows Dam was back on the table.[33]

The Army Corps of Engineers was at work on Los Angeles flood control even before Congress passed the Flood Control Act of 1936, building projects with federal relief funds, setting up a district office in Los Angeles, and studying regional flood control needs.[34] Just a week after Roosevelt signed the Flood Control Act, the corps issued a report endorsing retaining basins like Whittier Narrows. Although the Army Corps had long favored river channel improvements in Los Angeles, it now argued in favor of impounding floodwaters in large, shallow basins and releasing them slowly after river levels fell and after some of the water percolated into Los Angeles's extensive aquifers.[35] This should have cheered the Los Angeles Chamber of Commerce, which had long complained that the Army Corps of Engineers' dedication to concrete river channels wasted money and precious water resources.[36]

The 1936 report on retaining basins did not mention Whittier Narrows Dam by name. Whittier Narrows did not figure in the first plans to come out of the Los Angeles District Office under the Flood Control Act, either, because those plans focused on the Los Angeles River. The Los Angeles River Definite Project, as the Army Corps called final proposals submitted up the chain of command, did include Hansen and Sepulveda flood control basins, which were similar to Whittier Narrows, as well as river channel improvements and the completion of projects started in 1935 with funds from the Emergency Recovery Act.[37]

Only after the Los Angeles District finished redesigning Los Angeles River did the Army Corps turn to the San Gabriel and Whittier

Narrows. It took the Army Corps most of 1937 to draft plans for that river, but in the end the Definite Project for the San Gabriel closely resembled the Los Angeles River Definite Project. The Army Corps of Engineers envisioned two flood control basins, Santa Fe and Whittier Narrows, and river channel improvements from the mountains to the Santa Fe basin, and from Whittier Narrows to the Pacific. The Los Angeles District of the Army Corps submitted this Definite Project early in February 1938.[38] A month later, on 2 March 1938, yet another flood hit the Los Angeles basin. Existing flood channels and mountain dams protected most of the city from damage, but the deluge reinforced the Army Corps' new interest in retaining basins.[39] These two events, the 1938 flood and the release of the Army Corps' Definite Project for the San Gabriel River, earned the corps immediate support from the Los Angeles Chamber of Commerce, the Long Beach Chamber of Commerce, the city governments of Long Beach and Whittier, and water companies throughout the county. With so much support, dam advocates expected Congress to appropriate funds quickly for Whittier Narrows and the rest of the San Gabriel River works.[40]

The Definite Project for the San Gabriel River sparked a flurry of activity among those living just above the Narrows. The El Monte City Council and administrators from three school districts immediately protested that the dam would displace some five thousand residents from the area and put valuable facilities, including El Monte's sewage treatment plant, under water.[41] By the middle of March, El Monte's representative in Congress, Jerry Voorhis, had received so many letters from worried constituents that he wrote to the Army Corps of Engineers to alert it to this opposition.[42] At the end of the month, a public meeting attended by homeowners from the proposed flood control basin, the superintendent of the El Monte Elementary School District, the publisher of the *El Monte Herald*, the El Monte city engineer, a former state senator and a future assembly member, and representatives of the Temple School District led to the creation of the El Monte Citizens Flood Control Committee to fight the dam.[43] The group protested that the dam would demolish "hundreds of homes of hardworking citizens with their gardens and fruit trees to make an enormous reservoir and Dam for which there is no need."[44] In addition, the dam would ruin

The March 1938 flood was one of the largest in Los Angeles's recorded history and did considerable damage, as this photograph of the Los Angeles River in Burbank suggests. This flood reinforced the Army Corps' determination to build flood-retaining basins on the Los Angeles and San Gabriel rivers. *Report on Engineering Aspects, Flood of March 1938*. Special Collections, Oviatt Library, California State University–Northridge.

"some 4700 acres of the best agricultural land in the county... which is a high state of development and use" and would "cause a serious business depression" in the region.[45] These objections to the dam all hinged on the concentration of homes and farms in the territory to be taken for the "uneconomic, unnecessary" dam; the tension between working-class subsistence and big industry lay at the heart of El Monte Citizens Flood Control Committee arguments.

The El Monte Citizens Flood Control Committee struggled for legitimacy in the larger arena of Los Angeles flood control planning. Even its name conveyed its determination to define itself as the voice of the public. The group understood that key decision makers in Congress and in Los Angeles would defer to the Army Corps' expertise and that the Army Corps' would not hesitate to use its own reputation to dismiss its opposition. So the committee hired James Reagan, F. J. Safley, and John A. Bell to design an alternative to Whittier Narrows Dam. This was not a very astute choice. These engineers had spent much of the previous decade criticizing the flood control district, and they had little professional or political cachet. Reagan's reputation had suffered following his ouster from the Los Angeles County Flood Control District and the scandalous end of his pet project, the Two Forks Dam. That scandal also tainted Safley and Bell because they had served as consulting engineers for the doomed project.

On 14 April 1938, Los Angeles County supervisors voted to return Whittier Narrows Dam to the LACFCD's comprehensive plan. This realigned the county's planning documents with materials submitted to the Army Corps of Engineers several years earlier and with the corps' strategy for the San Gabriel River.[46] County supervisors' inconsistency on the dam reflects the importance of financial considerations and the opinions of their designated experts in county decision making. The Army Corps of Engineers' preference for Whittier Narrows Dam and the federal money that the Army Corps brought to the county made the county supervisors and the LACFCD predisposed to dismiss alternative designs and the residents who opposed Army Corps' activities.[47]

The supervisors' support for the dam provoked an immediate reaction in El Monte. At the next meeting of the county supervisors, the El Monte Citizens Flood Control Committee pleaded with county officials to build river channel improvements instead of Whittier Narrows Dam.[48] To support its petition, the committee presented a report by J. A. Safley in which he argued that Whittier Narrows Dam was unnecessary and that river channelization would provide better flood protection for the coastal plain below the Narrows. Safley also asserted that the Army Corps' arguments for the dam were based on overestimations of the size of and maximum rainfall in the San Gabriel watershed. Specifically, Safley claimed that a flood of the magnitude the Army Corps used as the basis for its designs would take place only with "a sustained rainfall for 2 hours and 46 minutes, at the rate of 2 inches per hour" throughout the entire San Gabriel watershed. But, according to Safley, "no rainfall of such intensity has ever been recorded in this section" over such a large territory.[49] Oddly, Safley did not cite Robins's May 1934 report favoring river channels over retaining basins.[50]

The Army Corps disputed Safley's flow estimates, his understanding of the flood control in the Los Angeles basin, and his skill and motivations as an engineer. In correspondence with Safley and the county supervisors over the next two years, the corps explained that it used flow estimates that exceeded measured floods in Los Angeles history because urban development of open and agricultural land that absorbed and slowed flood waters would inevitably lead to bigger, faster, more dangerous floods in the future.[51] Experience has confirmed this calculation; urbanization has been a major factor in increasing peak floods in cities around the world.[52] Within a year, Safley reversed himself and attacked the dam on the grounds that the corps had underestimated peak floods.[53]

Safley, Bell, and Reagan escalated their criticism throughout the fall of 1940. In newspaper interviews and in reports forwarded to Congress, they insisted that the Army Corps' reservoirs would not control Los Angeles floods.[54] In September, they called for a congressional investigation "of the many ill-planned projects as well as the wasteful expenditure of many millions of Federal funds thereon."[55] The dissident engineers derided the Army Corps for its "inexperience" and "lack of knowledge concerning the functioning of reservoirs in the control of major flood discharges."[56] The Army Corps countered by accusing Safley of writing his reports to get "a job defending the people who, he claims, will be damaged by the proposed project" and by dismissing Safley, Bell, and Reagan as cranks. In correspondence with the San Francisco office, the Los Angeles District of the Army Corps noted that the three had opposed nearly every LACFCD plan since Reagan's resignation.[57] When Safley, Bell, and Reagan persisted, the Army Corps and the Los Angeles County Flood Control District complained that they could not even evaluate their proposals because Safley and his associates refused to share their hydrological data.[58]

The Army Corps' reactions to the dissident engineers' reports as well as the opposition from El Monte prove just how politically adept the army engineers were and how much their participation shaped Los

Angeles flood control politics. The corps' reactions to Safley, Bell, and Reagan's reports varied by audience. To the dissident engineers, the corps wrote more or less collegial responses requesting data so that the Army Corps might replicate their analysis. To the county board of supervisors and to their own supervisors in San Francisco and Washington, the Los Angeles District army engineers rejected Safley, Bell, and Reagan as incompetent and countered Safley, Bell, and Reagan's specific assertions with detailed reports clearly intended to persuade their readers of the corps's engineering superiority.

Their reactions to lay opponents likewise depended on the Army Corps' audience. So, in response to U.S. Representative Voorhis's inquiries, the Army Corps insisted that it had designed Whittier Narrows Dam with the needs of El Monte in mind. It also reassured Voorhis that "much of the present opposition" to the retarding basin would "disappear after a full understanding of the construction and operation features of the project are known."[59] When corresponding with the Long Beach water commissioners, however, the Army Corps implied that it would modify the design of Whittier Narrows Dam to reduce opposition. Then, to mobilize proponents of the dam, the corps added that it did not pursue congressional appropriations for Whittier Narrows Dam because of local opposition.[60]

The Authorization of Whittier Narrows Dam

Local opposition to Whittier Narrows Dam showed no sign of disappearing. Between August 1938 and April 1940, the Army Corps received a steady stream of letters opposing the dam or inquiring nervously about the fate of homes and property in the El Monte area.[61] Some of these letters argued that the federal government should not sacrifice "rich 'self sustenance land'" or "hundreds of homes of hardworking citizens with their gardens and fruit trees" for an unnecessary dam.[62] In April 1938, Voorhis wrote the Army Corps to request a public hearing on the dam. The head of the Los Angeles District Office of the Army Corps of Engineers, Theodore Wyman, responded that such a hearing was not "proper procedure" and that he would hold a public hearing only "if such hearing is found to be required, after local interests have submitted factual data and statements giving reasons for desiring a hearing."[63] Wyman did not indicate what type of data might prove a hearing necessary. More important, because the Army Corps did not recognize the El Monte opposition as a "local interest," it were unlikely to convene a public hearing even if the El Monte group did submit the kinds of factual data and statements Wyman described. Without such a forum, the opposition remained fragmented and weak.

The relationship between the Army Corps of Engineers and its supporters contrasts sharply with Wyman's response to Voorhis and the El Monte coalition. While the Los Angeles District replied to letters from opponents and discussed the merits of the dam with the El Monte Citizens Flood Control Committee, the Army Corps actually helped organize supporters of the dam. This collaboration showed in the supporters' correspondence and activities. The Long Beach Board of Water Commissioners passed resolutions in April 1938 and again in February 1940 calling the dam the best means to protect the population and property below the Narrows. Although Long Beach originally eyed the Whittier Narrows as a source of municipal drinking water, neither of these resolutions mentioned water conservation. The 1938 resolution used not only the Army Corps' data on flood sizes and runoff rates but also Army Corps's wording. The resolution stated, "The erection of said Whittier Narrows dam will create no engineering problem that cannot be solved to the entire satisfaction of residents of that area" and that "any economic problems affecting the residents of that area can also be solved without working a hardship upon such residents";[64] nearly the same language appeared in the Army Corps' responses to Voorhis's 1938 enquiries on Whittier Narrows Dam.[65]

A 1938 resolution passed by the Norwalk Chamber of Commerce repeated the Long Beach Board of Water Commissioners' resolution almost verbatim.[66] These petitions and reports suggest considerable coordination among coastal plain groups. Both the Norwalk and Long Beach resolutions mention the Army Corps' warning that, in view of the El Monte opposition, the corps would not seek congressional appropriations without a stronger show of local support for Whittier Narrows.[67] The *Los Angeles Times* carried no statements blaming delayed funding on the opposition the way the Army Corps did. Rather, the *Times* consistently described Whittier Narrows Dam as one of a list of projects that would surely secure federal funding in the next round of congressional appropriations.[68] So neither Long Beach nor Norwalk derived their very similar resolutions from Los Angeles's major newspaper. The LACFCD and the Army Corps of Engineers actively sought to "drum up support" for the dam, leading to "a very close relationship between the District and the Long Beach Chamber of Commerce."[69] It is likely that the Army Corps itself alerted the LACFCD, the Long Beach Board of Water Commissioners, or Long Beach Chamber of Commerce to the threat posed by the El Monte opposition in order to mobilize the coastal plain groups the Army Corps considered "interested parties." This suggests all supporters had access to Army Corps of Engineers' documents and shared information among themselves and that the El Monte interests' persistence forced government officials and supporters of the dam into a closer alliance, much as criticism of the Air Pollution Control District drove county officials to rely ever more on the Los Angeles Chamber of Commerce. Also as in the air pollution case, the relationship between the Army Corps of Engineers and the Long Beach interests excluded the opposition.

In the spring of 1940, Los Angeles County supervisors escalated their lobbying efforts for federal flood control appropriations.[70] The Army Corps of Engineers, the LACFCD, and the Long Beach Harbor and Water Commissions joined in, arguing that the small population near El Monte should not block a project that would protect the larger population and valuable property of the coastal plain.[71] The Army Corps also defended the Whittier Narrows Dam as a water conservation measure, an astute nod to both congressional and Southern California preoccupations with multiple-purpose water projects.[72] The Army Corps continued to dispute Safley, Bell, and Reagan's calculations, as well as the data used by the El Monte flood control committee. As Safley, Bell, and Reagan persisted in their criticism of Whittier Narrows Dam, internal correspondence revealed flood control officials' mounting frustration. The Los Angeles County Flood Control District's chief engineer, H. E. Hedger, began referring to El Monte's statements as "propaganda,"[73] while the Army Corps dismissed Safley, Bell, and Reagan as a joke and "out of date and decrepit in mind as well as in body."[74]

The El Monte Citizens Flood Control Committee reacted by sending letter after letter to Congress citing Safley's assertion that channel improvements would cost less and work better and accusing the Army Corps of sacrificing relatively rural El Monte for the industrial coastal plain. The committee "earnestly recommend[ed]" to Congress "that no funds for flood control be appropriated for Los Angeles County except funds . . . for channel protection only" until Whittier Narrows Dam was more thoroughly investigated.[75] But the El Monte coalition had fractured. In February 1940, the board of supervisors received petitions signed by ninety-six residents of the unincorporated Garvey Acres who supported the dam because condemnation would help them move out of the Rio Hondo flood plain and farther away from El Monte's sewage disposal plant. These petitions protested that the "self-appointed leaders of the City of El Monte" had only "mercenary reasons" for opposing Whittier Narrows Dam. As one of them put it, "They are afraid of losing a few dollars in business, not caring whether we drown here or not."[76] Garvey Acres residents distrusted El Monte's leaders because El Monte tried to annex Garvey Acres over residents' objections and because El Monte was eighteen months into a campaign to recall the mayor, city clerk, and two city councilors tainted by a scandal over poker rooms and poor record keeping.[77] The recall had nothing to do with flood control, but because El Monte's mayor helped lead opposition to the dam, her fall widened the rift between El Monte and Garvey Acres. Some of those who signed the petition had spoken out against the dam on other occasions, but the ongoing debate over the dam cost them dearly. As long as Whittier Narrows Dam loomed, they could neither improve their property or sell it property at a fair price.

Over the objections of El Monte and Representative Voorhis, Congress authorized Whittier Narrows Dam in August 1941. Congress would not have approved the dam had the Army Corps been unable to show that local interests supported the project. Because Congress required the Army Corps to show this local support, the engineers cultivated "interested parties" to help them secure congressional appropriations. In the case of Whittier Narrows, the Army Corps consulted as interested parties the Long Beach Chamber of Commerce, Water Commission, and Board of Harbor Commissioners and the San Gabriel Valley Protective Association, a consortium of irrigation companies on the coastal plain. These groups all welcomed federal spending on flood control and had all lobbied for Whittier Narrows Dam. The Army Corps did not treat the El Monte city government, chamber of commerce, or Citizens Flood Control Committee or the Anti–Whittier Narrows Dam Association as interested parties because they opposed the dam. The relationships between the Army Corps and the San Gabriel River valley community as a whole grew organically from the corps' dependence on local endorsement of Army Corps projects, but they also defined the public in Los Angeles flood control to exclude opponents of Whittier Narrows Dam.

Jerry Voorhis and the Battle over Congressional Appropriations

Once Congress approved the dam, the Los Angeles District of the Army Corps of Engineers redoubled its efforts to convince El Monte to drop its objections. To this end, in September 1941, the Army Corps finally sat down with the El Monte Chamber of Commerce.[78] But this did not amount to the kind of public hearing that Voorhis or the El Monte interests desired. By the end of 1941, moreover, America's entry into World War II halted flood control projects in Los Angeles.[79] The Los Angeles District of the Army Corps continued to refine the Definite Project for the San Gabriel River in 1942. Although wartime growth significantly increased flood hazards along the San Gabriel River, Voorhis now used congressional debate over flood control appropriations to force the Army Corps to reckon with El Monte.

In 1944, the Los Angeles County supervisors, the Army Corps of Engineers, and opponents of Whittier Narrows Dam all prepared for a postwar boom in federal spending.[80] Congress took up flood control appropriations in early 1945. The *Los Angeles Times* marked the occasion with an editorial cheering federal flood control and Whittier Narrows Dam.[81] In March 1945, Voorhis, who had urged the Army Corps to consider El Monte's concerns, now declared his unequivocal opposition to the dam.[82] The El Monte Chamber of Commerce organized a protest meeting at the El Monte Union High School in August 1945. Several hundred people attended. Jerry Voorhis and two longtime leaders of the opposition, the Reverend Dan Cleveland and F. M. Thurber, outlined the impact of the dam on 5,000 residents, 2 schools, and more than "37,000 acres of good land." Emery Metcalf of the LACFCD presented the official perspective on the dam, which doubtless did little to sway the audience.[83]

Opponents continued to paint the dam as a fight between the people and special interests. El Monte resident Ralph Becker, for example, wrote President Harry Truman complaining that Los Angeles County supervisors sided with "the people with money" to deprive "the poor class" of their land.[84] Allegations that the construction industries and the cement manufacturing companies had illegally dictated flood control policy surfaced around this time as well. This was a recurring theme in public works controversies; similar allegations surfaced about the Bureau of Reclamation's Salt River Project in 1903 and Los Angeles Airport improvements in 1945.[85] A earlier scandal over a cement quarry lent particular credibility to these assertions in Los Angeles County. In 1929, Alphonzo Bell sought a zoning variance to open a lime and shale quarry near a residential subdivision that he had developed in the Santa Monica Mountains. The county rejected his permit, so Bell tried to put the issue on the city ballot. When opponents of the quarry countered with their own petition, Bell's hirelings forged signatures on the opposition petition to void them.[86] In spite of the many accusations, however, there was no direct evidence of cement company manipulation of flood control on the San Gabriel or Los Angeles rivers.

Opposition appeared, too, from more potent quarters than El Monte. The area that Whittier Narrows Dam was to transform into a flood control basin contained a small oil field, a stretch of Union Pacific Railroad track, wells and intake canals for several irrigation companies, and a three-hundred-acre Audubon Society sanctuary. When the institutions that owned these facilities raised objections to the dam, the Army Corps acted quickly to satisfy them. In 1944, the Army Corps realigned a section of the dam away from the oil field in the Rio Hondo channel. Then it shifted the east end of the dam "to avoid costly relocation of the railroad" and made similar alterations to protect the irrigation companies' installations and the Audubon Sanctuary.[87] The oil, railroad, and water companies and the Audubon Society all dropped their opposition to the dam after the Army Corps promised these changes.

The Army Corps would later deny redesigning the dam to "protect any special interests."[88] It described the 1944 and 1945 design alterations as reasonable efforts to reduce the cost of the dam, but these changes also divided opposition into two classes. The first was composed of the El Monte Chamber of Commerce, the school districts and city officials from the El Monte area, and the homeowners whom the Army Corps regarded as stubborn but inevitable victims of progress.[89] The second had far more legitimacy and power. In contrast to its accommodation of the second group, Army Corps dismissed the concerns of the first, noting that a large flood "probably would destroy most improvements in the reservoir area even if Whittier Narrows Dam were not constructed."[90]

Voorhis tried to use his position to convince the Army Corps to treat his constituents more like it treated the Audubon Society. In February and March 1945, he urged the Army Corps to build the dam a mile farther downstream. This location, he claimed, would reduce the impact of the flood control basin on his constituents and the danger that the dam would raise groundwater enough to damage agriculture in the basin. He also expected moving the dam to reduce local opposition to the dam.[91] The Army Corps rejected Voorhis's suggestions and denied that the dam would affect groundwater levels.[92] Congress reauthorized Whittier Narrows Dam in October 1945 as part of a package that included the Santa Fe Dam and river channel improvements for the Los Angeles River and for the San Gabriel from the mountains to the Santa Fe Dam, but it did not appropriate funds for the controversial dam.[93]

When Congress took up flood control funding again in January 1946, the chambers of commerce from Gardena, Hawthorne, and Compton sent Congress resolutions dismissing the El Monte interests as a small minority directly affected by neither the dam nor floods.[94] Long Beach Harbor commissioners argued that uncontrolled floods filled harbor channels with silt, delayed millions of dollars in essential port improvements, and threatened some $30 million worth of navy, port, and oil facilities.[95] In an interesting twist, their chief engineer argued that the mountain dams built in the 1930s increased flood problems by turning seasonal rivers into year-round streams "dangerously obstructed by willows and undergrowth."[96] Dam proponents on the coastal plain, Long Beach among them, continued to dismiss El Monte's all-channel plan as less effective and so much more expensive than Whittier Narrows Dam that even suggesting it endangered federal funding for all of Los Angeles County flood control.[97] According to this coalition, sacrificing "a limited number of homes and ranches" should not outweigh the danger of uncontrolled floods, reduced federal funding, and damage to Long Beach's harbor and oil industries.[98]

The El Monte Chamber of Commerce reacted by creating a new organization, the Anti–Whittier Narrows Dam Association, to unite the opposition throughout the San Gabriel River valley and lobby for channel improvements instead of the dam. Individuals who owned property in the proposed flood control basin sent worried letters to the Army Corps and Congress inquiring about the fate of their homes and lamenting the difficulties of relocating. One typical letter read, "We live here near the Rio Hondo, in a small community known as Garvey Acres . . . and we would like to know how we are going to be affected when that Whittier Narrows Dam is built. The newspapers are now saying that this dam will be finished by next summer. . . . It seems to me, that we here could stay on—as the dam . . . would be more than 4 miles downstream. Am I right?"[99]

In January 1946, Voorhis blocked appropriations for Whittier Narrows Dam again. Using his position in Congress, he continued to pressure the Army Corps of Engineers to address some of the El Monte interests' concerns. Even so, the Army Corps of Engineers did not reconsider its approach to flood control or seriously engage El Monte's concerns. In April, Congress requested that the Army Corps restudy San Gabriel river flood control to end the deadlock; the Army Corps' assistant chief, General Roscoe C. Crawford, responded, "I can see no objection to restudying the Whittier Narrows program."[100] The restudy took only two months; the Army Corps' report outlined six possibilities for the San Gabriel River, three dam-based and three channel-based plans. But the corps still strongly preferred its original design for Whittier Narrows, designated "Plan A" in the 1946 report. The House Flood Control Committee now ordered the Army Corps to hold a public hearing, something that Voorhis had urged and the Los Angeles District of the Army Corps refused in 1938. Coming so late in the game, the public hearing did not provide a real opportunity for El Monte to reshape the Army Corps' priorities. If anything, it reinforced the ties between the Army Corps of Engineers and its supporters.

The Public Hearing

Although Congress may have intended the hearing to give opposition groups a belated opportunity to participate in flood control planning, the Army Corps feared it would undermine support for the dam. So, once again, the corps worked to bolster support, this time by delaying the hearing until the Long Beach coalition was fully prepared. Like Randall Dickey's air pollution hearings in 1950, the public hearing on Whittier Narrows Dam gave marginalized groups a forum to voice their concerns but had no significant impact on policy. The transcript of the hearings reveals more about the conflicting and contradictory ways in which participants understood the controversy over the dam, and their relationships to each other, than it does about flood control.

The chief of the Army Corps of Engineers forwarded Congress's order for a public hearing to the Los Angeles District in June 1946. The Los Angeles District requested a delay, warning its Washington supervisors that a "hasty" hearing would be "unwise" because proponents of Whittier Narrows Dam needed time to prepare for the event. In September, the Army Corps announced a public hearing on Whittier Narrows Dam to take place on 12 December 1946. The official notice contained a summary of the six plans described in the 1946 restudy and a pro forma request for alternatives.[101] The Army Corps sent notice of the hearing to nearly everyone who had written to the corps, the LACFCD, or Congress about Whittier Narrows Dam since 1940. The Army Corps also invited public officials and civic leaders from communities in the San Gabriel River watershed that had taken little notice of the controversy; it calculated that "Plan A" would receive more support from a wider audience.[102] These preparations challenged the army engineers' claim that they "did not themselves institute projects" but merely carried out congressional orders based on local desires.[103]

Supporters of the dam made good use of the delay. The Long Beach Chamber of Commerce named a flood control committee to distribute "authentic information" about the dam to coastal plain communities and water companies "in order that they may be intelligently represented at the public hearing."[104] This committee also arranged for a dinner meeting at which Army Corps representatives could make presentations on the dam and the alternative plans to the Long Beach Chamber of Commerce, the Los Angeles County Flood Control District, and "representatives of Coastal Plain communities and water users."[105] Supporters also succeeded in mobilizing groups such as the Palos Verdes Corporation to join the pro-dam lobby, even though floods on the San Gabriel River had no direct impact on their holdings.[106] Meanwhile, the Anti–Whittier Narrows Dam Association passed out postcards to schoolchildren in El Monte urging their parents to attend the public hearing or, failing that, to write letters that the association could present at the hearing.[107] The opposition group collected information about school bonds, improvements, and populations from El Monte High School and other districts.[108] Its efforts were now assisted by a growing sense that the "everlasting threat of placing this territory under water and making out of it a place fit only for the habitation of frogs and mud turtles" had kept El Monte from "humming with industry"[109] and that the dam would forever cast a pall on the area.[110]

The fall of 1946 also saw challenger Richard Nixon defeat the incumbent Jerry Voorhis for a seat in the House of Representatives. Whittier Narrows was not a primary focus of the campaign, although Nixon did criticize Voorhis for not opposing the dam earlier, which distorted Voorhis's record and his early attempts to intervene. But both candidates reassured voters that they would protect them from the dam. Nixon won because Voorhis did not take him seriously as a challenger and because he associated Voorhis with the "blundering" administration in Washington and suggested that socialist labor unions had corrupted Voorhis.[111]

The final weeks before the December 1946 public hearing saw extensive public discussion of alternatives to Whittier Narrows Dam. Some of the ideas submitted to the Army Corps of Engineers reiterated Safley, Bell, and Reagan's river channel plan.[112] Others recommended moving the dam, making it smaller, damming the San Gabriel's tributaries upstream from El Monte, diverting floodwaters into abandoned gravel pits, or placing threatened homes on stilts.[113] In one of the oddest, a dentist from Long Beach suggested replacing all the bridges along the San Gabriel with small dams to create a string of reservoirs from the mountains to the sea.[114]

In all, however, the hearings reprised the debates and claims that had begun nearly a decade earlier. The opposition maintained that the dam cost too much, damaged too much property, displaced too many people, and sacrificed small holders for big industries. It accused the Army Corps of breaching its responsibility for impartial engineering and of using economic sleight of hand to make the dam seem more cost-effective than it was. It tried to show that the corps had inflated the expense of river channel improvements by including the cost of replacing decrepit bridges that had to be rebuilt whether the river channels were changed or not and had underestimated property values in the flood control basin to make the dam look cheaper by comparison.[115] The coastal plain coalition emphasized, as it always had, the small numbers of people displaced by the dam and the enormous value of the property that the dam would protect. An array of powerful spokespersons appeared in support of the dam: county supervisor William Smith; LACFCD chief engineer Harold E. Hedger; the supervising engineer of the California Division of Water Resources; and W. F. Rosecrans, who was both the chair of the Los Angeles Chamber of Commerce Flood Control Committee and the chair of the state board of forestry.[116]

The hearing did not alter the Army Corps' analysis of the San Gabriel River. Each alternative, according to the corps, harmed more people and property and cost more than its Plan A for Whittier Narrows Dam.[117] The corps did concede that one alternative, known as Plan B, was "competitive" with Plan A. Plan B also combined a dam and flood control basin but moved the dam about a mile downstream of the dam in Plan A. In fact, Plan B closely resembled Voorhis's 1945 proposal that the Army Corps had dismissed. Moving the dam downstream even as little as a mile did increase the cost of land acquisition and, if anything, added to the protests against the dam.[118] Not only did the El Monte interests reject a dam in either location, but the city of Whittier, nine water companies, and the citrus growers of Whittier, Montebello, Pico, Downey, and Rivera objected that the alternative dam location threatened their water rights and water quality.[119]

After the public hearing, the Army Corps concluded that "all local interests affected by San Gabriel River, except those ... within the area of the proposed reservoir," unanimously supported the corps' original plans for the dam. But those within the basin continued to plead for a reprieve. One fourteen-year-old girl wrote President Truman to ask if the dam was really necessary, given drought and the success of flood control channels.[120] Thomas F. Hoult and Lois C. Hoult wrote letters to the Army Corps and to the *El Monte Herald* describing the "real tragedy" of losing their home. The Hoults had arrived in El Monte after seven years in the armed forces; they described their community as one "peopled by families who are building their houses as they can afford them" whose homes "represent great financial sacrifice and the belief in the sanctity of the American home." Like many other small landowners in danger of losing their property, the Hoults protested that the relocation of these residents was "not an adequate solution to the entire problem" because "feeling toward a home is not wholly concerned with the structure of the building, but is also connected to the land, the neighborhood, the neighbors. Yes, love *is* a factor."[121]

During and after the hearings, the Army Corps continued to emphasize that by displacing 5,000 people it could protect 40,000 acres and 850,000 people.[122] After the hearings, the Army Corps escalated its rhetoric, accusing the Anti–Whittier Narrows Dam Association of using the public hearing "for the purpose of confusing the issue." The army engineers also refused to reply to a list of questions from the Anti–Whittier Narrows Dam Association because they felt responding would merely feed the opposition's "tactics of confusion and delay."[123] In contrast, the Army Corps regarded letters from "private individuals who have not been swayed by organization effort" as worthy of more "considerable weight" than those influenced by the opposition's campaign. The corps ignored the role of the Los Angeles County Flood Control District and Long Beach in soliciting and shaping these letters.[124]

The Compromise of 1948

The public hearing did not resolve the Whittier Narrows Dam controversy; the stalemate stretched into 1947. The city of Whittier and the LACFCD tried to break the deadlock by asking Secretary of the Navy James Forrestal to support the dam. He wrote the secretary of war that the dam would protect the Los Alamitos Naval Air Station and Seal Beach Naval Ammunition Depot from flooding on the San Gabriel River.[125] The Anti–Whittier Narrows Dam Association proposed that the city of El Monte annex the flood control basin in the belief that the federal government would have a harder time taking land from an incorporated city.[126] The Army Corps, meanwhile, surveyed the residents of Garvey Acres to see whether they preferred staying in their homes behind a ring dike to selling their property for the flood control basin. Of the ninety-three homeowners who responded, only fifteen wanted to stay under these circumstances.[127]

Richard Nixon's position as congressional representative from El Monte now became important. Nixon had opposed Whittier Narrows Dam during his campaign because his constituents opposed it and because some employees in Los Angeles District of the Army Corps regarded Whittier Narrows Dam unnecessary in light of the Santa Fe Flood Control Dam and the mountain dams already in place.[128] But under pressure from Senator William Knowland, Nixon negotiated a compromise that closely resembled Plan B; the Army Corps would move the dam downstream to accommodate the Audubon Sanctuary, the irrigation companies, and some seventy oil wells and to affect fewer homeowners. In addition, the army engineers would build ring dikes to protect a Texaco oil refinery and the Temple School building.[129] The compromise plan still displaced more than 2,000 residents, 560 homes, and much of the Temple School District's population.

A new opposition group, the San Gabriel River Conservancy, mounted one last effort to block the dam in 1949. It alleged that test boring by the Army Corps in preparation for dam construction caused a sudden drop in water levels in local wells. The conservancy attempted to persuade the Pasadena Metropolitan Businessmen's Association to pass a resolution against the dam[130] and wrote letters to President Truman, Bess Truman, and Los Angeles newspapers protesting placement of a dam "over large quicksand deposits and on a major earthquake fault" and the diversion of water to "millionaires" in Long Beach.[131] In the end, however, the compromise held, and Congress finally appropriated funds for the dam in 1949.[132]

Construction at Whittier Narrows began in 1950, more than twenty years after the controversy began. Because of the fortuitous location of congressional district boundaries, opponents of Whittier Narrows Dam were able to force the Army Corps to make small changes in the Definite Project for the San Gabriel River. Even so, the flood control basin and park replaced hundreds of homes. After the Temple School closed, the Army Corps of Engineers moved into the building. As the final protests in 1949 illustrate, lingering suspicion remained among those displaced that the Army Corps' project had benefited large special interests at their expense. The corps' relationship with the city of Long Beach, the Los Angeles County Flood Control District, and water and oil companies clearly contributed to this perception. Likewise, the corps' dismissal of the engineering and fiscal arguments for channel proposals and of the value of the semirural community in the basin area fed suspicions about the influence of special interests.

The question of special interests and political legitimacy remained a source of conflict for all sides. This played out in the association Garvey Acres and El Monte residents saw between bigness, illegitimate self-interest, and support for the dam. In a variation on this argument, a homeowner in the flood control basin protested in 1947 that some "pull" or special interest supported the dam "to get our properties" and the oil she was certain lay under her land.[133] Even Los Angeles County Supervisor Herbert C. Legg believed that the idea for the dam originated with "the big land interests" south of Whittier and that "the whole scheme was to keep from building channels down through the properties owned and controlled by the ranch interests to the south" that "put considerable pressure on the County Flood Control Department and the Army Engineers."[134] Richard Nixon's political patron Herman Perry concurred: "Whittier Narrows Dam is being promoted by big interests

The Whittier Narrows flood control basin displaced people, farms, and businesses and left considerable resentment in its wake. "Briano Legion Store Closed after 64 Years," 20 July 1953. Jensen, photographer. *Los Angeles Examiner* Negatives Collection. Courtesy of Doheny Memorial Library, University of Southern California, Los Angeles, California.

which do not wish, in one instance their property damaged by channels and in the second place, large interests to the north who do not wish the dams created above their property in the foothills."[135] But the rhetoric of bigness proved very flexible, applying equally to the citrus growers of Whittier, the industries of Long Beach, and even El Monte itself. So, for example, in 1947, a Garvey Acres resident described the El Monte opposition as a group of large landowners who stood to gain from future subdivision and development while the threat of both dam and flood depressed property values for less prosperous homeowners like him.[136]

Conclusion: Federal Programs and Antigovernment Sentiment

The story of Whittier Narrows Dam illustrates a number of important trends in twentieth-century American politics. The language that each side used to promote its position reveals the deep-seated conflicts in American political ideology over whether government should enact the will of an industrial majority who, in this case, lived on the coastal plain or protect the much smaller population of El Monte who saw themselves as upholding the nation's agrarian traditions. The politics of Whittier Narrows Dam, and in particular the way federal agencies interacted with local powerbrokers and institutions, has important implications for understanding both how the American federal system worked in the mid-twentieth century and why criticism of federal authority and political retrenchment flourished in the years after World War II. At Whittier Narrows Dam, the Army Corps of Engineers did not override local desires or weaken local government institutions. But even as the Army Corps pursued projects endorsed by local leaders, it contributed to the rejection of federal programs.

The Army Corps of Engineers engineered the politics of flood control on the San Gabriel River as surely as it engineered the river itself. It increased the political influence of the coastal plain interests from the Whittier area and the city of Long Beach by meeting with these groups regularly, providing them with information for their lobbying efforts, and, more explicitly still, delaying the 1946 public hearing to prepare the coastal plain interests. Meanwhile, the Army Corps fragmented and weakened the opposition to the dam by appeasing potentially powerful opponents like oil, railroad, and utility corporations and the Audubon Society and by isolating other opponents from each other. This political engineering neither fundamentally changed the balance of power along the San Gabriel River nor resulted in the construction of an ill-conceived or excessively costly project. Whittier Narrows Dam made sense in both hydrological and economic terms: the river channel plan, at least as sketched out by Safley, Bell, and Reagan, did not offer as much flood protection as the flood control dam and would have cost more to build, at least in part because the property values along the river in the coastal plain exceeded those in the flood control basin.[137] The dam protected far more people than it hurt: the flood control basin displaced 2,000–3,000 people to protect 500,000.[138] By measures of economics, engineering, and social costs, then, Whittier Narrows Dam was a good project. But this does not render the Army Corps of Engineers' political intervention irrelevant.

Throughout the twentieth century, proposals for increased federal intervention in local government affairs raised concerns that federal agencies would interfere with local politics and threaten home rule and autonomy. Political historians and policy analysts observing the workings of the American federal system have argued that a change in policy venue alters the distribution of power in policy disputes, usually by creating political opportunities for excluded groups. At Whittier Narrows Dam, however, federal flood control reinforced the existing power structure, which suggests that other twentieth-century federal programs have likewise reinforced local politics. In broader terms, the Whittier Narrows Dam episode suggests that creating new political institutions or moving a policy dispute from a local government to a state or federal arena can have more nuanced impacts on American politics than historians or activists have generally assumed.

Also more nuanced than mid-twentieth-century political speech suggests was the impact of federal programs on local political autonomy. Opponents of dozens of federal programs over the decades have protested that increases in federal authority undermine local governments' independence. They have made these claims regardless of whether the federal activities in question replicated local priorities, as they did at Whittier Narrows Dam, or bypassed local government, as did many of the Great Society social programs in the 1960s. The next two chapters illustrate some of the ways that fear of centralization and the appeal of local control limited federal authority. Nevertheless, the record at Whittier Narrows Dam suggests that fear was sometimes misplaced: many federal programs threatened neither local governments' autonomy nor the influence of local powerbrokers. Rather, opponents of specific projects raised the specter of dangerous centralization of power because home rule and local autonomy were such powerful political tropes.

Opponents did not try to defeat Whittier Narrows Dam by arguing that the Army Corps's project threatened Los Angeles's autonomy, perhaps because the Los Angeles County Flood Control Board had failed to build effective flood projects or secure funding to expand flood protection. But the El Monte interests did appeal constantly to another, related theme in American politics and culture: the threat of economic centralization. In their descriptions, residents of Garvey Acres emphasized community, self-sufficiency, and the importance of the land. The Anti–Whittier Narrows Dam Committee echoed this imagery in its sentimental appeals for protection of small farms and family homes. Likewise, the El Monte Citizens Flood Control Committee repeatedly contrasted the small farms threatened by the dam with the greedy "special interests" and industries that endorsed the project.[139] The opposition consistently represented its position as a defense of small business and modest truck farms, the twentieth-century embodiment of Jefferson's agrarian vision of the nation, threatened by the self-interested, large-scale forces of modernization.

Neither El Monte nor Garvey Acres bore much resemblance to the mythic American homestead. The El Monte interests all viewed the region in diverse and complex ways. Many of the "farmers" displaced by the flood control basin used their large gardens to supplement industrial wages and described their property as both a home and a business. Either way, they paid the highest price of any of the groups involved in the debate, and not just because so many of them lost their homes to the dam. The dispute over Whittier Narrows Dam left them and their property in a decade-long limbo during which they could not sell or improve their property. The El Monte Chamber of Commerce, the heart of the opposition, saw Garvey Acres as a market and a base for local industrial development and a site for real estate speculation but also the ideal location for El Monte's sewage treatment plant. As it made clear numerous times, replacing farms and homes with an empty flood control basin undermined its own economic interests.

The Army Corps of Engineers' political engineering was the kind of activity that alienated Americans from the federal government. The early and mid-twentieth century was a period of great increases in, and vehement rejections of, federal power. Some of the episodes of retrenchment grew from changes in circumstance: the end of World

War II did render many wartime institutions irrelevant. Some of them grew from concerted public relations campaigns on the part of private enterprise to turn voters against government regulation or activities that private companies viewed as competition. The private utility corporations' campaigns against government hydroelectric power, discussed in the next chapter, were typical of these efforts. But political activism by federal agencies like that seen during the Whittier Narrows Dam controversy contributed to frustration, mistrust, and disempowerment of those whom federal officials marginalized. This experience surely made residents of Garvey Acres and El Monte more receptive to calls to limit federal power.

The federal government failed El Monte and Garvey Acres not by building the dam but because the Army Corps of Engineers refused to treat them seriously as legitimate participants in flood control policy debates. The Army Corps did not simply reject the river channel alternative that the El Monte interests favored but denied them standing in the policy debates over San Gabriel River flood control. Because the Army Corps and the LACFCD decided whom to include in policy discussions, and because both these agencies needed constituent support to secure congressional funding, they favored groups that agreed with them. The coastal plain interests, for all intents and purposes, became the only public involved in San Gabriel River flood control discussions. In a very real sense, the El Monte opposition lost before the debate even began. The development of air pollution policy similarly revealed how close alliances between civic groups and policy makers shaped environmental policies and excluded dissenting groups. The story of San Gabriel River flood control goes even further, suggesting that opposition groups face greater barriers to political participation than Americans expect. Federal government intervention can raise the threshold to participation, making political exclusion worse. In the case of flood control, this is an ironic result of a well-intentioned effort on the part of Congress to ensure that local communities did, in fact, have a voice in federal flood control policy.

CHAPTER FOUR

PRIVATE POWER AT HOOVER DAM

Utilities, Government Power, and Political Realism, 1920–1928

When approached by road from the Nevada side, Hoover Dam appears first in glimpses. Its 726-foot-high mass, its triumphant sandy arched face, its art nouveau details are revealed slowly; the final impressions are of majesty and an unproblematic celebration of technology so tangible it can make one nostalgic. This impression is not accidental. The physical design of the dam and its carefully planned approach roads were intended to inspire not only confidence in the Bureau of Reclamation but patriotic pride in the nation's ability to conquer nature even in such a remote and forbidding place as the Black Canyon of the Colorado River.[1]

Hoover Dam, known as Boulder Dam before it was built, is widely regarded as the archetype of American high dams. Because American engineers have participated in overseas assistance projects, Hoover Dam has been emulated not only across the West, but also around the world.[2] Just as Whittier Narrows Dam reflects Long Beach's desires, Hoover Dam bears some imprint of the Imperial Valley irrigation interests that spawned it. Much of Southern California receives drinking water and electricity from the dam, but the Imperial Valley receives more benefits than any other region. Nearly three-quarters of California's allotment of the Colorado River flows to the Imperial Irrigation District; urban electricity consumers subsidize irrigation costs. The dam also controls floods on the lower Colorado River, preventing the kind of catastrophe that originally inspired the project. The rest of Southern California reaps substantial benefits, too, in the form of water and electricity. In all, Hoover Dam is a model of early twentieth-century multiple-purpose river development. It was intended as a

Colorado River basin and the All-American Canal

The highway winding over Hoover Dam in 1940. "View of Hoover Dam," ca. 1940. Los Angeles Area of Chamber of Commerce Collection. Courtesy of Doheny Memorial Library, University of Southern California, Los Angeles, California.

practical monument to American technological know-how and public enterprise. It was proposed at the height of both the public power movement and efforts to define federal authority over federal waterways and electric utilities in America. It is surprising, therefore, that half of the electricity delivered to Southern California from the dam is generated and sold by Southern California Edison.

The prominent place of Southern California Edison's generators in the bowels of Hoover Dam reflects the political influence of the electric utility industry. This influence had different origins from either the Los Angeles Chamber of Commerce's on Los Angeles's air quality regulations or Long Beach's role in Whittier Narrows Dam. In those cases, key decision makers recognized a few, specific interest groups as the legitimate representatives of the public interest. These groups secured their influence by defining policy problems and recommending solutions early in the policy-making process or by mobilizing political support for government programs by assisting government officials with vexing public problems. Colorado River development does not follow this mold: Southern California Edison never enjoyed this kind of relationship with Congress or the Bureau of Reclamation. Instead, the utility led an aggressive political campaign against both federal dam building in general and Hoover Dam in particular. So how did Southern California Edison secure its unique position on the Colorado River?

The answer to this question lies partly in the contested history of the public power movement in the United States and partly in the interstate contest for water resources in the West. This latter issue led to a showdown in Congress, during which the Arizona, Utah, and Nevada delegations filibustered the Boulder Canyon Dam Act three times in two years and stalled the dam for nearly a decade. The Arizona, Utah, and Nevada delegations mixed their warnings about the dangers of California's water greed with even more dire warnings about the dangers of government-owned electricity development at the dam. The private utility industry, for its part, did a great deal to encourage this particular objection to Hoover Dam. In the face of such determined opposition, California had to compromise. In Congress, supporters of the dam yielded on the power issue to save the project. As a result, Hoover Dam stands as a compromise between the Progressives' desire for comprehensive, public development of natural resources and conservative fears of excessive federal power. Southern California Edison's generators both demonstrated and enhanced the power of business in twentieth-century American politics because the compromise itself was trumpeted as the acme of public-private cooperation, rather than a stinging defeat of the public power movement.

Imperial Valley, Los Angeles, and the Origins of Hoover Dam

The story of Hoover Dam begins in the Imperial Valley, in the Sonoran Desert of southeastern California. An unlikely place for agriculture, the region has cold winters, very hot summers, and an annual rainfall of about three inches. But in 1901, Charles R. Rockwood's California

Development Company built a canal that sparked a land boom there.[3] When silt clogged the diversion works, the company built a new canal intake south of the Mexican border. Rockwood had to promise Mexican farmers rights to half of the water in the canal to get permission to build in Mexico. In February 1905, a massive flood breached the canal at the new diversion, swamping fields under silt and mud, tearing up railroad tracks, and surging into the Salton Sink. The California Development Company could not close the breach because Mexican authorities, to protect Mexican water rights, refused the company permission to make repairs, and when the Mexican government finally did allow work to proceed, it levied exorbitant duties on the equipment the irrigation company tried to bring across the border.[4] Political unrest in Mexico in the early part of the twentieth century delayed canal repairs and maintenance still further.[5]

Imperial County farmers resented equally Mexican water claims and Mexican "interference" with canal repairs. They wanted a new canal that would deliver water without crossing the Mexican border, but the so-called All-American Canal cost far more than Imperial County irrigators could afford. As a result, in 1919 they sought federal assistance. Arthur Powell Davis, the director of the Bureau of Reclamation, convinced Imperial Valley interests to package their pet project with a multiple-purpose dam to generate hydroelectric power and control floods on the lower Colorado River. U.S. Representative Philip Swing, former chief counsel for the Imperial County Irrigation District, recognized the advantages of this approach; revenue from hydropower would reduce the amount of construction costs that his constituents would have to repay the Reclamation fund and might increase support for the dam in California and in Congress.

In April 1922, Swing and Senator Hiram Johnson introduced a joint bill to authorize the Bureau of Reclamation to build the All-American Canal and a multiple-purpose dam at Boulder Canyon.[6] At the time, Los Angeles not only was the sole market for Boulder Dam's electricity but also desperately needed more electricity. Three years earlier, in 1919, the city of Los Angeles had purchased Southern California Edison's power grid but no generating plants. This did nothing to increase energy supplies because Los Angeles still had to buy power from Southern

California Edison.[7] Los Angeles tried to develop hydroelectric power but found that private utilities owned all the best dam sites in Southern California. Northern California streams were out of the question, too, because of northern water needs, sectional rivalries, and lingering resentment over Los Angeles's actions in the Owens Valley. Frustrated, the city of Los Angeles tried to take a Southern Sierras Power Company plant in the Owens River Gorge by eminent domain. This, too, failed; the U.S. Appeals Court ruled against the city in 1922.[8] By 1922, when Swing and Johnson introduced their bill, the Los Angeles Department of Water and Power seemed out of options and could no longer guarantee power supplies to new factories or refineries.[9]

A hydroelectric dam at Boulder Canyon offered the Imperial Valley the irrigation water and canal system it needed and promised Los Angeles all the electricity it wanted. Energy was so important that Los Angeles offered to contract for all of Boulder Dam's power before Congress even approved the dam.[10] Publicly supplied electricity from Boulder Dam garnered support, too, from other Southern California cities.[11] The mayor of Riverside, California, celebrated the great things that "Government development and Government construction and Government sale" of water and power would bring his community.[12] The Los Angeles Board of Public Service Commissioners, including the prominent reformer John R. Haynes, hired a silent film star to produce a film promoting a city-owned dam on the Colorado River.[13] But the Swing-Johnson bill, also known as the Boulder Canyon bill, inspired immediate, determined opposition because it required the federal government to operate a massive power plant in competition with private utilities and because it established California's rights to so much of the Colorado River. In Los Angeles, the prospect of vastly increased power supplies ultimately trumped the importance public ownership, particularly as the Swing-Johnson bill came under attack from Arizona.

Interstate Conflicts over the Colorado River

While Los Angeles contemplated the hydroelectric potential of the Colorado River, the other states in the region feared what California-focused development might mean for them. In the arid Colorado

River basin, water made the difference between economic growth and stagnation. All seven of the states in that basin—Arizona, California, Colorado, Nevada, New Mexico, Utah, and Wyoming—assigned water rights according to the principle of prior appropriation. This meant that the first person or institution to use water from the Colorado River would own the most secure rights to the river. The main stem of the Colorado was prone to massive, powerful floods, as Rockwood had learned so vividly, so this jealous interest had not yet translated into actual projects. Outside the Imperial Valley, residents of the Colorado River basin relied on groundwater and smaller streams. These practices did not create substantial rights in the Colorado itself. But in the 1920s a number of proposals for large projects, including the proposed dam at Boulder Canyon, threatened to vest California, in particular, with substantial rights in the river. In other words, by the 1920s California's ambitions threatened the water rights and therefore economic futures of the remaining states in the basin.[14]

Concern over water rights surfaced as soon as the Swing-Johnson bill reached Congress. Fears that Hoover Dam would give California senior rights to the river undergirded much of the opposition to federal development of the Colorado River. But interstate disputes represented only part of the water rights picture. By the 1920s, hydroelectric utilities and entrepreneurs had submitted twenty applications to dam the Colorado. Neither the states nor Congress could simply overlook these claims, but these private hydroelectric power projects threatened to further compound competition for water rights.[15]

In the face of intractable disputes between the states and over the ownership of hydroelectric power, Secretary of Commerce Herbert Hoover proposed an interstate compact to distribute water rights among the seven Colorado River basin states. First, he convinced President Warren G. Harding to halt approval of new hydroelectric dam permits on the Colorado. Then he convened delegates from all seven states as the Colorado River Commission. In 1924, the commission sent the Colorado River Compact to the states for approval. The agreement guaranteed the so-called upper basin states of Colorado, New Mexico, Utah, and Wyoming rights to half of the flow of the river, or 7.5 million acre feet per year. The lower basin states of Arizona, California, and Nevada split the other half. This more or less allayed the upper basin's fears of a California monopoly but not Arizona's. The compact did nothing, in Arizona's eyes, to prevent California from using the whole of the lower basin's allotment. When Arizona refused to sign the compact, Hoover and the Colorado River Commission wrote a new compact that required approval by only six states.[16] The Six-State Compact, as it became known, only compounded Arizona's fear of California's power and thirst.

Arizona's suspicions of its larger neighbor figured prominently in debate over the Swing-Johnson bill. In the House of Representatives, Elmer O. Leatherwood of Arizona called the dam "an attempt by the State of California to gain special privileges and advantages in the development of the greatest resource in the Southwest at the expense of other States in the Colorado River Basin."[17] His colleague in the Senate, Henry F. Ashurst, agreed that the dam disproportionately benefited California, and he accused California of negotiating the Colorado River Compact in bad faith.[18] The Arizona state legislature labeled Boulder Dam "a menace" to its state.[19] The Bisbee, Arizona, Chamber of Commerce declared itself "unalterably opposed" to Boulder Dam because "it discriminate[d] against Arizona," sent Arizona's water to California, and permitted federal water projects for the upper basin states even as it denied Arizona these benefits.[20]

Los Angeles's interest in the Colorado River became a particular sore point for Arizona. As early as 1921 Los Angeles municipal officials began eyeing the river as a source of new electrical supplies. Arizona's representative on the Colorado River Commission pointedly questioned "the authority of the City of Los Angeles, as a municipality, to invade another State in quest of power."[21] The *Los Angeles Times*, opposed to public development at Boulder Canyon, cautioned that "Arizona will want to know by what authority the City of Los Angeles intends to jump the State of California line and develop hydroelectric power in another State."[22] The Los Angeles Taxpayers Association also cautioned that "Los Angeles agitation" would prejudice Arizona against the Colorado River Compact and thus interfere with a project Los Angeles desperately needed.[23] The Taxpayers Association was right, of course. Los Angeles's interest in the dam did alarm Arizona. In fact, even though Arizona's elected officials frequently cited the dangers of federal enterprise in their arguments against Hoover Dam, they were no more friendly to Southern California Edison's proposed hydropower monopoly.[24] This suggests that in the welter of claims Arizonans made about the Colorado River, the protection of Arizona's water rights trumped everything else.

A minority in Arizona saw federal development as the only way to counter California's influence. Arizona's delegation to the American Association of Engineers, for example, projected that the Colorado River Compact would promote Arizona agriculture, mines, and industry by increasing energy supplies.[25] Others expected the compact to bring much-needed federal flood control, irrigation, and hydropower projects to Arizona that the state could not afford on its own.[26] Behind these reassuring claims lay an implicit acknowledgment that California could build projects on the Colorado right away and that, unless Arizona took aggressive steps to secure its rights, California would monopolize the river. To protect Arizona's future rights, its leadership pressed Congress to substitute a federal dam at Glen Canyon with "high line canal" to Arizona farms for the Boulder Canyon and All-American Canal complex.[27] This would have placed federal construction squarely within the boundaries of Arizona and so far away from Southern California as to make water or power deliveries there impractical.

Arizona's governor regarded Boulder Dam "the course planned by California for our destruction."[28] By the mid-1920s, Arizona's opposition blocked all progress, and the Swing-Johnson bill stalled in Congress. California withheld its approval of the Six-State Compact as a bargaining chip in Boulder Dam negotiations, causing what little support there was for the Six-State Compact to waiver. Colorado, New Mexico, Utah, and Wyoming still had to decide whether to side with California to promote a dam that would set the stage for federal projects in the upper basin or with Arizona to oppose a dam that would surely give California incentives to block upper basin development and thus reserve more of the river for itself.[29] Even though it was essentially a regional dispute, the conflict over water rights ultimately trumped the national question of who should develop interstate resources and, in particular, hydroelectric power.

Hydro(electric)phobia

Early supporters of Boulder Dam presented public ownership of utilities as crucial to defeating the "power trust's" stranglehold on energy resources in the United States. Opponents like the *Los Angeles Times* countered by citing the benefits of private enterprise, the dangers of big government, and the hysteria of public power advocates. The "rabid politician" (bottom left) is a caricature of Senator Hiram Johnson, the main sponsor of Boulder Dam in the U.S. Senate and a longtime champion of public utilities. "Hydro(electric) phobia" by Edmund Gale, 15 Apr. 1927. Copyright © 1927, *Los Angeles Times*. Reprinted with permission.

The Public Power Question

Phil Swing included federal hydroelectric power development in the Boulder Canyon bill to help his constituents but also because the Water Power Act of 1920 required it. The Water Power Act of 1920 mandated that all federal agencies sell hydroelectric power generated at federal dams to rural electrical cooperatives or municipally owned utilities before they sold power to private, for-profit utility corporations.[30] The legislation had its roots in the expansion of municipal ownership of gas and light networks, waterworks, and even icehouses in the nineteenth century; in the Populists' and Progressives' critiques of large-scale capitalism as a threat to American democracy, equality, and opportunity; and in the inconsistencies of federal water and hydroelectric policies. But Swing introduced the Boulder Canyon bill to a Congress already in a stalemate over federal operation of a dam and power plant on the Tennessee River and to a nation deeply divided over the merits of federal operation of utilities. The hydroelectric provisions in the Swing-Johnson bill ensnared the Colorado River project in that debate.

Federal jurisdiction over hydroelectric power development began in the 1880s when Congress, citing federal authority over public lands, interstate commerce, and navigable rivers, began issuing issue licenses for private hydroelectric power projects and transmission systems on federal lands and streams. During the Theodore Roosevelt and Woodrow Wilson administrations, the Department of the Interior attempted to establish uniform rules to limit the amount of time that a private utility could operate a power plant on public lands or claim water in a navigable stream, to increase federal income from private use of these public resources, and to curb the activities of speculators.[31] In the early twentieth century, the Army Corps of Engineers, the Bureau of Reclamation, and, to a lesser extent, the U.S. Forest Service built dams on public lands in the United States. In keeping with the principles of conservation, and in recognition of scarce of water resources and expensive construction, Congress began to require these agencies to design multiple-purpose rather than single-purpose dams. Federal river agencies could comply with this requirement by installing power plants at their dams.[32] The ensuing growth in federally funded hydroelectric power projects complicated national debates over water policy and excited the concern and opposition of the private utility industry.

The Bureau of Reclamation, in particular, recognized in the multipurpose mandate a solution to one of its greatest challenges. The Reclamation Act of 1902, which created the Reclamation Service (renamed the Bureau of Reclamation in 1907), required irrigators to repay the federal government for the costs of Reclamation projects. Very quickly, however, it became obvious that irrigators on Reclamation projects could not meet repayment requirements. Reclamation responded by extending repayment deadlines and by integrating nonfarm water uses such as urban water supply, flood or silt control, or hydroelectric power generation into its dam designs. Then, Reclamation subtracted the portions of dam construction associated with these other uses from the total costs of these projects to make the irrigators' repayment obligations less onerous. Electricity generation was a special case; Reclamation used revenue from power sales to directly subsidize dam and canal construction costs. By the mid-1920s, this use of power revenue became routine, but the Swing-Johnson bill took this practice one step further by requiring the Bureau of Reclamation to sell enough hydroelectric power to pay for the Boulder Canyon dam.[33]

Niagara Falls and Muscle Shoals

Disputes over public power were heated in the 1920s. When the New York State Water Power Commission approved a proposal for private hydroelectric development of the Saint Lawrence Seaway and Niagara Falls in 1926, accusations of corruption exploded in the New York newspapers. The company seeking the hydroelectric power license was linked to Secretary of the Treasury Andrew W. Mellon. Opponents of private development at Niagara argued that the New York Water Power Commission was intended to promote public utilities and should not give public resources to private interests.[34] The connections between Mellon and the utility company seemed to confirm the public power advocates' assertions that private utilities monopolized vital resources, charged excessive rates, corrupted government, and stifled economic opportunity. The contest gave national exposure to arguments against private development of public resources.

The battle over hydroelectric resources that had the greatest bearing on the Colorado River debate focused on a dam and power plant at Muscle Shoals, Alabama. During World War I, naval warfare impeded U.S. imports of nitrates for fertilizer and explosives. Congress responded with the National Defense Act of 1916, which authorized federal construction of a cyanamid plant to manufacture nitrates, with coal-fired and hydroelectric generating plants to provide power. In 1919, when the war ended, work on the hydropower dam had barely begun; the cyanamid plant had not begun operating either. Although the National Defense Act specifically prohibited privatization of the Muscle Shoals facilities at the end of the war, the Wilson administration wanted to sell it.[35] Swing introduced Boulder Dam at the height of the ensuing battle over public ownership of the Muscle Shoals complex.

Proposals to deaccession Muscle Shoals pitted agricultural interests that wanted inexpensive fertilizer from the cyanamid plant against power companies that wanted to add the coal-fired and hydroelectric generating facilities to their networks, and both of these groups against those who demanded public ownership of the Muscle Shoals complex. In 1922, Henry Ford offered to lease the whole complex for a century for $5 million, about 6 percent of the $85 million that the federal government had already spent on the Muscle Shoals complex.[36] Ford's proposal brought agricultural interests and public power advocates together into an unlikely coalition.[37] Farmers in many parts of the United States had been counting on subsidized fertilizer production after the war; they did not believe Ford would produce enough cheap nitrates to help them. For their part, public power advocates such as Gifford Pinchot, Nebraska senator George Norris, and California senator Hiram Johnson saw in Ford's scheme the embodiment of the very excesses of private capital that gave birth to the public power movement in the first place.[38] They pointed to two federal laws mandating public operation of the Muscle Shoals power plants—the Water Power Act of 1920 and the National Defense Act of 1916—and called private exploitation of Niagara Falls and aspirations for Muscle Shoals a larceny of public assets that would foster monopoly, raise electricity rates, and stall economic growth.[39] They used much the same language in defense of Boulder Dam.

The conflict over Muscle Shoals, and public power generally, grew steadily more strident. The utilities and their laissez-faire allies began denouncing public hydroelectric power as socialism, a tactic that resonated in this Red Scare era.[40] They also pointed to the Teapot Dome scandal as proof that direct federal administration of natural resources opened the way for bribery and corruption at the highest levels of government. Advocates of public ownership countered that "entrenched power companies" in state government would "cause a local scandal comparable to the national scandal that has developed out of the Teapot Dome mess."[41] Similarly, the *Labor News* decried proposals to lease the Muscle Shoals power plants to private utilities as a giveaway of natural resources comparable to Teapot Dome.[42] In an article titled "The People of the United States Do Not Want Another Teapot Dome Scandal," the *American Globe* magazine warned that private utilities sought to create a "system of depriving the people ... from sharing equally in the public domain resources."[43] In a backhanded way, this contest between public and private utilities, with their competing models for America's future, reinforced Americans' suspicion of concentrated power in all its forms. Certainly, the constant references to Teapot Dome helped undermine confidence in the federal government.

Congress debated Muscle Shoals to an impasse that lasted until the creation of the Tennessee Valley Authority in 1933.[44] Meanwhile, proponents of publicly owned utilities continued to argue that inexpensive electricity from government-owned dams would foster economic growth and opportunity and protect the nation from the corrupting influence of big corporations. The other side warned that big government threatened prosperity and that private development of hydropower protected the nation from graft, inefficiency, and high taxes. The conflicts between the public power movement and the utilities over Niagara Falls, Muscle Shoals, and the Colorado River touched on fundamental and still unresolved questions about the roles of government and private enterprise in America.

Public Power and Boulder Dam

Private utilities did not simply oppose government operation of a Boulder Dam power plant on principle. Southern California Edison also had a vested interest in the river. In 1902 and again in 1921, the Bureau of Reclamation and Southern California Edison had jointly surveyed the lower Colorado River.[45] Based on the first trip, the utility began planning comprehensive hydropower development of the river. First, Southern California Edison applied to the Federal Power Commission in November 1920 for a license to build a 500-foot-tall rock-fill hydropower dam at Glen Canyon. Applications for a 410-foot dam at Boulder

Boulder Dam

Politics, namely Arizona's determination to protect its water rights, did indeed block construction on the Colorado River for many years. "Boulder Dam," by Edmund Gale, 15 Jan. 1928. Copyright © 1928, *Los Angeles Times*. Reprinted with permission.

Canyon, a 200-foot structure in nearby Pyramid Canyon, and a fourth, smaller dam near Needles, California, followed in 1921 and 1925.[46] Together, these four dams would have given Edison a near monopoly of the hydroelectric power generating capacity of the river.[47] These ambitious plans made Southern California Edison just as antagonistic to the Swing-Johnson bill as Arizona was.

Southern California Edison and its allies mobilized the same Red Scare rhetoric that was directed against public operation of the Muscle Shoals facilities. Southern Sierras Power called federal dam building defective and costly and warned that "political engineering, political banking, political railroading and general public utility operating is usually unsound and dangerous."[48] Other utilities also denounced public development at Muscle Shoals and Boulder Dam as "'socialistic' and 'dangerous,'"[49] while still other opponents called Boulder Dam a "wide crack in the door for the entry of state socialism" and a "typical instance of the increasing centralization of authority and expenditures in federal bureaus."[50] During the 1920s, a significant number of powerful federal officials shared this opinion, including Secretary of the Interior Albert Fall, who deemed municipal public power systems "socialistic," and executive secretary of the Federal Power Commission Oscar C. Merrill, who so blatantly advocated private hydropower development that Phil Swing eventually accused him of using his office to "discredit government ownership."[51]

Both direct lobbying against Boulder Dam by Southern California Edison, Southern Sierras Power Company, and other utilities and the arguments against public ownership by individuals like Merrill and Fall caused proponents of the dam no end of frustration. Franklin Hichborn, for example, accused private power corporations of "blocking Boulder Canyon as [a] public ownership project," much as they had brought about the defeat of "other public ownership projects in California."[52] Senator Norris criticized the power companies for "dirty, disreputable politics" when Southern California Edison ordered employees to flood Congress with prewritten telegrams criticizing Boulder Dam and the industry orchestrated a $200,000 citizen telegram drive against the Swing-Johnson bill. "These telegrams," he complained, "were sent at the command of the power trust" by citizens who had little or no understanding of the Boulder Canyon bill itself.[53] In the late 1920s, the Federal Trade Commission investigated the utility industry for its political activities, among other things, and even though the commission found no evidence of a monolithic "power trust," its revelations about the utilities' long and aggressive campaign against public power provided fodder for proponents of Boulder Dam.[54]

Supporters of the dam came to see the power question as the major barrier to congressional approval and began to treat the dam and hydroelectric generation as separate issues.[55] According to Secretary of the Interior Hubert Work, for example, "The sale of power by the government, which was paramount in the discussions in Congress, is only incidental to the more important features of the project."[56] Likewise, as secretary of commerce, Hoover insisted that using power revenue to offset construction costs did not require "the entrance of the Federal government into either the generation or the distribution of electric power."[57] Bertrand H. Snell, a Republican representative from New York, took a different tack, declaring support for Boulder Dam "as it pertains to flood control" but disputing the notion that the federal government had to "generate and distribute electric current in competition with private industry in order to give those people the flood protection they are entitled to."[58] Even Hiram Johnson, the sponsor of Boulder Dam in the Senate, softened his position on public power.

Boulder Dam in Congress

The final showdown in Congress began four years after Swing and Johnson introduced the first Boulder Dam bill and stretched over two years and three Senate filibusters. For much of that time, Boulder Dam enjoyed the support of a slim majority of Congress, President Coolidge, and Secretary of Commerce and chief architect of the Colorado River Compact Herbert Hoover. But the determined opposition of Arizona's congressional delegation, with occasional help from its counterparts in Nevada and Utah, successfully delayed one floor vote after another.[59] By framing its objections as the defense of private enterprise and state sovereignty against a power-hungry federal government and imperial California, Arizona's congressional delegation secured enough support to force California to make the concessions. This was an astute strategy, but one that ultimately failed to block the dam.

The first filibuster of the Swing-Johnson bill came in February 1926. Arizona had thus far refused to sign the Colorado River Compact; meanwhile, California had also refused to sign to keep pressure on the upper basin states to support Boulder Dam. But this strategy now threatened to unravel the whole Colorado River Compact. In January 1926 the Coolidge administration tried to push the compact forward by announcing support for amendments to the Swing-Johnson bill that would have denied benefits from Boulder Dam to any state that did not sign the compact.[60] A few weeks after Coolidge's announcement, Senators Ashurst and Ralph H. Cameron, from Arizona, assisted by Reed Smoot and William H. King, of Utah, initiated a filibuster of Boulder Dam that ended the Senate's consideration of the Colorado River for the year.

In June 1926 the *Los Angeles Examiner* polled U.S. representatives and senators about the Swing-Johnson bill. The vast majority of those who responded dismissed the poll as a naked attempt by the *Examiner* to force a vote on the bill but nevertheless spoke in favor of both Boulder Dam and public power.[61] A Nebraska Democrat, for example, accused the Coolidge administration of "murdering every piece of legislation which does not have advance approval of the Morgan Mellon group," the private utility interests that by then controlled hydropower at Niagara Falls.[62] One of Wisconsin's representatives, who described himself as an "anti-administration Republican," announced, "In my judgment [the] so called Swing Johnson Boulder Dam project should be completed by government and protection given and power used by [the] Federal government." He went on to emphasize, "If proper safeguards are not incorporated to prevent private power corporations from obtaining control of the power [at Boulder Dam], . . . I cannot support the bill."[63] One of the few respondents who opposed Swing-Johnson rejected both public ownership of the power plant and any projects to expand agriculture as long as U.S. farmers produced record surpluses.[64] The *Examiner* poll revealed two things to its Southern California readership: first, that a majority in Congress favored Boulder Dam; and second, that the fate of the Swing-Johnson bill was hopelessly entwined with the public power question. The fact that most of the letters to the *Examiner* defended public power did not signal a national consensus on government ownership of hydroelectric facilities.

In October California governor Friend Richardson entered the fray. Richardson blamed California's continued refusal to sign the Colorado River Compact for the stalemate in Congress, so he called a special session of the California legislature to approve the compact.[65] He may have done this in response to pressure from the governors of the upper basin states. Wyoming governor Nellie T. Ross, fearing that California's continued reticence would hurt her state's interests in the Colorado, had already threatened to withdraw her state's support for the Boulder Canyon project if California did not sign.[66] Richardson's special session prompted Utah governor George H. Dern to convene a Colorado River conference, with the optimistic forecast that California and Arizona would now settle their differences.[67] Hiram Johnson and Phil Swing, in contrast, rejected the special session as meddling. Johnson suspected that Richardson actually wanted to kill the Boulder Canyon project.[68] Swing fumed because he believed that the threat that California might reject the compact, and that threat alone, ensured the upper basin states' support for Boulder Dam in Congress.[69] Things got heated even before the special session began as Johnson and Swing denounced Richardson as a dupe of Harry Chandler and the private utilities, while Richardson accused Hiram Johnson of sacrificing the needs of the Imperial Valley to promote "the Johnson political machine."[70] The California legislature did not approve the compact during the special session.

Congress reconvened in early December 1926, with the Swing-Johnson bill prominent on the calendar. The day Congress resumed, the *Los Angeles Times* reported that Governor George W. P. Hunt of Arizona planned to request the Arizona legislature to "withdraw opposition" to Boulder Dam if the federal government would promise Arizona "sufficient water to irrigate lands which can be practically developed" and a share in power revenue generated at the dam. Hunt claimed that Nevada concurred. This represented a big change from Hunt's previous, determined opposition to Boulder Dam and his insistence that any dams on the lower Colorado be built within Arizona, where his state could better control them.[71] In Congress, the House Irrigation Committee struggled to resolve Arizona's objections to the Swing-Johnson bill, first by trying to persuade Arizona, California, and Nevada to settle water allocations in conference and then by considering a variety of amendments to Swing-Johnson to enumerate water rights and the distribution of power revenues from the dam. These suggestions expanded on earlier proposals made by the Colorado River Commission to mediate between Arizona and California but went somewhat further.[72] In spite of Hunt's assurances and the efforts of the House Irrigation Committee, Arizona continued to block both the Swing-Johnson bill and the Colorado River Compact.

As the House Irrigation Committee debated amendments to the

Swing-Johnson bill, F. A. Reid of Arizona's Colorado River Commission announced that Arizona would withdraw its objections to Boulder Dam if guaranteed exclusive rights to all the tributaries to the Colorado within its borders and half of the unallocated water in the main stem the Colorado minus three hundred thousand acre feet for Nevada. Reid also urged the United States to ignore all Mexican claims to the Colorado. Reid wanted more than water for Arizona; his plan also would have given Arizona and Nevada control over the hydroelectric power generated at the dam and would have allowed these two states to own the dam itself if they repaid construction costs.[73] Finally, Reid promised that Arizona would sell surplus electricity to California if the two states could agree on a price. The water rights provisions of Reid's proposal were not new, and they still guaranteed California the lion's share of the lower basin's portion of the river because the Imperial Valley held vested rights to 2,280,000 acre feet of water a year, six times more than the 325,000 acre feet that Arizona communities could claim at the time. But Reid's plan still set aside more water for Arizona than any other proposal on the table, and would have given Arizona both a steady stream of income from the dam, and a certain power over its larger neighbor.

Throughout December 1926 and January 1927, the House Irrigation Committee urged Arizona, California, and Nevada to compromise on water allocations. Representative Carl Hayden of Arizona attacked federal plans for the Colorado River as a "violation of the Federal Constitution and an illegal invasion of the rights of the State of Arizona."[74] Hayden argued that Los Angeles could get all the water it needed from the Sierra Nevada, ignoring the growing competition for water within California itself, and proposed that the seven Colorado River basin states create a Colorado River authority rather than cede control of the river to the Bureau of Reclamation. He objected most strongly to any plan for structures in one state that might "create prior rights to use of water which may thereafter prevent needed agricultural development in another."[75] In this telling statement, Hayden made his state's priorities clear. All of Arizona's representatives cited the dangers of excessive federal authority, of government ownership of hydroelectric power resources, and of California's desire to claim other states' resources in order to protect Arizona's water rights.

Legislators seemed unwilling to impose a water distribution scheme on the lower basin states or to try to override Arizona's determined opposition to Boulder Dam. Meanwhile, public power provisions of the Swing-Johnson bill attracted powerful allies to Arizona's side. W. M. Whittington of Mississippi, for example, joined Utah's Elmer O. Leatherwood and Hayden in their minority report from the House Irrigation Committee on the Swing-Johnson bill because he opposed federal hydroelectric development and saw Boulder Dam as an invasion of states' rights.[76] Charles Eaton of New Jersey criticized Swing-Johnson as a "socialistic Russian Scheme of having the Federal Government go into the power business in competition with its own citizens."[77] Senator Cole Blease of South Carolina joined the May 1928 filibuster against Swing-Johnson citing the same states' rights and public power issues that turned Whittington against Boulder Dam.[78]

Although Arizona's officials fretted more about their water rights, the public power issue and, to a lesser extent, the question of states' rights dominated debate over the Swing-Johnson bill during the Sixty-ninth Congress. In the House, the Senate, and the press, opponents criticized Boulder Canyon dam as a public power scheme masquerading as an irrigation or flood control project. Leatherwood frequently made this the focus of his attacks. At a speech before the California Taxpayers Association, for example, he criticized the Swing-Johnson bill for setting a dangerous precedent "for the Government to go further into business and development" that every interest group in the Colorado River basin would exploit to its own advantage. Public ownership of hydroelectric facilities, he said, was paternalistic and "inimical to the best interests of the United States."[79] On the floor of the House, he called the Boulder Canyon bill "a gigantic Government power project masquerading in the more appealing clothing of flood control and needed water for irrigation."[80] While the House Irrigation Committee considered the bill in December 1926, he had proposed amendments to eliminate federal funding for power plant construction and to give the secretary of the interior broader discretion to license private or municipal utilities to carry out hydropower development at Boulder Dam. These amendments would have enabled Congress to "avoid adoption of any provision that would place the Federal government in the power business."[81]

In January 1927, when the Rules Committee seemed poised to send Boulder Dam to the House floor, prospects for the Swing-Johnson bill were grim. Coolidge urged congressional approval of the bill "at the earliest possible moment" but would not promise to sign it.[82] Hoover, in spite of his years of effort on the Colorado River Compact, refused to comment.[83] Meanwhile, opponents of public power inundated Congress with telegrams demanding private power development at Boulder Dam.[84] When pressed, the Utah and Arizona congressional delegations and other critics of the government hydropower blamed Phil Swing and Hiram Johnson for delaying vital southwestern development by insisting on a federally owned power plant at the dam. When major flooding threatened the Imperial Valley in February and then devastated the Mississippi Valley in April, these accusations grew more strident and pointed.[85]

Norris saw the swarm of telegrams that arrived in Washington in mid-January not as a public rebuke of an unpopular project but as a sign of utility industry propaganda.[86] Swing also blamed the slow progress on the influence of private utilities. Johnson warned colleagues that they played into the hands of the power trust if they voted against the Swing-Johnson bill and fretted that the utilities would fight Boulder Dam to a standstill just as they had Muscle Shoals.[87] He tried to redefine the dam as a flood control project that used power revenue to defray public expenses, but this tactic was probably weakened when he and Phil Swing resisted emergency flood appropriations for the Imperial Valley because they feared the smaller flood projects would weaken support for Boulder Dam.[88]

In January, the *Los Angeles Times* predicted that the Sixty-ninth Congress would not approve Boulder Dam with a government-owned power plant.[89] Then, the House Rules Committee began considering another round of amendments from Leatherwood and finally decided to put off sending the Swing-Johnson bill to the floor until the lower basin states settled their differences over water allocations and hydropower revenue.[90] In the Senate, the bill faired no better. The upper house took up Boulder Dam as unfinished business in mid-February, but even Hiram Johnson admitted the bill would not pass. On the floor in the Senate, the Arizona and Utah delegations promptly filibustered the bill. After more than thirty hours, Johnson lost the cloture vote, and the Senate moved on to other business and adjournment.[91]

The second Boulder Dam filibuster aroused considerable ire in Los Angeles. John R. Haynes took his frustration out on the press, criticizing the *Los Angeles Evening Express* for suppressing facts about Boulder Dam to protect the interests of its owner, whom Haynes described derisively as a "power company man" who selfishly kept the benefits of publicly owned power from Angelenos.[92] Haynes also accused a number of Congress members of conflict of interest in the Boulder Dam debates. Lawrence C. Phipps, the chair of the Senate Irrigation Committee and senator from Colorado, he revealed, had invested in Southern Sierras Power Company. Representative Charles A. Eaton from New Jersey, who promoted "a permanent, sane, economic policy" of water resource development "featured by the Government keeping out of the field of private business," Haynes noted, had edited General Electric Company's publication, *The Lamp*, for years before running for Congress.[93] Haynes was not the only one making these accusations; the *New Republic* blamed the filibuster on the "menace of the holding company interests which contributed large sums toward the election of a former utility commissioner as Senator from Illinois."[94]

Of course, not all opponents of the Swing-Johnson bill had formal ties to the utility industry,[95] but the power companies did escalate their lobbying efforts in the months leading up to December 1927. They now tempered their position and focused on removing language from the Swing-Johnson bill that mandated public hydropower development at the dam rather than defeating the federal dam project itself.[96] Other groups now joined the chorus for private hydropower development. The American Engineering Council, for example, challenged the engineering and economic feasibility of the dam in the midst of Senate debate in the spring of 1928.[97] A pamphlet circulated among southern Congress members warning that Boulder Dam would hurt their constituents by expanding cotton production in the Southwest.[98] With so many voices raised against the bill, Representative Leatherwood boasted that William Randolph Hearst's newspapers were "the only substantial support" the Swing-Johnson bill had.[99] Of course this was not true. The American Legion endorsed Boulder Dam, as did the Las

Vegas Chamber of Commerce; the cities of Pasadena, Long Beach, Riverside, and San Diego; and many in Congress.[100]

The Swing-Johnson bill did not reach the floor of either the House or the Senate until quite late in the spring of 1928. For months leading up to the floor debate, the Arizona delegation, with support from Utah and Nevada, pressed for more water. It no longer attacked Boulder Dam as a "socialistic" adventure into public power but instead demanded that Arizona receive compensation for hydropower sent to California. California's legislators rejected Arizona's demands and tried to direct their colleagues' attention to the importance of Boulder Dam for flood control and development in Imperial County.[101] The majorities on the House and Senate Irrigation committees, joined by the *Los Angeles Times* and civic groups as varied as the National Association of Insurance Agents and the Phoenix Real Estate Board, urged compromise and pressed the lower basin states to settle their differences through negotiation.[102] No one really wanted to override Arizona's fervent objections.

In the face of this intractable opposition, Hiram Johnson tried to cultivate allies for cloture votes, if not for the Swing-Johnson bill itself, by stepping aside so that the Senate could address other pressing business instead of insisting that the Senate turn right away to the Colorado River.[103] Appropriations, the Norbeck migratory bird refuge bill that was filibustered to delay debate on McNary-Haugen farm relief bill, the farm relief bill itself, and a last-minute twenty-hour filibuster of a Muscle Shoals bill that Coolidge later vetoed delayed Senate debate on Boulder Dam until late May and the very end of the congressional session.[104] After all these delays, Missouri senator James A. Reed threatened to filibuster a tax bill to put more pressure on Johnson.[105] Meanwhile, Senator Ashurst persisted with his threat to filibuster rather than "engage in any compromise to bargain away the rights of Arizona and thus make our State a vassal and servile thing."[106]

As the time to debate or filibuster the Swing-Johnson bill approached, Carl Hayden, elected to Ralph H. Cameron's Senate seat in 1927, and Utah's senators claimed not to have decided whether they would join with Ashurst.[107] Their apparent ambivalence signaled some willingness to negotiate over the Colorado River. In fact, it had been obvious for some time that only negotiations between California and Arizona could settle the stalemate. Ashurst's obvious pleasure that Boulder Dam had "lost considerable ground in the last few weeks" and that "influential Republican newspapers through the country" now opposed congressional action in the absence of a seven-state compact added to the pressure on California to concede to Arizona's demands.[108] Several senators from other Colorado basin states also tried to delay Senate action on the Swing-Johnson until Arizona and California could come to an agreement. Senators King of Utah and Phipps of Colorado called for new engineering and economic studies of the Colorado River.[109] King also disputed the need for flood control on the lower Colorado, sparking a series of angry descriptions of the dire threat that the river posed to Imperial County and western Arizona.[110] While Ashurst tried to amend Swing-Johnson to delay construction on the dam until all seven states ratified the Colorado River Compact, Phipps proposed allowing the project to proceed with a six-state compact, but with private power development. Meanwhile, Key Pittman of Nevada threatened to filibuster if his amendments granting power royalties to Nevada and Arizona and giving the lower basin states preferential rights to contract for power at the dam did not reach the Senate floor. The Senate Irrigation Committee approved Phipps's and Pittman's amendments over Johnson's objections.[111]

When the Swing-Johnson bill finally went before the full Senate a week before adjournment, it contained Phipps's and Pittman's amendments: it provided for federal construction of Boulder Dam after yet another engineering study, power royalties for Arizona and Nevada, and private hydroelectric development and gave California, Arizona, and Nevada preference in power contracts. The filibuster began immediately, with Ashurst, Hayden, and their allies urging the Senate to protect Arizona's rights and to force California and the federal government to compensate Arizona and Nevada for the use of Arizona's and Nevada's power resources. During the Senate filibuster, the possibility that Boulder Dam would increase Mexican rights to Colorado water, rather than the public power question, dominated debate, probably because Coolidge was in the middle of water negotiations with Mexico.[112] Of course, the power question did not disappear. The *New York Times* political correspondent Richard V. Oulahan, for example, described both

Boulder Dam and Muscle Shoals "as an entering wedge for government ownership of public utilities."[113] Hiram Johnson, for his part, continued to insist that his bill included hydropower development "only [as] the instrument for financing" the dam without burdening the general treasury; Swing noted that even this idea had come from Secretary of the Interior Hubert Work, not the sponsors of the bill. Johnson also dismissed power generation as purely incidental to flood control, irrigation, solving "the Mexican water problem," and supplying water for domestic use in Southern California.[114] Presenting the public power provisions of the bill thus may have been the only way to counter the opposition's description of Boulder Dam as an entering wedge for socialism or government ownership, but because it severed power ownership from the dam itself, it ultimately facilitated private development of the Colorado River's power resources.

While Ashurst and Hayden filibustered the bill in the Senate, an amended version of Swing-Johnson passed in the House of Representatives. Swing accepted an amendment that required a new engineering study of the dam and the dam site because it seemed to have no real teeth. The more important amendment, identical to Pittman's in the Senate, granted Arizona and Nevada each just under 18 percent of the surplus power profits from the dam.[115] The House rejected several additional changes to the bill in the final days of debate, including one that would have allowed Arizona to block construction indefinitely simply by refusing to sign the Colorado River Compact.[116] Meanwhile, in the Senate, Johnson attempted to rally support for cloture. When this failed, he tried to delay adjournment. Finally, with assurances that the Senate would take up Boulder Dam before anything else when it reconvened in December, Johnson agreed to let the Senate adjourn. By then, the Senate had grown so contentious that even adjournment required a dramatic tie-breaking vote by Vice President Charles G. Dawes.[117]

In December 1928, the lame duck Seventieth Congress resumed for a short session scheduled to last only until March, with Boulder Dam at the top of the Senate's agenda. Hoover waited in the wings to take office, promising to convene an extra session of Congress to complete unfinished business including treaties with Europe, farm aid, manufacturing tariffs, new cruisers for the navy, and, if necessary, Boulder

Dam.[118] This reduced the likelihood of yet another filibuster of the Swing-Johnson bill, but the Senate resumed debate on Boulder Dam in early December as though uninterrupted. Carl Hayden now led the opposition, reiterating Arizona's objections to losing revenue to federal hydropower development and demanding 400,000 acre feet of water more than California wanted to concede. Johnson claimed to be willing to compromise but rejected Hayden's demand for power royalties, arguing that "if the Federal Government financed the project the State should not have the right to tax it," and refused to reduce California's water allocation below 4.6 million acre feet.[119] Senators from New Mexico, Colorado, Utah, and Nevada finally brokered a compromise that split the difference between Arizona's and California's water allocation demands. This amendment reduced California's allocation to 4.4 million from 4.6 million acre feet and increased Arizona's allocation from 2.6 million to 2.8 million acre feet. Johnson accepted the deal to end Arizona's opposition, but when Ashurst demanded power royalties and exclusive rights to the Gila River for Arizona, Johnson changed his mind. Nevertheless, the Senate approved the water allocation compromise by a vote of 48 to 29 and subsequently gave Arizona the power royalties and Gila River rights it also wanted.[120]

As Boulder Dam ground its way through Congress, the intractable disagreements over the Colorado River forced each side to pare its position back to its essentials. For Arizona, this meant focusing on water allocations and preserving state revenues from natural resource exploitation. For California, it meant securing water and energy supplies and federal construction of the All-American Canal. The representatives from the upper basin states focused on protecting water rights and future federal development in their communities. At the same time, all those involved sought to connect their concerns to larger, national policy questions such as states' rights, government hydroelectric development, private enterprise, and even comprehensive water resources planning. They hoped that by drawing a connection to national policy debates they might secure support from legislators or constituents otherwise unaffected by a dam in the southwestern corner of the United States. But the congressional delegations from Arizona, California, and the other basin states quickly dropped larger policy objectives when they burdened the bill. Most significant, when pressed by Arizona's intractable opposition, California's congressional delegation jettisoned its insistence on the public power provisions of the bill. As long as Los Angeles could get power to pump water over the mountains and to run its factories, it did not really care who generated or profited from the electricity.

The Senate finally approved Boulder Dam on 14 December 1928; Coolidge signed it a week later.[121] By the time Boulder Dam was complete, Southern California was guaranteed 58 percent of the lower basin's water and, directly or indirectly, 80 percent of Hoover Dam's power. Most of California's share of the water flows to the Imperial Valley, but greater Los Angeles also received nearly everything it wanted. Arizona, in contrast, had to wait until 1993 for the Central Arizona Project and has had to fight California again and again for its promised water allocation.

Conclusion: The Celebration of Public-Private Cooperation

The final Boulder Canyon Act required the Bureau of Reclamation to sign power contracts with parties that could guarantee enough power revenue to underwrite the project before any construction began.[122] But the Boulder Canyon Act neither mandated public hydropower nor specified who would generate or distribute electricity from the dam. Instead, Congress gave the Bureau of Reclamation three options: wholesale power from federally operated turbines, lease machinery in a federally constructed power plant, or lease the *right* to generate power in a power plant built and operated by leaseholders.[123] Arizona and Nevada were each guaranteed a block of power for their future use and 18 percent each of the power revenue from the dam.[124] The Metropolitan Water District, created to deliver water from the Colorado River to urban Southern California, obtained fully half of the electricity generated at the dam to pump water into the Los Angeles basin. This left 30 percent of the dam's power output to be allocated by the secretary of the interior, Ray L. Wilbur.

When Herbert Hoover first convened the Colorado River Commission and when Phil Swing introduced the first Boulder Canyon dam bill, it was practically a foregone conclusion that a multiple-purpose dam on the Colorado River would include a government-owned power plant. The scale of the project, the high cost of irrigating the Imperial Irrigation District, and the requirement that irrigators repay the Bureau of Reclamation for construction costs made the sale of hydroelectricity power to a large, urban market like Los Angeles absolutely essential. It was not essential that the Bureau of Reclamation itself operate or even build the power plant, however. So Wilbur split the available electricity between the Los Angeles Department of Water and Power and Southern California Edison, even though the Los Angeles Department of Water and Power had offered to purchase all available power.[125]

Historians have argued that legislators intended to leave the public power question open and that the requirement that the secretary of the interior have power contracts in hand before construction began pushed Wilbur to select the most financially viable bids. This makes private utility presence in the power plant seem more incidental than it was. By December 1928, backers of the Boulder Canyon project knew that Hoover would be the next president and that, although he supported the dam, he did not favor public power.[126] They could not have been shocked that a compromise on hydropower resulted in contracts for a private utility corporation. In fact, Swing, Johnson, and the other champions of Boulder Dam expressed neither outrage nor surprise at Wilbur's decision. Even John R. Haynes accepted Southern California Edison's contract at Boulder Dam as useful for preventing public agencies from taking on too many financial burdens.[127] More to the point, as Phil Swing explained to the Imperial Irrigation District in 1930, any fracturing of California interests would have reduced the amount of water and power California received.[128] Southern California Edison was one of those California interests.

Once Congress approved the dam, the utilities that had fought the Swing-Johnson bill abruptly changed their stance. Southern California Edison, for example, still denied that the dam would "emancipat[e] ... an oppressed people from the tentacles of an imaginary power trust octopus" but now trumpeted the benefits of federal "flood protection, irrigation, and the disbursement of hundreds of millions of new money for material, labor and supplies" in the Southwest.[129] The utilities' new enthusiasm galled the champions of public ownership. Even years later, critics raged that private corporations "claim[ed] the right to install their own generators in public dams, build transmission lines and retail the power."[130] They complained that the utilities had duped the American public, opposing the Boulder Canyon bill only to ensure that they profited from dams built with the taxpayers' dollar. But as growth and ready supplies of water and power overshadowed other possible benefits from the dam, the basis for excluding private utilities crumbled.

Reactions to Boulder Dam in Congress and in the press revealed deep ambivalence about the relationship between government and private enterprise in the 1920s. On the one hand, voters elected three presidents in a row—Harding, Coolidge, and Hoover—who favored private over public enterprise. A great deal of ink was used in describing public concern about the inefficiencies and corruption inherent in government operation of enterprises like power plants. At the same time, revelations about industry misdeeds fueled an impulse toward public ownership and regulation. Advocates of Boulder Dam tried to mobilize this by accusing energy holding companies of evading state regulations by combining into multistate enterprises, by citing the propaganda that the utilities employed to dupe Americans into opposing government ownership, and of course by referring to the Teapot Dome scandal.

The ambivalence about utilities companies played out differently in local and national politics. At least in Los Angeles in the 1920s, rhetorical appeals to public rights had more success in local than national politics. After all, a campaign based in part on references to the public interest and public rights resulted the purchase of the municipal power grid in 1919 and the construction of the ill-fated Saint Francis Dam and power plant. This same language was used to justify the industrial zoning regulations that moved oil wells out of residential neighborhoods and beaches and to challenge private beach clubs around this same time. It is important not to oversimplify Los Angeles's record of business regulation or municipal ownership. As the other chapters in this volume demonstrate, business interests as a whole were intimately involved in all aspects of policy making in Los Angeles. Nevertheless, campaigns for public ownership in Washington faced greater resistance from a potent coalition of disparate business interests that rallied the merits of private enterprise and states' rights to their cause. In the case of Boulder Dam, this coalition consisted of electric utilities, insurance companies, the American Federation of Labor, banking organizations, and chambers of commerce from all over the country.[131] They spoke out even if—like the Ohio Chamber of Commerce, which called government ownership of the Boulder Dam power plant "a far cry from the ideas of the founders of this government"—they could expect Boulder Dam to have little direct impact on their pockets.[132]

The ambivalence about roles of private enterprise, regulations, and government authority makes the compromise on hydropower at Hoover Dam all the more poignant and important. The compromise was born of political necessity but was celebrated as the solution not just to development on the Colorado River but also to the problems with both private enterprise and government ownership. The public sector was expected to check the private sector, and the private sector to balance the public, even as they both supplied the Southwest with important public services. When Southern California Edison and the Bureau of Reclamation signed contracts for Boulder Dam power, they all but settled the debate over public power in the United States. The public power movement seemed to have exhausted itself passing the Water Power Act of 1920 and blocking private development of Muscle Shoals. Even during the New Deal, proponents of government ownership and comprehensive planning failed to replicate the Tennessee Valley Authority. More important, the hybrid of public and private enterprise that grew out of the bitter conflicts over the Colorado River came to be portrayed as the acme of effective government, subject to far less criticism even than the participation of industry leaders in designing industrial regulations. By the time the dam was completed, few regarded Southern California Edison's role there as controversial or odd. This type of cooperation was one of many forces that shaped the postwar ideology of political economy emphasizing public-private cooperation over public enterprise and that kept private industry central to American public policy.

CHAPTER FIVE

THE TRIUMPH OF LOCALISM

The Rejection of National Water Planning in 1950

In December 1928, in an editorial announcing that the Senate had finally passed the Boulder Canyon dam bill, the *New York Times* lamented that Congress had missed an opportunity to plan the development of all the Colorado River's resources for the benefit of the entire region and nation. Instead, Congress, "torn by conflicting desires and expediencies of the moment," had responded piecemeal to the competing demands of Imperial Valley irrigators, utility corporations, cities, and the states.[1] Two decades later, another opportunity for comprehensive water resources planning arose. This time it was defeated less by the "conflicting desires and expediencies of the moment" than by fear of federal power. In some ways, debate over national water resources planning in 1950 echoed the Colorado River controversies of the 1920s. The midcentury debate, however, concluded with an even more ringing endorsement of business influence in American government. More even than Los Angeles's public beach, air pollution, flood control, or electric power controversies, the defeat of the 1950 federal water resources planning proposal demonstrates that Americans now looked to business to direct and contain the power of government.

(OPPOSITE) Boundaries of the major river basins in the United States, prepared for a study of national water resources in 1937. The President's Water Resources Policy Commission's proposals for river basin planning echoed a number of earlier proposals for comprehensive, coordinated river development. U.S. National Resources Committee, Water Resources Committee, "Basin Subdivisions for Drainage Basin Study," 1937. Reproduced by permission of The Huntington Library, San Marino, California.

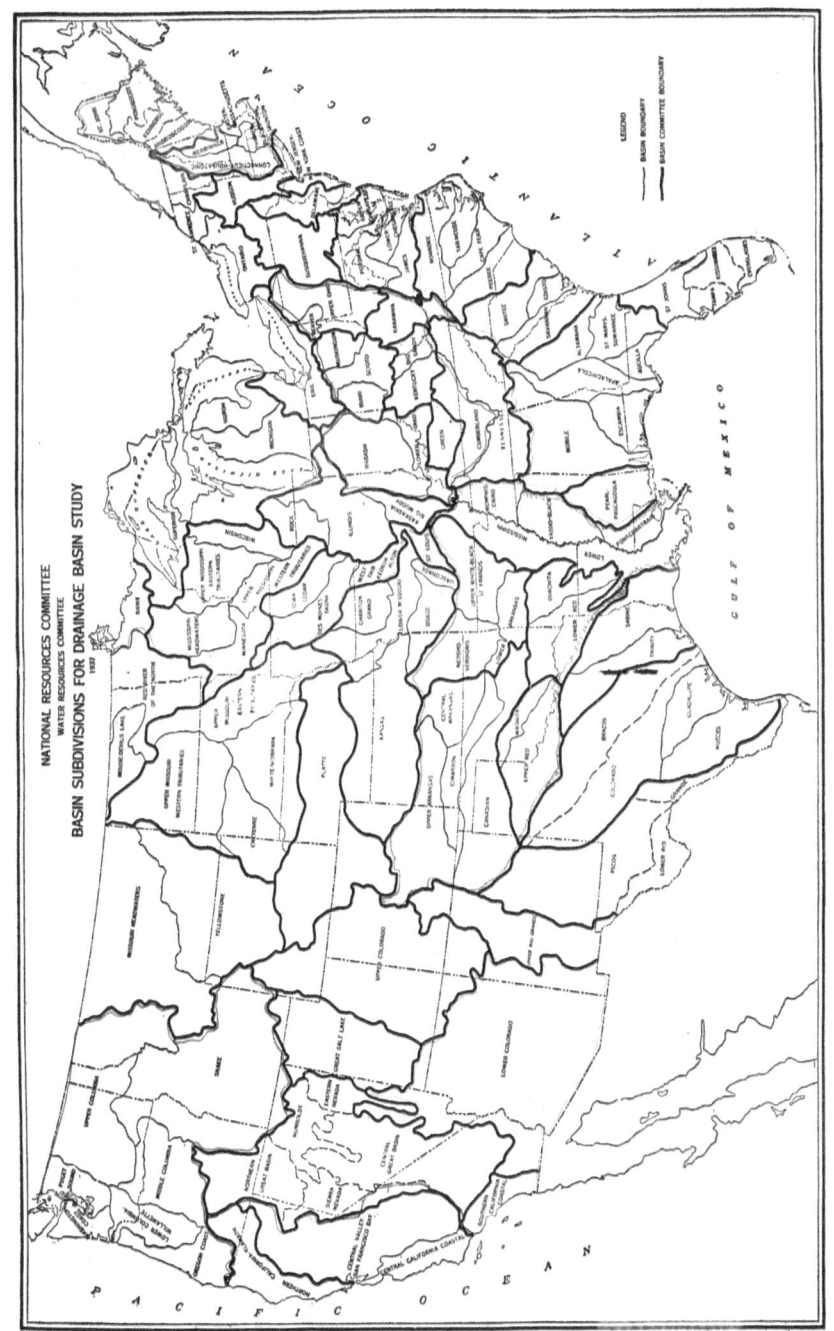

The issue of water resources planning arose after World War II because of a paradox. Because of wartime growth, cities like Los Angeles were desperately short of jobs, housing, roads, sewers, drinking water, and electricity. Local officials lobbied for and expected federal spending to help remedy these problems, some of which had plagued their cities since well before the war. After the war, however, many of the individuals who sought federal funds for their communities also joined a national campaign to curb federal spending. Frustration with wartime economic restrictions fed this campaign, but many opponents of federal spending also worried that programs intended to rebuild the civilian economy in one region would undermine the stability and prosperity of their own communities. Decades of positive depictions of public-private cooperation, including the celebration of Southern California Edison's role at Hoover Dam and the hoopla that surrounded the Dollar-a-Year men's roles in the war bureaucracy, shaped public assessments of government after World War II. The political influence of America's business communities and decades of industry campaigns against government regulation and public ownership of utilities played a role, too. In practice, the drive for federal retrenchment meant that community leaders sought federal spending for themselves but lobbied against federal investments elsewhere. In the late 1940s, Americans continued to see federal programs as essential to their own communities even as they feared federal spending in general as a threat to free enterprise and democracy. Herein lay the paradox.

Congress was ill equipped to resolve this paradox. Congress members recognized that they served their constituents better by securing more spending for their own districts than by rejecting new federal projects. In other words, each Congress member judged his or her constituents' desires for federal projects in their communities as greater than their opposition to federal spending in general. Outside Congress, executive agencies responsible for actually implementing federal initiatives, such as the Army Corps of Engineers and the Bureau of Reclamation, had their own institutional incentives to build and spend more. So the federal budget expanded. Meanwhile, critics blamed ballooning budgets on outdated New Deal visions of an activist federal government and on federal agencies' own desires for larger budgets. As a group of faculty members from Stanford University put it, federal spending was growing "like Topsy, under the influence of local and sectional pressures, competition among different Federal agencies," and obsolete ideas.[2] The Stanford group was correct, of course, and in no policy arena was that clearer than water resources management.[3]

President Harry Truman found himself caught in the middle of this conflict, under pressure both to accede to local demands for specific projects and to reduce federal spending. Analysts argued for federal dams to assist with postwar reconversion, industrial decentralization, and agricultural expansion and to reduce regional poverty. But new irrigation projects might just as easily add to ruinous agricultural surpluses and industrial competition. Moreover, neither the federal agencies nor Congress used consistent standards to evaluate the costs and benefits of even the simplest federal dams. Truman recognized that demands for ever more dams "naturally . . . resulted in conflicts, inconsistencies, and wastes that the Nation [could] ill afford."[4] So in January 1950 he created the President's Water Resources Policy Commission to "study and make recommendations . . . with respect to Federal responsibility for and participation in the development, utilization, and conservation of water resources."[5] The PWRPC was charged with injecting logic, clear national objectives, and standards for project evaluation into this highly political process. The commissioners themselves hoped to replace piecemeal development with comprehensive planning. They failed.

Although national planning might have resolved interstate conflicts, reduced federal spending, improved military preparedness, and brought prosperity to impoverished communities, Americans soundly rejected the PWRPC's proposals. In so doing, they ensured that federal water policy would continue to reflect the logic of local politics rather than national or even state priorities. The resolute rejection of the PWRPC's proposals protected the influence of the local powerbrokers discussed in previous chapters. The history of Los Angeles's beaches, air pollution, and flood control revealed how these groups secured their influence. The story of the PWRPC illustrates how they kept this influence in the face of growing federal power after World War II and how locally driven federal policy came to be defined as essential to preserving not only local authority but also American democracy itself.

Problems with Federal Water Development

By the time Truman appointed the President's Water Resources Policy Commission, public dissatisfaction with federal water development centered on two closely related problems: waste of federal funds and the concentration of power in federal hands. These criticisms reflected fear of overproduction and economic competition on the one hand and the anger of communities denied new resources and federal aid on the other. At the same time, the competition between the Bureau of Reclamation and the Army Corps of Engineers seemed to lead them to build superfluous projects. In this competition, the agencies seemed more concerned with expanding their construction portfolios than with serving national or local needs. Voters, Congress, and even the Office of the President seemed powerless to halt even those projects that cost more to build than they would ever yield in economic benefits for the country.

One of the most egregious examples of wasteful competition emerged in 1944 when the Bureau of Reclamation and the Army Corps of Engineers released competing plans for the Missouri River. When ordered to coordinate their efforts, they combined nearly all the elements of the competing plans into the Pick-Sloan Plan. The resulting scandal made Pick-Sloan a watchword for the failure of federal water resources planning in the late 1940s. The conflict over the Missouri also culminated decades of rivalry in which the Bureau of Reclamation and the Army Corps of Engineers sought to outdo each other in funding and prestige. Congress had inadvertently added to their competition as water conservation mandates blurred the distinctions between the two agencies' missions. Beginning the 1920s, Congress required federal agencies to build multiple-purpose rather than single-purpose dams. Specifically, to ensure efficient use of water resources and maximum yield from federal investments, Congress authorized the Army Corps of Engineers to incorporate irrigation into its flood control projects and the Bureau of Reclamation to design irrigation projects to assist in flood control. Both outfits were permitted to incorporate hydroelectric power and other components into their dams as well; this mandate spurred much of the conflict over Hoover Dam. By the 1940s, the responsibilities of the Army Corps of Engineers and the Bureau of Reclamation clearly overlapped, but the formulas they used to identify projects and the rules they imposed on those who received water or other benefits from their projects did not.

In the 1930s and 1940s, both Congress and the White House attempted to rationalize federal water construction. The Roosevelt administration's first attempt, the 1939 "tripartite agreement," was intended both to increase coordination between the Bureau of Reclamation and the Army Corps of Engineers and to enhance the cost-effectiveness of federal dams. When this failed, the Roosevelt administration created the Federal Inter-Agency River Basin Committee and the National Resources Planning Board.[6] The National Resources Planning Board did provide some coordination for a time, but Congress dissolved it in 1943. Meanwhile, in Congress, efforts to foster cooperation foundered because different committees reviewed Bureau of Reclamation and Army Corps of Engineers project proposals.[7]

The Pick-Sloan scandal originated with the Army Corps' and the Bureau of Reclamation's ambitions for comprehensive, multiple-purpose water resources development on the Missouri River. The Missouri River basin had two major water resource problems: highly variable rainfall in its upper reaches periodically bankrupted farmers in the Dakotas, while enormous floods on the downstream stretches of the river threatened cities, shipping, and great swaths of agricultural land. In the late 1930s, the Bureau of Reclamation began planning a series of dams in the upper Missouri basin to irrigate North and South Dakota wheat fields. The agency argued that controlling the upper stretches of the river would reduce flooding downstream, but the Missouri project marked an important opportunity for Reclamation to bring irrigation to regions not traditionally served by the agency.

The Army Corps of Engineers disagreed with the Bureau of Reclamation's approach to flood control on the Missouri but initially did little in response to Reclamation's planning efforts. This all changed, however, when three floods roared down the Missouri in the spring of 1943. These floods inspired Lewis Pick, the regional director for the Army Corps of Engineers, to draft a flood control plan for the Missouri. This plan consisted mostly of levees, which the Army Corps preferred for flood control on long, large rivers.[8] Reclamation immediately complained that the Army Corps would squander the river's hydropower and irrigation potential. The Army Corps, for its part, regarded Reclamation's Sloan Plan as an undisguised attempt to usurp the Army Corps' responsibility for flood control. In 1944, conflict between the agencies halted the Missouri River projects completely. The Bureau of Reclamation and Army Corps of Engineers agreed to compromise only when President Roosevelt cited the deadlock as a prime justification for the creation of a Missouri Valley Authority modeled on the Tennessee Valley Authority.[9]

After much fanfare and negotiation, Reclamation and the Army Corps announced the compromise Pick-Sloan Plan in late 1944. But it was a compromise in name only; Pick-Sloan preserved most of both the original plans, even when this authorized Reclamation and the Army Corps to build dams and reservoirs so close together that they could never operate properly.[10] The obvious duplication in the plan galled a public determined to wring the most out of every federal dollar. The waste seemed even worse in light of predictions that the projects, expensive though they were, would not control the Missouri's floods. Even the agricultural benefits caused as much concern as celebration, first because irrigating arid land in the Dakotas required the inundation of profitable farms on rich Missouri Valley bottom lands, and second because the main result of irrigation in the Dakotas would be to increase the nation's wheat surplus. Finally, the fact that the Bureau of Reclamation and the Army Corps could label a proposal that merely folded together two conflicting plans a "compromise" incensed their critics and made the agencies look all the more committed to pursuing their own goals irrespective of public opinion, cost, or logic.[11] Critics pounced, calling Pick-Sloan a prime example of wasteful and ineffective federal spending and ineffective water resource planning.

The compromise over the Missouri River did nothing to abate the competition between the Army Corps of Engineers and the Bureau of Reclamation. By 1950, the nation's water resources development seemed more disorganized, inconsistent, and costly than ever. Unresolved conflicts between these agencies hindered development in nearly every major western river basin, including California's Central

Valley.¹² Piecemeal flood and power projects interfered with multiple-use, coordinated development in New England and the Northwest.¹³ Meanwhile, opposition to massive federal expenditures mounted. Record agricultural surpluses and falling farm profits challenged the logic of huge federal expenditures on irrigation. A growing number of eastern and midwestern taxpayers felt they were being asked to underwrite their own competition and, potentially, their own economic decline. Moreover, the laws that seemed to direct endless streams of money to rural and western Americans for water projects provided no similar benefits to those eastern and midwestern cities facing serious water shortages of their own.¹⁴ Together, the inefficiency caused by interagency rivalry and congressional logrolling, the agricultural surpluses, the uneven distribution of benefits from federal water projects, and fear of economic competition undermined support for federal river projects nationwide.

River Basin Planning

Truman decried duplication and economically unsound river projects almost as loudly as the critics of Pick-Sloan had. The president agreed with the Bureau of Reclamation that "spasmodic" responses to flood and drought, undertaken with "little attempt at coordination . . . usually failed."¹⁵ In 1950, he savaged the Omnibus Flood Control and Navigation Authorization Bill even as he signed it because it perpetuated piecemeal flood control and hydroelectric power development in New England and the Pacific Northwest.¹⁶ He continued to sign water project bills because vetoing them meant denying congressional delegations and constituents projects that they wanted and needed. Truman appointed the President's Water Resources Policy Commission to diffuse public anger and perhaps to generate a new mechanism for directing federal spending.

Truman charged the PWRPC with studying the nation's water resources policy and needs and devising new standards for evaluating water projects. His appointments to the PWRPC reveal a faith in expertise, planning, and conservation more in keeping with the Progressive Era or the early years of the New Deal than postwar America. Four of the seven appointees to the PWRPC had worked for federal planning agencies during the 1930s and 1940s, and all believed in the conservation precept that planning could replace conflict and scarcity with harmony and plenty.[17]

The New Deal veterans on the commission included Morris Cooke, Gilbert F. White, Leland Olds, and Samuel B. Morris. Cooke, the chair of the commission, had headed the Rural Electrification Administration and remained committed to public hydroelectric power. He insisted that the commissioners reach consensus on each element of their water policy report because this would protect all interests and generate a plan that voters would accept.[18] Gilbert F. White, the vice chair, was a geographer and the president of Haverford College who served on the water resources committees of the National Resources Committee and National Resources Planning Board.[19] In PWRPC correspondence, White proved particularly sensitive to the impact of federal construction on nearby communities.[20] Samuel B. Morris consulted with the National Resources Committee, the National Resources Planning Board, and the American Water Works Association's National Water Policy Committee.[21] He began his career with Pasadena Water Department and the Los Angeles Department of Water and Power; he advocated for policies that met urban needs, including protections for domestic water supplies and low power rates.

Leland Olds, by far the most controversial appointee, served on the National Resources Planning Board's water committee with White. He earned more notoriety, however, as the most outspoken advocate of public utilities on the Federal Power Commission. In 1949, the Senate blocked his reappointment to the Federal Power Commission because he was too "ardent for the extension of Federal power in every direction."[22] The private utility industry excoriated Olds as an extremist and a "leftist" who wrote articles for the *New York Daily Worker* allegedly "arguing that capitalism was dying fast in the United States and must be replaced by collectivism."[23] His association with the socialist publication ultimately became a significant liability for the PWRPC.

The final three appointees, Lewis Webster Jones, Roland Renne, and Paul S. Burgess, brought to the PWRPC economic and agricultural expertise from distinguished careers at public universities. Jones, an economist and the president of the University of Arkansas, viewed well-planned resource development as essential to the Cold War and blamed ill-considered, piecemeal development for resource degradation. The nation could ill afford such waste, he argued, given its "Titanic contest of economic strength . . . in defense of human freedom everywhere."[24] Renne, president of Montana State College, was a land economist who cautioned the commission that publicly operated power plants did not always deliver cheaper electricity or stimulate more economic growth than their privately owned counterparts. He worried, correctly as it turned out, that excessive emphasis on public enterprise would kill the PWRPC's proposals.[25] Burgess, dean of the College of Agriculture at the University of Arizona, represented one of the most important traditional constituencies for federal water development. His fellow Arizonans praised him for "serving the interests of irrigation and agriculture."[26] His presence on the commission balanced the New Dealers' preoccupation with hydroelectric power generation. Given the ongoing conflict over the Colorado River, Truman may have chosen the Arizonan to balance Morris's Los Angeles affiliations. Jones, Renne, and Burgess shared neither their colleagues' New Deal connections nor their confidence in the federal administration. They often challenged Cooke's, White's, Morris's, and Olds's assumptions about public enterprise and water use priorities, but they still embraced large-scale planning as the panacea for national water problems.

In the spring of 1950, the seven commissioners began their work with a review of dozens of earlier government studies, an ambitious calendar of public hearings, and surveys of experts in universities and federal, state, and local water and land management agencies. The PWRPC wanted to know how academic experts and government resource managers weighed national against regional interests, and urban and industrial versus rural needs. The surveys revealed the importance of standardization and economic efficiency to the PWRPC; they asked what economic criteria federal officials should use in evaluating water projects, what kinds of reimbursable and nonreimbursable costs the federal agencies should include in their cost-benefit analyses of proposed projects, and what minimum ratio of benefits to costs all federal projects should meet. These questions about the economics of water resources development, the use of hydropower to subsidize development, and the distribution of benefits from federal water projects came up during the debate over Hoover Dam and nearly every other major river project since. There were other questions, too, that revealed Morris Cooke and his colleagues as groping for a consensus on water resource development priorities for the nation. The surveys and hearings raised questions about the acreage limitations and repayment schedules imposed on farmers receiving water from Bureau of Reclamation projects, the balance of upstream versus downstream interests, the dangers of policies that created short-term food surpluses to ensure adequate long-range food supplies, and the merits of decentralizing American industrial production. But at the heart of the surveys lay an attempt to identify national priorities for irrigation, industry, conservation, and transportation.[27]

The surveys did not yield the consensus that the commission had hoped for. But the government studies that the PWRPC consulted offered a solution to the conflicts: using the river basin or watershed as the basic unit of planning. This was not a new idea. In 1922, Arthur Powell Davis and U.S. Representative John E. Raker of California had discussed the importance of comprehensive planning for the whole Colorado River basin to keep private companies from preempting key development sites and to ensure that the river's resources were put to the best possible use.[28] The Tennessee Valley Authority, created in 1933, offered a model of coordinated, watershed-wide planning. In 1934, the Mississippi Valley Committee demonstrated the benefits of basin planning, and the President's Committee on Water Flow proposed federally coordinated river basin planning for all the nation's waterways. Two years later, the federal Water Resources Committee issued a report titled "Drainage Basin Problems and Programs," which recommended creating a system of river basin planning committees to bring together federal, state, and local water programs. The National Resources Planning Board endorsed this approach, too. If he was not already aware of the arguments in favor of river basin planning, Samuel Morris's service on the Water Resources Committee of the National Resources Planning Board would have introduced him to the idea.[29] Duplication of effort, so vividly embodied by the Pick-Sloan Plan and a similar interagency dispute over the Columbia River, together with a long history of conflicts among communities and between public and private entities over water resources added to the appeal of river basin planning.

The PWRPC took less than a year to complete its surveys and research. In December 1950, the commission sent a three-volume report, *A Water Policy for the American People*, to President Truman. The report included an in-depth analysis of the history and potential of the nation's major rivers and a model bill for implementing river basin planning. The PWRPC proposed the creation of an independent river basin commission to implement "river basin planning" for each of the nation's largest watersheds. Confronted by the hydra of private companies, local and state governments, federal agencies, and congressional delegations that shaped the nation's waterways, river basin planning promised "unified . . . multiple-purpose, basin-wide programs" for the nation's rivers.[30] Comprehensive planning would curb wasteful, inefficient development by eliminating the competition among federal, local, and private water developers, including the now notorious conflicts between the Army Corps of Engineers and the Bureau of Reclamation. As the PWRPC saw it, river basin commissions would prevent waste by substituting unified planning for piecemeal development and eliminate conflict by including all interests and institutions in the planning process.[31]

River basin planning, however logical it seemed to the PWRPC, was controversial from the start because it implied a massive reorganization of the institutions managing the nation's rivers. This, both supporters and opponents quickly recognized, created an opportunity to introduce new goals into national water resources policy debates. Two groups in particular supported river basin planning: those who saw fragmented planning as the greatest barrier to good use of resources, and those who felt excluded from national water policy discussions. In the 1950s, those who indicted fragmentation included Secretary of the Interior Oscar Chapman; he blamed the "present difficulties in the field of water resources" on legislative barriers to basinwide planning.[32] In contrast, those with a vested interest in the status quo and those who feared river basin planning as a federal power grab fought river basin planning whenever and wherever they could. They succeeded, even during the New Deal years, in defeating proposals to implement the river basin planning recommendations of the National Resources Planning Board and to apply the Tennessee Valley Authority model to the Columbia and Missouri watersheds.[33]

Legitimacy and Participation in Policy Making

The PWRPC received support for river basin planning from labor and conservation organizations, the most notable of which were the Congress of Industrial Organizations and the Isaak Walton League. These labor and conservation groups criticized existing policies as "everywhere and always place[ing] personal, political and special class interests before the general welfare."[34] The Pick-Sloan debacle and the other consequences of the competition between the Army Corps and Bureau of Reclamation also inspired the CIO and Isaak Walton League to dismiss the Army Corps and Reclamation themselves as special interests. In other words, groups like the Isaak Walton League and the CIO sought to transform federal water resources development by challenging the legitimacy of the groups that had, thus far, spoken for the public in water policy debates.

The Congress of Industrial Organizations' endorsement of river basin planning began even before the PWRPC first convened, during debate over the Columbia River. The CIO advocated for the Columbia Valley Authority—or, at the very least, a comprehensive river development plan to ensure that projects served "the good of the valley as a whole, not on the special interests of the Army Engineers."[35] It believed that well-planned federal development could secure for "the first victims . . . of callous industrialism" a higher quality of life, more leisure, and more "space for living."[36] The CIO criticized the Army Corps of Engineers, the Bureau of Reclamation, and Congress for overlooking the importance of camping, fishing, hunting, scenic resources, and "heritage of the frontier" in their rush to promote industry and agriculture.[37] The Department of Agriculture and regional planning agencies joined the union in pushing for greater consideration of outdoor recreation in river development.[38] The CIO's demand that river basin planners preserve "beautiful recreational country" in national parks reflected its membership's participation in the postwar surge in outdoor recreation.[39]

The union's preoccupation with outdoor recreation did not overshadow labor's interest in healthy economic growth, but the CIO insisted that it was not the "proper function of the trade union movement to support the ballyhoo of Chambers of Commerce and Real Estate Boards."[40] This was a direct attack on the influence of business in public policy. It was also a specific challenge to more conservative labor groups like the American Federation of Labor that resolutely defended private enterprise in river development. The AFL tended to deride public water development as a flirtation with socialism, the danger of which far outweighed any benefits from enhanced outdoor recreation.[41] The CIO's interest in the victims of industrialization and its skepticism of chamber of commerce boosterism prompted the union, like the PWRPC, to endorse dispersed economic development. The CIO, in short, sought "a program which will help get our union people out of the noise and dirt and dust of the big metropolis."[42] But most of all, the union wanted more recognition as a legitimate participant in policy debates so it could "present its point of view and get it adopted as part of the regional program."[43]

The Isaak Walton League voiced a similar desire to unseat the "super-engineering" agencies that enjoyed "omnipotence in decreeing what happens to other natural resources."[44] When the league blasted the Army Corps of Engineers and the Bureau of Reclamation for spending billions of tax dollars to build uneconomical projects that destroyed "existing values," it meant that these agencies overlooked such things as the "aesthetic value of the mountain river."[45] Like the CIO, the Isaak Walton League did not oppose all river construction, but it did object to widespread destruction of fisheries and other natural resources. The Colorado Council of Sportsmen and the Department of Agriculture joined this critique of river development, identifying recreation as the highest use of some resources and suggesting that demand for recreation justified projects designed specifically to preserve fish, wildlife, and recreation.[46] The Upper Colorado River Commission likewise criticized existing policies for sacrificing national parks, wildlife, and obligations to Native Americans in order to promote hydroelectric power generation, industry, and agriculture.[47]

This confidence that river basin planning would yield better protections for recreation was, perhaps, misplaced. Cooke and the rest of the PWRPC endorsed "continuous use" of rivers by fish and wildlife only if "higher uses" did not dictate otherwise.[48] But the CIO, Isaak Walton League, and similar groups including the Upper Colorado River Commission, American Public Power Association, and the Missouri Division of Natural Resources saw basin planning as the kind of bureaucratic change that would allow them to speak for those Americans who wanted to end the omnipotence and single-mindedness that allowed the Bureau of Reclamation and Army Corps of Engineers to ignore federal mandates to protect Indian reservations and preserve wildlife, as well as public demands for preservation and recreation.[49]

This kind of animosity toward the Bureau of Reclamation and the Army Corps of Engineers did not always manifest as support for basin planning. In fact, many powerful organizations saw the PWRPC itself as the greater threat. Newspapers and business groups decried river basin planning as a dangerous concentration of federal power.[50] The Chamber of Commerce of the United States warned that the PWRPC's changes in water policy would give the president control of the national economy, making him, in effect, the "czar of Natural Resources Development and use" and allowing him to act without consulting state or local agencies or Congress. "Government by Authorities" like the PWRPC's river basin commissions, the chamber insisted, was "a program of socializing our economy at the source by controlling all natural resources."[51] The Engineers Joint Council, a consortium of engineering associations, argued that basin commissions violated the principles of democracy, giving too much power to individuals subject to neither electoral nor congressional review.[52] Even the National Reclamation Association, an organization that endorsed basin planning at least in principle, protested the PWRPC's ideas as part of "the trend that is . . . making the United States government the proprietor and total authority" in water development.[53] These groups rejected the PWRPC's proposals as a threat to local autonomy and private enterprise, but it should be noted that their number included many organizations that enjoyed a great deal of influence and legitimacy in water policy debates.

Rumors that the PWRPC's river basin plans would supplant state authority over water rights followed quickly from critiques of basin planning as an increase in federal power. States, not the federal government, administer water rights; this artifact of federalism was one of the things that so complicated authorization of Hoover Dam in the 1920s. The fear that changes at the federal level would undermine either specific water claims or state administration of those rights remained strong in the 1950s. For this reason, the California Farm Bureau warned that river basin planning would invalidate established water rights and cautioned that the PWRPC's plans would increase competition for water by expanding the list of uses approved for federal funding.[54] The *San Diego Union* acknowledged the need for better water conservation and hydropower development but insisted "there is no reason" that the states could not work together without "surrendering their just rights" to federal planners.[55] The *Oregon Journal* complained that the PWRPC showed little or no commitment to local participation in water planning.[56]

Civic leaders in many western towns feared that river basin planning would harm their interests either by interfering with projects they saw as essential or by diverting water to a competing community. The PWRPC's own discussions of this subject demonstrate that this concern was not entirely unwarranted: Roland Renne believed that "national interests supercede regional interests" and refused to accept language in the PWRPC's final report that seemed to place regional interests at the center of national water resources planning.[57] The Los Angeles Chamber of Commerce clearly disagreed with Renne. The chamber rejected the PWRPC's proposed basin commissions because they would limit the chamber's ability to protect local interests.[58] The Pacific Northwest Development Association shared the chamber's fear that basin planning would reduce local influence.[59] Likewise, the Engineers Joint Council protested that the PWRPC would reduce local, state, and private roles in "water project programming, execution, and financing."[60] The American Society of Civil Engineers also labeled river basin commissions an invasion of states' rights.[61]

Others opposed the PWRPC because they saw little need for change. One Idaho newspaper, for example, published an editorial that asserted that the Army Corps and the Bureau of Reclamation had "proven in the test of time" that they could build all the dams the nation needed "if the Government boys will give them the chance."[62] Among supporters of the status quo, this odd distinction between the "Government boys" and the Army Corps and Bureau of Reclamation was unique, but the defense of the two great river construction agencies was not. The Idaho newspaper reflected the common conviction that basin planning collided with local control[63] and that any changes in federal planning or new scrutiny of federal river construction would undermine carefully honed strategies for protecting local interests.[64] In this at least, opponents and supporters of the PWRPC agreed.

Although basin planning had much to recommend it in the abstract, it fell victim to the rhetoric of local control and the Cold War. The PWRPC intended basin commissions to coordinate all river construction, whether funded by federal, state, or private revenues, and to eliminate the "patchwork of plans by separate agencies for separate purposes."[65] In this way, the PWRPC's plan directly addressed the problems that sparked public complaint in the late 1940s. By 1950, however, the public saw basin planning as something else entirely. Or, rather, when confronted with the PWRPC's solutions to waste and competition, Americans changed their priorities. In practice this meant that the Los Angeles Chamber of Commerce, the National Reclamation Association, and the Pacific Northwest Development Association might have regarded specific federal projects as wasteful, but they accepted that waste as long as it seemed to serve local interests. They did not protest river basin planning as excessive federal power because comprehensive planning necessarily increased federal authority or spending. Rather, they objected because the PWRPC's proposals had the potential to eliminate precisely that patchwork of political authority that allowed them to influence federal policy. Recreation, conservation, and labor groups like the CIO, Colorado Council of Sportsmen, and Isaak Walton League, which saw federal administration as a solution to political exclusion rather than a problem, could not counter this interpretation. Thus the pervasive public impression held river basin planning as an expansion of federal authority inconsistent with the political environment of the postwar era.

Irrigation and the Power Subsidy

Neither river basin planning nor its implications for state authority and political influence were the only things to excite opposition to *A Water Policy for the American People*. Three other extremely contentious issues also undermined support: whether the federal government should use revenue from hydroelectric power generation to subsidize irrigation, what benefits should be included in the economic calculations used to justify new construction, and whether government or private utilities should generate and sell power at federal dams. None of these conflicts were new in the 1950s; they had bedeviled major water projects for decades. Unsurprisingly, in raising these issues explicitly, the PWRPC aroused vehement opposition to its proposals.

In the postwar years, one proposed river project after another bogged down in discussions of hydroelectric power rates and irrigation subsidies. Should the Bureau of Reclamation, for example, use electricity income to underwrite irrigation, thus reducing irrigation repayment costs but raising power prices? Or should the agency leave farmers to fend for themselves, to keep power prices low for urban consumers? This conflict arose in the first place because Congress ordered federal agencies to include hydroelectric facilities whenever possible. Reclamation had adopted this multiple-purpose doctrine enthusiastically and had relied on electricity revenues to subsidize irrigation.[66] Power sales covered three-quarters of the construction costs of Hoover Dam, Grand Coulee Dam, and California's Central Valley Project.[67] By 1950, the bureau operated twenty power plants, producing 18 billion kilowatt hours of electricity and more than $31 million in revenue; thirty-six more power plants, either under construction or authorized, would soon double Reclamation's total generating capacity.[68]

The PWRPC challenged the bureau's dependence on hydroelectric power to cover the costs of irrigation projects. Among the PWRPC's goals for federal water policy were decentralization of industry and the establishment of greater economic stability throughout the country.

Most of the commission believed that the nation could attain these goals only by ending the practice of using power revenues to subsidize irrigation.[69] Samuel Morris initially proposed that the federal government end the irrigation subsidy to lower power rates and slow the expansion of irrigation. He argued that high electricity rates interfered with industrial growth and that cheap irrigation projects promoted irrigation of new lands rather than the implementation of good farming practices on lands already under the plow.[70] Although entirely consistent with congressional intent to create a self-supporting reclamation fund, the diversion of power revenues to cover irrigation costs pitted irrigators directly against industry by raising power rates to urban and industrial consumers.

Most responses to the commission's surveys supported Morris's analysis. Academics from Maryland, Pennsylvania, Indiana, New Jersey, Nevada, California, Washington, New Mexico, and Utah, for example, all rejected subsidies for agriculture because of overproduction. They agreed that industry, not agriculture, was the nation's future.[71] Many other Americans, urban and rural, shared Morris's preoccupation with power rates. Irrigators who used electricity to pump groundwater onto their fields wanted lower rates and resented subsidizing their agricultural competitors who received their water from federal irrigation networks while they received no similar federal assistance. Urbanites demanded, "How far should the consumers of electric energy in the cities, towns and farms... underwrite higher and higher cost irrigation projects?"[72] If irrigation was so important to the nation, they argued, the general fund, not power users, should bear the burden of national agricultural expansion.[73]

At least two members of the PWRPC, Roland Renne and Paul Burgess, defended irrigation's special status in U.S. water policy. Burgess argued that every irrigation project repaid the U.S. Treasury many times over by creating new taxable wealth.[74] To this Samuel Morris replied that industrial production yielded similar benefits without comparable assistance.[75] Burgess went on to justify federal investment in the West as compensation for extensive federal landownership there and to remind his colleagues on the commission that agriculture was the backbone and heritage of the nation.[76] Burgess spoke for the nation's irrigators when he insisted that national water policy should make land and water available to anyone who wanted them.

Roland Renne focused his defense of irrigation subsidies on an issue that had long plagued the Bureau of Reclamation: irrigators' obligation to repay the reclamation fund for irrigation construction costs. The Newlands Reclamation Act of 1902 gave irrigators ten years to repay the federal government for the costs of the projects that served them. The original ten-year deadline quickly proved unrealistic. Irrigators pressured the agency, and the Bureau of Reclamation lobbied Congress to alter repayment rules on the grounds that they placed an unfair burden on Reclamation clients. By 1939, Congress extended the repayment deadline to forty or more years.[77] Even so, many Reclamation projects never generated enough income for farmers to repay construction costs.[78] Ending the power subsidy, as Morris proposed, threatened to saddle some irrigators with impossibly high reimbursements to the Reclamation fund. But there was an additional problem: because the Army Corps of Engineers provided irrigation water to farmers for free, eliminating the Bureau of Reclamation's practice of diverting power revenue to subsidize irrigation would further increase the disparity between Bureau of Reclamation and Army Corps of Engineers irrigation projects. By proposing to end the power subsidy, the PWRPC threatened to exacerbate the competition between Reclamation and the Army Corps. At the same time, it highlighted the resource conflicts between irrigators who wanted cheap water and industrial and domestic power users who wanted cheap power. The PWRPC hoped to resolve both of these conflicts once and for all.

Cost-Benefit Analysis and Nonreimbursable Benefits at Federal Dams

The power subsidy was but one question affecting the economics of dam building and the distribution of river resources. The PWRPC quickly found that it could not resolve questions about irrigation costs and the power subsidy without taking up the problem of "nonreimbursable" benefits. Nonreimbursables were benefits from dams that no one expected to generate income and for which beneficiaries did not have to pay. They entered project authorization debates in response to language in the Flood Control Act of 1936 that required the Army Corps of Engineers to show that all proposed flood control projects would yield benefits in excess of actual construction costs. Congress did not enumerate legitimate benefits. As a result, the new requirements for feasibility analysis inspired the Army Corps to identify all possible fiscal, nonfiscal, direct, and indirect benefits to justify new dams. The Reclamation Project Act of 1939 extended cost-benefit analysis, and hence the practice of identifying nonreimbursable benefits, to the Bureau of Reclamation proposals. In reaction to the Flood Control Act, however, the Reclamation Project Act restricted the Bureau of Reclamation's eligible nonreimbursable benefits to flood control, navigation, and fish and wildlife management. Like the reimbursement requirements, the Reclamation Project Act increased the economic differences between Army Corps of Engineers and Bureau of Reclamation projects. Nonetheless, Reclamation seized on nonreimbursables to prove the economic feasibility of its projects and to reduce irrigators' repayment obligations by attributing a portion of construction costs to flood control or fish and wildlife management.

Reclamation's ongoing efforts to decrease repayment obligations attests to the uneven playing field created by federal water policy. In addition to the differences in the rules governing nonreimbursable benefits and repayment, farmers who received water from the Bureau of Reclamation had to repay construction costs and, at least theoretically, could not irrigate more than 160 acres of land with Bureau of Reclamation water. Farmers receiving water from Army Corps of Engineers projects faced no similar limitations.[79] The inconsistencies between these policies stemmed from the agencies' distinct origins. The Army Corps engaged in irrigation as a by-product of flood control, navigation, or other public purposes for which the federal government assumed full fiscal responsibility. In contrast, the Bureau of Reclamation was intended to be a self-supporting irrigation agency, drawing on the revenue and repayments from one project to build the next without burdening the general fund. The differences between the rules governing the two agencies also made federal water policy look arbitrary, illogical, and inconsistent and were a constant source of irritation to the Bureau of Reclamation and its clientele.[80]

By the late 1940s, lists of benefits used to calculate the viability of federal projects routinely included "general welfare, national defense, recreation, salinity and sediment control, improvement of public transportation, protection of public health, and fulfillment of international obligations."[81] Congress accepted these nonreimbursable benefits because members knew that federal construction helped their constituents, because Congress relied on the Army Corps' and Bureau of Reclamation's expertise in designing federal projects, and because Congress, like the Army Corps and Reclamation, needed to justify expensive projects as economically sound. The PWRPC found this last point particularly troubling. Nonetheless, the commission was not willing to eliminate nonreimbursables entirely, and it considered valuable such intangibles as improved public health, recreation, resource conservation, and economic security. It concluded that projects that did not meet strict economic tests might still merit federal funds because of these nonmonetary contributions to the general welfare.[82] Nevertheless, its final report advocated restricting nonreimbursables as part of its larger effort to rein in federal water spending.

A number of groups felt that even this did not go far enough. According to the Isaak Walton League, "The Commission's views as to 'nonreimbursable' features of dam projects appear so liberal that almost any kind of project could be justified before Congress." They also complained that some nonreimbursable benefits appeared "elusive and uncertain."[83] The fact that the PWRPC specifically listed resource conservation and fish and wildlife preservation as general welfare benefits offered little comfort. The Isaak Walton League feared that the PWRPC's recommendations on nonreimbursables would still allow the Bureau of Reclamation and the Army Corps to "fatten on power production, and any other 'benefits' that can be maneuvered into the plans to justify them."[84] The head of the Interstate Commission on the Delaware River Basin also worried that the new approach to nonreimbursables gave federal officials too much latitude. He called for placing "definite limitations" on intangible benefits, and even then, he felt project authorization must rest "solidly on economic feasibility."[85]

Of all the members of the PWRPC, Roland Renne advocated the most unrestricted use of nonreimbursables. He argued that including intangibles in their deliberations allowed Congress to consider the social as well as economic benefits of water development.[86] Morris countered by reiterating that expansive calculations of project benefits fostered an unjustifiable expansion of irrigation.[87] Their exchange struck at the heart of the debate. Nonreimbursables and extended repayment schedules privileged irrigation insofar as federal funds, water, and reservoir sites used for irrigation could not be used for other things. With Burgess and Renne advocating for the future of American irrigation and Morris worried about industrial expansion, the PWRPC strove to protect irrigation even as it opened the way for future construction to promote industry. To help agriculture the commission recommended directing federal funds to rehabilitate existing public and private irrigation systems and to provide direct financial assistance for farmers during emergencies, instead of building new irrigation dams.[88] While the PWRPC refused to eliminate the irrigation repayment requirement that had caused so many problems for the Bureau of Reclamation's clients, the commission did recommend applying identical repayment rules to all projects and to drainage and watershed management as well as irrigation. Finally, the PWRPC proposed eliminating the strict repayment deadlines that had so burdened Bureau of Reclamation projects. The commissioners suggested instead that repayment reflect a beneficiary's "ability to pay, without interest, measured by the resulting increase in the land operator's net earnings."[89] These changes to federal policy would have eliminated the special burdens faced by Bureau of Reclamation farmers. They also would have placed eastern needs on an equal footing with those of the arid West.

Not all irrigators cheered the proposed changes to repayment rules or the compromise on nonreimbursables. New Mexico's Economic Development Commission, for example, wanted to keep nonreimbursables, subsidies, and anything else that would bring in federal money because it blamed the dearth of water in New Mexico for everything from slow urban and industrial growth to declining livestock production.⁹⁰ The PWRPC's insistence that irrigation receive no more consideration than "other water resources projects for which full reimbursement is not required" also excited considerable opposition.⁹¹ The commission lost still more support from farmers for insisting that acreage limitations remain an integral part of federal irrigation. Cooke and his colleagues saw the 160-acre limits as the best way to "prevent large landholders from monopolizing the benefits of Federal irrigation projects."⁹² The irrigation community was not mollified by a compromise allowing owners of larger farms to purchase water at rates that covered all costs of supplying that water.⁹³

Government Ownership, Comprehensive Planning, and Cold War Fear

The objections to nonreimbursables in benefit-cost analysis were mild compared with the storm over public hydropower development at federal dams. In its discussions of hydroelectric power generation, the PWRPC focused on the balance between irrigation and industry. But commentators and critics of *A Water Policy for the American People* were far more likely to accuse Cooke and his colleagues of seeking to replace the nation's private utilities with a massive federal hydroelectric system. Unsurprisingly, given the Cold War context in which it worked, the PWRPC's emphasis on public enterprise and on federal initiatives sparked many accusations that the PWRPC advocated socialism. Leland Olds's association with the *New York Daily Worker* made these Red Scare tactics worse. The result was a spate of red-baiting and attacks on the public power movement that made the fury over Hoover Dam seem mild in comparison.

The PWRPC claimed to have no interest in eliminating the private power industry, and it described its proposals as perpetuating "the mixed system of public and private operation which has characterized the power industry for more than a generation."⁹⁴ However, it did want federal hydropower development to take precedence over local or private construction. The commission imagined federal investments and public utilities delivering ample, inexpensive electricity to regions where monopolies artificially raised power prices or where high transportation costs and other obstacles impeded "a sound balance of agriculture and industry."[95] It also advocated shortening the terms of private hydroelectric generation licenses on federal streams so that the federal government could "recapture" valuable natural resources after a reasonable period of time and at reasonable cost.[96] The PWRPC suggested that private power development proceed only where it would not interfere with federal plans for "comprehensive multiple-purpose development of river basins," including the distribution and marketing of electricity.[97] This amounted to significant curbs on private power generation.

The utility industry did not view the PWRPC's proposals as benign. The utilities disputed the PWRPC's claim that only federal generation and distribution of electricity would keep rates low, and they bridled at the commission's suggestion that private utilities should have access to natural resources only when this helped keep power rates down.[98] As the industry newsletter, *Electrical World*, put it: "The idea that 'issuance of such licenses to private power interests would have far-reaching effects upon federal water resources programs . . .' might better read that federal water programs have had 'far-reaching effects' upon private water power development."[99] Power companies objected to being characterized as "intruder[s] in water resources development,"[100] and they lambasted the PWRPC for promoting policies favored only by "public power boosters."[101] *Electrical West* called the PWRPC's report "completely at variance with public sentiment."[102] *Electric Light and Power*, meanwhile, dismissed the report as the "subterfuge" of "public powerites" that would "virtually ban private hydroelectric development."[103] The power industry was not alone in this critique. At one public hearing, the Oxford Paper Company declared, "We are unalterably opposed to the socialization of the power industry . . . and to any and all legislation which brings us nearer to that result."[104] Letters from the University of Southern California and New Mexico A&M University likewise insisted that any federal water plans should "encourage private enterprise and discourage government competition with private institutions, whenever possible."[105] Ultimately, it proved too easy for the utilities to dismiss the commission's work as "federal socialization of the water resources of the Nation's principal rivers."[106]

Just as New Mexico's Economic Development Commission had evaluated the PWRPC's proposals in terms of New Mexico's desire for subsidized water projects, Arizona's newspapers invariably measured the commission's recommendations in light of their most pressing concern: the Central Arizona Project. So, Arizona newspapers trumpeted, "the commission's recommendations as a whole will be helpful to the development of irrigation and reclamation in the West and will further the interests of the [Central Arizona] project."[107] Arizona senator Ernest W. McFarland believed that the PWRPC's Reclamation reimbursement terms would eliminate opposition to the Central Arizona Project by easing farmers' concerns about repayment.[108] Los Angeles newspapers more frequently objected to the PWRPC's proposals, their positions likewise influenced by the battle over the Colorado River. The *Santa Monica Evening Outlook*, for example, criticized the new reimbursement terms as "strange and uneconomic" precisely because they might give "the Arizona project a better chance than ever."[109] In its eagerness to criticize the PWRPC, this same article misreported that the commission recommended such strict standards of economic feasibility that the federal government would build only those projects "able to pay their own way," a telling error.[110]

Southern California newspapers did not limit their criticism to the presumed implications of proposed water policies for the Central Arizona Project. In a large number of articles, they resorted to a rhetorical defense of capitalism to explain their objections to *A Water Policy for the American People*. Thus they rejected river basin planning and federal hydropower alike as "hostile ... toward independent enterprise"[111] and "contrary to the American tradition of development by free and competitive enterprise."[112] It is not at all clear from the news coverage which came first—the concern that the PWRPC's proposals would weaken California's grip on the Colorado or the fear that new policies would promote socialism and constrain private enterprise.

Of course, not everyone rejected public utilities as dangerous flirtations with socialism. Indeed, some found it extremely disturbing that the private utilities assumed "that when ... spokesmen for electric corporations testified at Commission hearings ... they voiced the opinions and desires of the people of the entire United States, with perhaps the exception of a few public ownership cranks."[113] Yet very few newspapers published this sort of explicit critique of business groups' influence. More commonly, the media interpreted the commission's proposals in light of local needs. This tended to reinforce business and industry groups' claims that they could protect local interests better than federal bureaucrats.

Cooke and his colleagues envisioned a federal water policy that could eliminate both the kind of economic instability that shook the nation in the Depression and the kind of industrial bottlenecks that had plagued production during the war. The former New Dealers on the commission saw public dissatisfaction with federal agencies, the Korean War, and the political crisis that had prompted Truman to convene the commission in the first place as an opportunity to fulfill the promise of Progressive conservation and the New Deal. But they also discussed the importance of mobilizing natural resources to defeat communism. They were unprepared for either the Cold War backlash against river basin planning or opponents' claims that the commission wanted to displace local needs as the driving force behind public policy. This miscalculation let loose the virulent anticommunist rhetoric that ultimately defeated the PWRPC's proposals.

Conclusion: The Triumph of Localism

When the PWRPC released *A Water Policy for the American People* in early 1951, the Truman administration simply shelved it. Comprehensive planning was still tainted by wartime frustrations and newly discredited by association with Stalin's Five-Year Plans. River basin authorities, the core of the PWRPC's recommendations, were easily portrayed as a "step backward" that would concentrate "all water resource development in Federal agencies to the inevitable exclusion of local and state agencies."[114] Opponents warned that basin planning "imperil[ed] the water rights system upon which irrigation depend[ed] and deprive[d] those who pay the bill of any chance to own or control the facilities which their money would provide."[115] Because so many Americans rejected the commission's prescription for water development as contrary to American traditions of private enterprise and democracy, President Truman also ignored the commission's recommendations. In 1952, Cooke and Morris were still imploring the Bureau of the Budget to forward their draft bill to Congress.

But even if the Cold War had not made centralized planning such an easy political target, the commission's report would have generated controversy because of its complicated proposals for everything from balancing irrigation and industry to evaluating the nonreimbursable and quantifiable benefits of water resource development. As the commissioners quickly found, this made their report easy to attack and misrepresent. The PWRPC sought to discredit its most virulent critics by identifying its opponents' ties to private utilities, but Americans no longer seemed to fear corporate influence in politics.[116] Instead, the federal government seemed a greater threat to democracy. As a 1949 National Water Conservation Conference put it, although "a free democracy" ought to be able to develop natural resources efficiently, "a Federally centralized, super-planning agency with vast powers over individuals and state and local agencies" was "not in the best interests of the country."[117] That this development should include full participation by private corporations went without saying. Attendees at this conference, like so many others in the water policy debate, envisioned federally funded but locally controlled water development. This implied that they accepted the inefficiency and waste of the status quo as long as it continued to create opportunities for local influence. In fact, competition and fragmentation at the federal level now seemed the best guarantor of democracy.

Reactions to the PWRPC in Los Angeles provide an excellent example of this local perspective at work; in Southern California, debate over the *A Water Policy for the American People* focused on whether the PWRPC's proposals would interfere with local ambitions. The Los Angeles Chamber of Commerce endorsed federal investment directed by local priorities, as it had in harbor construction, flood control, water supply, and wartime mobilization. In response to the PWRPC's report, however, the chamber cautioned that the advantages of consolidating river construction in a single agency "must be weighed against the dangers of a bureaucracy which would ride roughshod over water users and state and local agencies."[118] It condemned federal spending that might hinder local economic expansion by raising taxes, by creating competition for local businesses or for Los Angeles as a whole, or by diverting federal spending to other communities.

The dangers of diverting federal monies to competitors arose frequently during the PWRPC's own deliberations. Some of the PWRPC's correspondents questioned whether residents of "submarginal" areas had the right to demand "the same level of income they might attain if they moved elsewhere."[119] They objected that industrialization of rural areas would require the "continual subsidization of uneconomic projects" and protested that aggressive, ill-considered federal spending would create new needs for federal assistance instead of rectifying existing problems.[120] These arguments drew on two main assumptions: federal funds would yield higher economic returns if directed to existing, productive industrial and agricultural ventures, and national interests were not simply an aggregate of local desires.

An undercurrent of anticommunism clearly runs through the reactions to the PWRPC's report. The PWRPC tried to draw a distinction between democratic centralization and socialism by arguing that improved planning would allow the United States to respond more effectively to the Russian threat.[121] Even so, it could not shake the red-baiting as newspapers and other commentators around the country repeatedly asserted that the proposed river basin commissions would cripple private enterprise and dangerously expand federal control. The mildest of these assertions still warned that centralized planning "should certainly be accompanied by close safeguards against socialistic control."[122] Apparently, no appeal to the country's need to end waste or mobilize to win the Cold War could overcome this fear of centralization.

There were other objections to the PWRPC's report as well. A representative of the Independent Engineers for Private Enterprise articulated one of these at a public hearing when he asked why the PWRPC expected uniform water laws to work any better than uniform land laws had.[123] But the paradox that faced Los Angeles and other American communities was more fundamentally about how to pursue regional interests in a political arena that defined these interests as simultaneously preeminent and dangerously narrow. Although critics argued that the status quo permitted "special interest groups" and self-perpetuating monopolies to pursue "their pet interest" rather than the "highest general welfare," the PWRPC never succeeded in defining the "highest general welfare" in concrete or compelling terms.[124] Thus local control over federal projects remained paramount.[125] What emerged from the water policy debates of the early 1950s, therefore, was a definition of democracy grounded not in an equal consideration of all public values, as the PWRPC imagined, but in a weak central government that served the needs and desires of local powerbrokers. Weakness in the federal government—including the very competition and conflicts that inspired Truman to create the President's Water Resources Policy Commission in the first place—was the core of the American system.

CONCLUSION

SMALL GOVERNMENT AND BIG BUSINESS IN THE MID-TWENTIETH CENTURY

The recommendations of the President's Water Resources Policy Commission of 1950 languished for many reasons. Among them was the fact that implementing river basin planning required Congress members who held the power to approve federal river projects to surrender this authority to an independent river basin commission. Congress had little incentive to make changes of this magnitude in the absence of widespread public demands. Such demands never appeared. If news coverage reflected as well as shaped public opinion on this matter, the PWRPC's proposals were widely perceived as a federal power grab, a threat to private and local initiative, and a flirtation with socialism. Behind the red-baiting rhetoric lay a deeper truth about American politics: localism.

By 1950, Americans criticized inefficiencies in the federal budget generally but defended the specific inefficiencies that created room for their own municipal and state leadership to shape policies to suit local desires. Public reactions to the competition between the Army Corps of Engineers and the Bureau of Reclamation exemplify this central irony of American localism. Americans criticized this interagency competition for wasting money and creating inconsistent policy. This same competition, however, allowed communities to pit one agency against another until they secured the projects they wanted; better coordination at the federal level threatened to undermine this local influence. As long as interagency competition created opportunities for cities and states to secure and shape federal spending, they preferred a wasteful federal government to an efficient one. Americans at midcentury did not really want a smaller, more efficient federal government. They wanted a federal government that drew its priorities from local government and gave municipal and state authorities great latitude in determining how and where to spend federal money.

Local influence over federal spending did not make federal policy making more democratic. The demands and proposals issuing from city halls reflected the priorities of the local powerbrokers who collaborated with municipal and county officials. While it is true that some federal government programs from this period created new political opportunities for excluded groups, even more did not. Under a great many federal spending programs from the New Deal to federal flood control, construction projects began with a petition and a detailed proposal from a local government. For this reason, the Los Angeles County Flood Control District submitted its comprehensive plan first to the Public Works Administration and then to the congressional committees considering the Rivers and Harbors Improvement Bill. Los Angeles's reaction to sewage pollution in Santa Monica Bay followed a similar pattern: when the city sought federal aid under the National Industrial Recovery Act and from the Public Works Administration to fix chronic sewage problems, the city submitted fully honed plans.[1]

When Congress required cities to submit completed project plans with their requests for federal aid, the resulting projects reflected cities' policy-making processes and power structures. At the very least, this meant that a great number of federal programs passively reinforced the local distribution of power. When the Army Corps of Engineers actively assisted supporters of Whittier Narrows Dam, it went much further. Congress member Voorhis could block appropriations, but he could not change the Army Corps of Engineers' relationship with El Monte. Nevertheless, local and national powerbrokers feared that institutional changes might undermine their power. This, of course, was why so many business and industry groups opposed the PWRPC's proposed river basin commissions and, conversely, why so many unions and outdoor recreation groups supported the creation of an entirely new river management system. The Whittier Narrows case, however, suggests that even the creation of the river basin commissions might not have shuffled political opportunity as much as unions and conservationists hoped. At the very least, the federal spending that did take place during the second quarter of the twentieth century posed little threat to the groups already established as the voice of the people. The record of federal involvement in Los Angeles outlined in these cases challenges the widely held assumption that changing institutions or political venues always redistributes influence.

If Americans preferred local control of federal spending, and if federal programs reflected the distribution of power at the local level, what, then, determined who had influence in city hall? These cases suggest that interest groups secured influence by assisting and defending public officials. The Los Angeles Chamber of Commerce clearly mastered this strategy. When smog descended on downtown Los Angeles in 1943, the Los Angeles Chamber of Commerce was among the first groups to respond. Over the next decade, it sponsored research, drafted legislation, organized voluntary smoke reduction programs, and defended the Los Angeles County Air Pollution Control District against complaints that the regulations did too little, unfairly targeted small businesses, or failed entirely to control the main industrial sources of smog. Controversy and public outrage only drew public officials and the business community closer together; eventually city and county officials explicitly referred to the Los Angeles Chamber of Commerce as the most legitimate and important of public voices on smog.

Although conflict strengthened the business community's influence, consensus did not undermine it. The business community exercised just as much influence over beach policies in Los Angeles as it did air pollution, although its proposals for the beaches prompted much less opposition. The Los Angeles Chamber of Commerce joined in the campaign to curb what was depicted as private, industrial exploitation of public, recreational resources, attacking real estate and commercial development along the shore.[2] When oil drilling on the beaches began to outrage Los Angeles residents, the Long Beach Chamber of Commerce joined the campaign to move oil rigs inland.[3] The Shoreline Planning Association, the group that wielded the most influence over coastal policy during this period, not only weighed in against oil wells on California's beaches but eventually orchestrated the postwar acquisition of hundreds of miles of beach lands by California state and local governments.[4] This organization initially derived its influence from connections to the larger business community; members of the Los Angeles Chamber of Commerce and the Los Angeles Realty Board made up its board of directors. But the association's steady presence in local politics and its pursuit of the uncontroversial goal of increasing public access to the beaches added to its political weight. Later, after World War II, the Shoreline Planning Association enshrined this influence by including in state beach acquisition laws the requirement that all coastal communities in California complete shoreline master plans at a time when the Shoreline Planning Association was the primary coastal and beach planning body in California.

One interesting feature of the Los Angeles beach policies was the blunt distinction between public and private uses of the shoreline. The coalition that opposed oil drilling on the beaches decried derricks and drilling piers as private exploitation of public resources. This same criticism was also levied against private developers who subdivided coastal lands for housing, exclusive beach clubs, and entrepreneurs who opened hot dog stands or peddled umbrellas on the sand. Significantly, these accusations of selfish exploitation were never levied either against members of the chamber of commerce who would earn more without competition from new, beachfront enterprises or against members of realty boards who would profit as recreational development drove property values up in coastal neighborhoods.

The Shoreline Planning Association and the Los Angeles Chamber of Commerce differed from less powerful groups in several ways. These influential organizations, and the chamber of commerce in particular, represented a significant cross section of Los Angeles's business community. The size of these organizations and the variety of economic sectors they represented, together with the importance of a healthy economy, made it easy for public officials to see these groups as legitimate representatives of the public interest. Their support for and assistance to public officials, especially when controversy erupted, made these groups valuable political allies. But convenience and reliability also contributed to their power; the Los Angeles Chamber of Commerce and the Shoreline Planning Association were long-lived institutions with a consistent record of political participation. In contrast, most of the opposition groups discussed in these chapters coalesced and dissolved in reaction to specific issues. This not only made them difficult to trace in the historic record but also reduced their legitimacy as political participants and ultimately their ability to shape in municipal policy debates. Smaller groups that organized around specific problems did not have the traits that gave business organizations their privileged, unofficial status as the voices of the public.

In general, Congress proved less ready than city and county officials, and some federal agencies, to accept business groups as proxies for the general public. While many members of Congress believed that only a robust private sector could counter government power, many others remained convinced that Americans urgently needed federal government programs and regulations to protect them from powerful corporations. The fundamental disagreement over the relationship between the public and private sectors surfaced repeatedly between 1920 and 1950 both in and out of Congress; the water resources conflicts in chapters 4 and 5 examine precisely these ideological debates. Furthermore, these two chapters reveal some of the ways that Progressive Era visions of public enterprise as the guardian of equality and democracy were eclipsed by Cold War era faith in private enterprise as the protector of liberty.

The defeat of public power development at Hoover Dam demonstrates how industry public relations campaigns and close political contests contributed to the nation's shift from commonwealth to corporate liberalism.[5] After the Water Power Act passed in 1920, the National Electric Light Association undertook a massive campaign to defend the private utility industry. The organization distributed curricular materials to schools and to civic and youth organizations touting the benefits of private ownership. Together with utility companies from around the country, the National Electric Light Association spent more than a million dollars to defeat public hydroelectric development at Muscle Shoals and Boulder Canyon.[6] Although some surveys found that Americans remained deeply suspicious of private utilities in the late 1940s, actual support for government ownership of electric power companies declined from 40 percent to less than 30 percent between 1936 and 1947.[7] The utilities clearly benefited from Arizona's vehement opposition to California's use of the Colorado River. Phil Swing and his allies in Congress could not overcome the combined opposition from the utilities and Arizona. Because they wanted a federally funded irrigation, flood control, and water supply dam more than they wanted public development of the hydroelectric power, proponents of the dam compromised and dropped the public power requirements in the Boulder Canyon Dam Act. This did not, in itself, increase the influence of business in American politics, but the celebration of Boulder Dam as a new achievement in public-private cooperation certainly did.

During the New Deal and World War II, American business gained political influence. Progressive suspicion of corporate power lapsed as business leaders played ever more prominent roles in the federal bureaucracy and as civilian frustrations with the federally managed war economy grew.[8] After the war, the rise of the consumer economy and increasing dependence on manufacturing jobs convinced more Americans that their interests aligned with those of major corporations.[9] Meanwhile, in Los Angeles, businesses took additional steps that contributed to this political and cultural realignment. Throughout the second quarter of the twentieth century, Southern California businesses blamed government for many of the problems and inconveniences that residents encountered in the growing metropolis. Backers of private utilities blamed the Saint Francis Dam disaster on Los Angeles's heedless rush toward public hydroelectric generation.[10] The oil industry journal, *Petroleum World*, blamed wartime shortages on federal policies and insisted that the industry did all it could in spite of federal "bungling" to provide for consumers.[11] The *Los Angeles Times*, the Los Angeles Chamber of Commerce, and the Los Angeles public even shifted the blame for air pollution onto the federal government, attributing smog to war production and warning that Washington-based officials might oppose air pollution regulations that threatened to interfere with war production.[12] Then, after World War II, the anticommunist crusade simply reinforced messages about the dangers of a powerful central government.

Ironically, this political realignment did not stop Americans from attacking large corporations. From the beaches of Los Angeles County to the canyons of the Colorado River, big corporations were criticized as seeking illegitimate and excessive advantages over smaller and therefore more meritorious firms. In Los Angeles, this sentiment figured prominently the oil fields as Los Angeles's small oil firms routinely criticized the Majors for promoting regulations that would force the Independents out of business.[13] The images of oil companies as selfish corporate giants also defined campaigns to limit oil drilling on and near the beaches. The threat of bigness appeared on both sides in the Boulder Dam debate: proponents of the dam warned that big utilities were manipulating American politics, while opponents fretted that the dam would allow big California to take resources from little Arizona. Even as the appeal of using government power to counter corporate influence faltered, the habit of lauding small businesses while criticizing larger firms persisted. So, for example, critics nearly always blamed smog on Los Angeles's biggest industries and complained that the APCD shielded big industry from regulation while cracking down on smaller firms. Opponents to Whittier Narrows Dam relied on their size, too, when they argued that flood control should not sacrifice the homes, acre-lot farms, and small businesses of El Monte to protect larger agricultural and industrial interests downstream. But by the 1940s, these arguments had greater rhetorical appeal than political force. They reflected American nostalgia for its agrarian past and culture of individualism, but they did not represent a significant challenge to business groups' pervasive political power or the localism that reinforced it and left so many citizens on the sidelines of American politics.

NOTES

ABBREVIATIONS

ACEC—Army Corps of Engineers Collection, National Archives and Records Administration, Laguna Niguel, California

CIO, "Magnificent Columbia"—Committee on Regional Development and Conservation, Congress of Industrial Organizations, "The Magnificent Columbia," CIO Department of Education and Research, Washington, D.C., 1949, 16, box 41, Morris Papers

Colorado River Hearings—U.S. Congress, Senate, Committee on Irrigation and Reclamation, *Colorado River Hearings and Miscellaneous Documents*, vol. 1, 68th Cong., 1st sess., 1924

FBC—Fletcher Bowron Collection, Huntington Library, San Marino, California

JAFP—John Anson Ford Papers, Huntington Library, San Marino, California

LAACC Collection—Los Angeles Area Chamber of Commerce Collection, Regional History Center, University of Southern California, Los Angeles

LAACC Minutes—Los Angeles Area Chamber of Commerce Board of Directors Minutes, Los Angeles Area Chamber of Commerce Collection, Regional History Center, University of Southern California, Los Angeles

LACA—Los Angeles City Archives

LAE—*Los Angeles Examiner*

LAHE—*Los Angeles Herald Express*

LAT—*Los Angeles Times*

NYT—*New York Times*

PWRPC Report—President's Water Resources Policy Commission, *A Water Policy for the American People*, vol. 1. Washington, D.C.: GPO, 1951

Steno Reports—Los Angeles Area Chamber of Commerce, Steno Reports, Los Angeles Area Chamber of Commerce Collection, Regional History Center, University of Southern California, Los Angeles

INTRODUCTION

1. The Los Angeles Area Chamber of Commerce is nearly always referred to as simply the Los Angeles Chamber of Commerce. The official title is reflected in the acronym LAACC. In most cases, I have used the more common name.

2. Einhorn, *Property Rules*. See also Pisani, *Reclamation Bureau, National Water Policy, and the West*, 202–34. Williams briefly describes the connection between waterworks and electric power generation and the private utilities' opposition to both in *Energy and the Making of Modern California*, 245–67. For more on the barriers to public enterprise generally, see Radford, "From Municipal Socialism to Public Authorities." For more on the relationships between business and government in Los Angeles, see Erie, "How the Urban West Was Won." See also Vietor, *Energy Policy in America since 1945*.

3. Hays, *Conservation and the Gospel of Efficiency*; Jacoby, *Crimes against Nature*; Warren, *Hunter's Game*. Cumbler, in *Reasonable Use*, discusses the transfer of resources from agriculture to industry and then to urban recreation in New England waterways. In contrast to these works, Judd traces the roots of conservation to New England communities seeking to preserve community rights; see *Common Lands, Common People*.

4. Broesamle, *Reform and Reaction in Twentieth Century American Politics*, 43–44.

5. See, for example, Link, "What Happened to the Progressive Movement in the 1920s?" and Koppes, "Environmental Policy and American Liberalism." Issel examined San Francisco and Los Angeles business leaders' efforts to counter the political power of labor and define public priorities in "'Citizens Outside the Government.'"

6. Brinkley has examined the transformation of American liberalism as a result of the integration of business executives into the federal bureaucracy in *End of Reform* and *Liberalism and Its Discontents*. Galambos and Pratt also note that labor unions and government were recognized as the protectors of the public good in the early twentieth century. Corporations, they argue, gained power as a result of political compromises and eventually proved themselves trustworthy; see *Rise of the Corporate Commonwealth*. Brock, in *Americans for Democratic Action*, blamed Dixiecrat influence for weakening liberalism under President Truman. Broesamle, in *Reform and Reaction in Twentieth Century American Politics*, attributes the decline of Progressive-style liberalism to the Progressives' own emphasis on special interests, which, he explains, intensified interest-group politics even during the Progressive Era and eventually sowed the seeds of a new politics based on interest-group competition. See also Issel, "Liberalism and Urban Policy in San Francisco from the 1930s to the 1960s" and "Business Power and Political Culture in San Francisco."

7. There is an extensive literature on "agency capture," the process by which regulatory agencies come to serve narrow private interests rather than regulate them. In environmental history, the bulk of these studies have treated the relationship between the timber and livestock industries and the U.S. Forest Service and the Bureau of Land Management. See, for example, Klyza, *Who Controls Public Lands*;

Raymond, "Localism in Environmental Policy; and Hirt, *A Conspiracy of Optimism*. Interest-group formation and influence has become an important field of study for political scientists since Dahl published *Who Governs?* See Moe, *Organization of Interests*, and Smith, *Interest Group Interaction and Groundwater Policy Formation in the Southwest*. Additional studies focus on the effectiveness, or lack thereof, of citizen participation in contemporary policy debates or on the difficulty that new groups experience in entering policy debates. See Beierle and Cayford, *Democracy in Practice*; Walter, "Critique of the Elitist Theory of Democracy"; and Lowi, *End of Liberalism*.

8. Hayden, *Power of Place*. Caltech and the University of Southern California have cosponsored the Los Angeles History Group in recent years.

9. Nicolaides, *My Blue Heaven*; Wild, *Street Meeting*.

10. Flamming, *Bound for Freedom*; Sides, *L.A. City Limits*; Deverell, *Whitewashed Adobe*.

11. According to Hise, Los Angeles's urban land use patterns grew out of a deliberate process of decentralization adopted by city and county officials and promoted by the Los Angeles Chamber of Commerce. See, for example, *Magnetic Los Angeles*, and Fogelson, *Fragmented Metropolis*.

12. Both Nash and Lotchin attribute much of California's industrial economy to wartime military production. See Nash, *Federal Landscape*; *World War II and the West*; *American West in the Twentieth Century*; *American West Transformed*; and *Crucial Era*. In *Bad City in the Good War*, Lotchin emphasizes that wartime spending merely accelerated California's industrial development. See also Starr, *Embattled Dreams*, and Johnson, *Second Gold Rush*.

13. Los Angeles's reform politics have received far less attention than San Francisco's. For good work on key figures in Los Angeles, see Sitton, *Los Angeles Transformed* and *John Randolph Haynes, California Progressive*. On San Francisco, see Issel and Cherney, *San Francisco*; Ethington, *Public City*; and Clark, *Defending Rights*.

14. California, Department of Public Health, Bureau of Sanitary Engineering, "Report on a Pollution Survey of Santa Monica Beaches in 1942," 6; "General Population by City, L.A. County, 1910–1950," ⟨http://www.laalmanac.com/⟩. The county grew at similar rates. Census figures show the following population for Los Angeles County: 936,455 in 1920; 2,208,492 in 1930; 2,785,643 in 1940; 4,151,687 in 1950. From 1930 to 1960, Los Angeles County made up 38–40 percent of the population of the entire state of California.

15. On flood control in Los Angeles, see Orsi, *Hazardous Metropolis*; Gumprecht, *Los Angeles River*; and Bigger, *Flood Control in Metropolitan Los Angeles*.

16. Two comprehensive works are Dewey, *Don't Breathe the Air*, and Krier and Ursin, *Pollution and Policy*.

17. The literature on water resources is among the most well developed in environmental history. Some of the best works include Hundley's comprehensive *Great Thirst*; Worster's classic *Rivers of Empire*; and Kahrl's *Water and Power*.

18. On the petroleum industry in Southern California generally, and on the so-called tidelands conflict specifically, see Freudenberg and Gramling, *Oil in Troubled Waters*; Clark, *Energy and the Federal Government*; Goldstein, *Politics of Offshore Oil*; and Nash, *United States Oil Policy*.

19. Boulder Dam, as most scholars refer to it, is officially known as Hoover Dam. I use "Boulder Dam" and "Boulder Canyon Dam" most often in this text because these names reflect archival documents and scholarly convention.

20. Webb, in "How the West Hungers for Federal Land," documented the transformation of the Bureau of Land Management's grazing advisory boards under pressure from national environmental organizations.

21. The Cuyahoga River burned regularly for decades before the 1969 fire that became a rallying point for the environmental movement. See Stradling and Stradling, "Perceptions of the Burning River."

CHAPTER ONE

1. Growth has been a major theme in Los Angeles historiography, from Fogelson's classic *Fragmented Metropolis* to studies of tourism, public infrastructure, race relations, and nearly every other possible topic. Works on boosterism and growth include Gish, "Growing and Selling Los Angeles"; Zimmerman, "Paradise Promoted"; and Ovnick, *Los Angeles*. In "How the Urban West Was Won," Erie examines the role of public infrastructure and the government institutions that ran them in Los Angeles's early twentieth-century growth. See also such varied works as Hise, *Magnetic Los Angeles*; Nicolaides, *My Blue Heaven*; Flamming, *Bound for Freedom*; and Wild, *Street Meeting*.

2. Quam-Wickham, in "Cities Sacrificed on the Altar of Oil," describes vividly the problems that oil development brought to Los Angeles's residential districts and the working-class movement to regulate the oil companies in the 1920s. See also Branch, "Oil Extraction, Urban Environment and City Planning."

3. Freudenberg and Gramling, *Oil in Troubled Waters*, 15; Yergin, *Prize*, 25, 28–29.

4. Abstracts of Articles of Incorporation for California Oil Companies on File in Alameda, Bancroft Library, Berkeley, California.

5. Linda Vista Oil, Articles of Incorporation, 1900, Abstracts of Articles of Incorporation for California Oil Companies on File in Alameda, Bancroft Library.

6. California Standard Oil Company, Articles of Incorporation, 1899, Abstracts of Articles of Incorporation for California Oil Companies on File in Alameda, Bancroft Library.

7. Freudenberg, *Oil in Troubled Waters*, 15, 72–73; Yergin, *Prize*, 25, 28–29; Quam-Wickham, "Cities Sacrificed on the Altar of Oil," 191.

8. Freudenberg, *Oil in Troubled Waters*, 17.

9. Ibid., 15, 72–73; Yergin, *Prize*, 25, 28–29; Quam-Wickham, "Cities Sacrificed on the Altar of Oil," 191.

10. Quam-Wickham, "Cities Sacrificed on the Altar of Oil," 191.

11. Yergin, *Prize*, 219–20.

12. The *Los Angeles Times* contains many descriptions of the chaos and filth that accompanied oil development. Another indication of the extent and persistence of oil problems may be found in the repeated efforts to curb noise, pollution, and other consequences of oil development by force of law. City ordinances, lawsuits, or other legal means to curb oil nuisances were recorded in 1901, 1926, and 1929. See "Measures to Stop the Oil Nuisance," *LAT*, 3 May 1901; "War to Bar Oil Leaks in Sea Starts," *LAT*, 9 Nov. 1926; and "Oil Pollution Evil Banished," *LAT*, 21 Mar. 1929.

13. For a description of the impact of oil booms on Huntington Beach, see Jim Combs, "Another Oil Boom Brings Chaos to Huntington Beach," *Fortnight*, 16 Mar. 1953, 13. *Fortnight* reported that most Huntington Beach residents were so money-struck that they welcomed even the chaos and filth. Quam-Wickham argues convincingly that many of these problems arose from the unusually high natural gas pressures overlying most of the oil deposits in the Los Angeles basin; see Quam-Wickham, "Cities Sacrificed on the Altar of Oil," 192–94.

Oil wells lowered residential property values, something oilmen acknowledged explicitly when they sought to transform oil fields into residential subdivisions. For example, in 1905, several oil companies asked the city council to force "holdouts" to give up their oil wells so that the majority could maximize profits from a residential development in the oil field. "Obsequies of Oiley Oozers," *LAT*, 19 Nov. 1905. A 1917 strike ten miles from downtown left even the "prominent oil operators" among home owners dismayed and "feel[ing] that they would rather make money out of oil in some other locality." "Oil Spoils Country Places," *Oil Age*, Mar. 1917, 17.

14. For more on the oil industry practices that created tension and resentment, see Olien and Olien, *Oil and Ideology*, and Tygiel, *Great Los Angeles Oil Swindle*.

15. For descriptions of some of these campaigns, see Quam-Wickham, "Cities Sacrificed on the Altar of Oil." See also Sabin, *Crude Politics*.

16. In 1932, the Huntington Beach City Council sought control over tidelands leasing. See "Tidelands Oil Battle Opens," *LAT*, 17 May 1932. For one example of an oil company purchasing land to block another company's access, see "News of Southern Counties: Stop Drilling on Tidelands," *LAT*, 16 Dec. 1927.

17. Downey, *Truth about the Tidelands*, 6.

18. On the Submerged Land Leasing Act of 1921, see "Origin and History of Tidelands Case," *Congressional Digest* 27:10 (1948): 233, and "Conflicting State and Federal Claims of Title in Submerged Lands of the Continental Shelf," 356.

19. C. C. Young, "'Save the Beaches' Is Plea Issued by Gov. C. C. Young," *Venice Evening Vanguard*, 4 Jan. 1928.

20. Ickes described the relations between independent and major oil producers in *Secret Diary of Harold L. Ickes*, vol. 2. For the political impact of America's largest oil companies on national politics, see Engler, *Politics of Oil*.

21. Young, "'Save the Beaches' Is Plea Issued by Gov. C. C. Young."

22. J. C. Rendler to Los Angeles City Council, 11 July 1930, box A453, commun.

6094, LACA. Rendler wrote on behalf of the Jonathan Club, still one of Los Angeles's most exclusive social clubs.

23. "A. A. Newton to Report on Harbor Probe," *Venice Evening Vanguard*, 20 Feb. 1936.

24. Guy W. Finney to John Anson Ford, 21 Aug. 1936, box 11, JAFP.

25. Ibid.

26. "A. A. Newton to Report on Harbor Probe." See also "Ordinance for Protection of Beach Pushed," *Venice Evening Vanguard*, 29 Jan. 1936; "City Planners Act Following Union Protest," *Venice Evening Vanguard*, 6 Feb. 1936.

27. "City Planners Act Following Union Protest."

28. Finney to Ford, 21 Aug. 1936, JAFP. Finney was one of the organizers of this movement.

29. Glanton Reah to John Anson Ford, 15 Sept. 1936, box 11, JAFP. Glanton Reah wrote this letter on behalf of the Shoreline Planning Association, a civic group that advocated public beach acquisition and the 2,500-foot drilling setback.

30. Los Angeles required oil companies to cover the sides of their derricks to reduce noise and to keep oil from spraying onto nearby property. These measures were not always very successful. For pictures of covered derricks, see Franks and Lambert, *Early California Oil*, 113.

31. J. A. Ford to Glanton Reah, 21 Sept. 1936, box 11, JAFP.

32. Glanton Reah to J. A. Ford, 15 Sept. 1936, box 11, JAFP.

33. Ibid.

34. Glanton Reah, "Warning! Our Beaches Are Threatened," undated broadside, box 11, JAFP. The ballot measure, known as Proposition 4, was narrowly defeated in Los Angeles, 451,191 to 434,859. See "City-County Vote," *LAT*, 4 Nov. 1936.

35. Some oil companies, unhappy with state leasing programs that seemed to give major oil corporations an unfair advantage, also argued that only city governments should issue drilling leases for nearshore oil. This, and a desire by the city government for oil royalties, prompted the Huntington Beach City Council to attempt to assert control over tidelands leasing in 1932. See "Tidelands Oil Battle Opens."

36. Elkind, "Public Oil, Private Oil," 131–34. See also "Origin and History of Tidelands Case," 233; "Conflicting State and Federal Claims of Title in Submerged Lands of the Continental Shelf"; and Bartley, *Tidelands Oil Controversy*.

37. "Ocean Front Site Is Purchased for New Clubhouse Project," *Long Beach Press Telegram*, 19 Jan. 1927.

38. Young, *Our First Century*, 122–23.

39. For more on real estate development of Los Angeles's beach communities, see Davidson, "Before 'Surfurbia.'"

40. Olmsted Brothers and Bartolomew and Assoc., *Parks, Playgrounds and Beaches for the Los Angeles Region*, 59.

41. George P. Larsen, "The Beaches Must Belong to the People: California's Statewide Program," *Shore and Beach*, Oct. 1946, 67.

42. In "New Director Named for Junior Chamber," *Redondo Reflex*, 25 Oct. 1935, the Hermosa Beach Junior Chamber of Commerce's new director identified the beach as his community's chief economic asset.

43. Steno Reports, 2 Dec. 1926, 11.

44. "Club's Beach Permit Stirs Wordy Battle," *LAE*, 29 June 1928. The Los Angeles Playgrounds and Recreation Commission was an advocacy group that advised and pressured the Los Angeles City Playgrounds and Recreation Department and the Los Angeles Department of Parks and Recreation. The Los Angeles Chamber of Commerce from time to time also convened commissions to investigate or lobby for the development of recreational resources in the Los Angeles region. For information on the Pacific Coast Club's breakwater proposal, see "Right to Build Groynes Said Not Refused," *Long Beach Press Telegram*, 26 July 1930. Neither the beach club phenomenon nor conflicts between locals and beach clubs over ownership and access to the beach were confined to Southern California. A similar dispute erupted in New York in June 1950 when a hotel fenced off a beach and access road for the exclusive use of its guests. Local property owners asserted that they owned the beach, and they stormed the disputed land armed with hack saws and hammers. See "Somebody's Trespassing: Citizens Storm Beach Claimed by Hostelry," *LAT*, 5 June 1950.

45. "Right to Build Groynes Said Not Refused."

46. Ibid.

47. "Private Beach Plan Is Given Opposition," *Redondo Reflex*, 22 Nov. 1935.

48. "Beach Club Plan Fought," *LAT*, 16 Nov. 1935.

49. "Surf and Sand Club Closing Threatened in Beach Row," *LAT*, 4 Oct. 1936. The Surf and Sand Club remained open, but in 1937 the Los Angeles Athletic Club leased out the unprofitable facility; the building was operated as the Hermosa Biltmore Hotel. The Los Angeles Athletic Club sold the building in 1945. See Young, *Our First Century*, 142–44.

50. "Acquisition of Beach Frontage for Public Use," Steno Reports, 24 July 1924, 10.

51. Los Angeles Chamber of Commerce, "Chronological Record of Accomplishments, 1927–1935," 96, LAACC Collection.

52. Harbor District Chambers of Commerce, Santa Monica Canyon Chamber of Commerce, and West Los Angeles Division of Los Angeles Chamber of Commerce, broadside, Nov. 1933, box A550, attachment to commun. 2829, LACA. See also "Rolph Fights Hot Dog Stand," *LAE*, 8 Dec. 1933; "Beach 'Refectory' May Go to Court," *LAE*, 14 Feb. 1934; and "Malibu Scores Business Plan," *LAE*, 8 Mar. 1934.

53. Letter to C. S. Lamb, 4 Sept. 1926, box A301, attachment to commun. 7429, LACA.

54. Olmsted Brothers and Bartholomew and Assoc., *Parks, Playgrounds and Beaches for the Los Angeles Region*, 63. For more on the Olmsted and Bartholomew plan, see Marguerite Shaffer, "Scenery as an Asset: Assessing the 1930 Los Angeles Regional Park Plan," *Planning Perspectives*, 16:4 (2001), 357–82.

55. Ibid.

56. Untitled memo to "JWA," 16 Apr. 1946, attachment to Walter Peterson, city clerk, to City Attorney, Police Commission and Playground and Recreation Commission, 23 Apr. 1946, box A893, commun. 23172, LACA.

57. "Two Beaches Planned as County Play Spots," *LAT*, 5 July 1946.

58. "Santa Monica C. of C. Takes Up Beach Plan," *LAT*, 9 July 1946; "Two Beaches Planned as County Play Spots." Jones Beach itself was touted as "one of the finest beaches in the United States, and almost the only one designed with forethought and good taste" because of attractive landscaping of facilities, ample trash cans, good lifeguarding, first aid, and inland swimming pool. See Edmund S. Fish, "New Swimmin' Hole," *Saturday Evening Post*, July 1941, 14–15.

59. The expectation that city parks offered respite from an increasingly industrial life is explored by Schmitt in *Back to Nature* and Cranz in *Politics of Park Design*, among others. This same idea also fed public interest in the national parks and western tourism in the 1920s. See Nash's classic *Wilderness and the American Mind* and Shaffer, "Seeing American First."

60. See, for example, Marjorie Meeker, "Color of Water," *Poetry: A Magazine of Verse*, Nov. 1927, 59–65; Freeman Lincoln, "Outer Beach," *Good Housekeeping*, Aug. 1928, 36–39, 212; Amanda Benjamin Hall, "Beach Party," *Commonweal*, 17 July 1929; Walter Beebe Wilder, "A Stroll on the Beach," *House and Garden*, July 1943, 73; Anderson M. Scruggs, "Beach Girl," *Hygeia*, Sept. 1943, 679; Eugene R. Guild, "Exploring America's Great Sand Barrier Reef," *National Geographic*, Sept. 1947, 325–50; "Fun on the Beach," *Life*, 19 July 1948, 64–71; and Dorothy Barclay, "First Encounters with the Sea," *New York Times Magazine*, 3 June 1956, 48. Architectural magazines emphasized the seclusion of the beach in their articles on beach resorts and beach houses, photographing buildings looking out onto windswept and empty strands, even when the structures themselves stood on busy, crowded beaches. See, for example, R. A. Schindler, "A Beach House for Dr. P. Lovell at Newport Beach, California," *Architectural Record*, Sept. 1929, 257–59; Donald Beach Kirby, "West Coast Beach House," *American Home*, Feb. 1941; and "Beach Clubs, Bath Houses, Swimming Pools, Boardwalks, Casinos," *Architectural Record*, Aug. 1931, 87–110. Many magazines also promoted the image of beaches as a fashionable tourism destination: Felix Isman, "The Accountings of a Real Estate Man: It's a Disease!" *Saturday Evening Post*, 18 Aug. 1923, 17, 40–42; "Life Goes on a Beach Vacation," *Life*, 28 Apr. 1947, 136–38, 140; Ray Josephs, "Winter Beaches," *Atlantic Monthly*, Feb. 1947, 110–11. Another expression of the ideal of a secluded beach appears in complaints about crowding or overdevelopment of the strand. For example, Joel W. Hedgepeth, in "A Century at the Seashore," *Scientific Monthly*, Sept. 1946, 194–98, blamed crowds of overenthusiastic amateur naturalists for a dramatic decline in the populations of marine creatures at public beaches. See also H. F. Ellis, "The Decline of Bathing," *Atlantic Monthly*, Sept. 1953, 31–33.

61. See, for example, "Westport Realizes Big Waterfront Project Designed to Pre-

serve Its Community Beach," *American City*, Feb. 1931, 89–91, and "Bathing Beaches and Bath Houses," *Playground and Recreation*, July 1930, 246. See also Ray Josephs, "Winter Beaches," *Atlantic Monthly*, Feb. 1947, 110–11.

62. "Shoreline Development Study for Los Angeles," *American City*, Aug. 1944, 11.

63. "Court Order to Open Beach Swimming Area," *LAT*, 2 Feb. 1946.

64. M. E. Diebold to Los Angeles City Council, "I Live in Venice Club," 1947, box 1924, commun. 27229, LACA.

65. Dean, *Against the Tide*, 44–45. Dean cites a 1923 article in the *Municipal Engineers Journal* on Coney Island erosion and beach improvements as the start of engineers' awareness that groins and other beach structures caused more erosion than they prevented. For more on the problems caused by groins, breakwaters, and seawalls, see Dean, *Against the Tide*, 36–91. Groins and breakwaters do not merely cause erosion by starving the beach of sand. Because a wave carrying little or no sediment has more energy, it will pick up more sand from the beach than a similar wave carrying a normal amount of sediment. Thus structures that impede the movement of sediment along the shore actually increase erosion nearby.

66. "Redondo Beach Waves Subside," *LAT*, 29 Dec. 1940.

67. For the attribution of erosion to yacht harbors, see A. G. Johnson, "The Vanishing Beaches of Southern California," *Western City*, May 1940, 23, and Griffin, *Coastline Plans and Action*, 14–15. See also Robbins and Tilton, *Los Angeles*, 157–58.

68. In 1935, the Los Angeles Department of Public Works added a sewage disposal plant on Terminal Island for wastes from the Wilmington, San Pedro, and Harbor City areas. In 1976 and 1985, the Los Angeles Department of Public Works added two water reclamation plants to treat sewage and produce reclaimed water for the San Fernando Valley. The Hyperion Point plant remains by far the largest and most important wastewater treatment facility for the city of Los Angeles.

69. R. F. Goudey, "Report on New Outfall Sewer," *Bulletin of the Municipal League of Los Angeles*, Aug. 1925, 12; California, Department of Public Health, Bureau of Sanitary Engineering, "Report on a Pollution Survey of Santa Monica Beaches in 1942," 26 June 1943, (Sacramento, 1943), 6.

70. California, Department of Public Health, Bureau of Sanitary Engineering, "Report on a Pollution Survey of Santa Monica Beaches in 1942," 26 June 1943, (Sacramento, 1943), 6.

71. California, Department of Public Health, Bureau of Sanitary Engineering, "Report on a Pollution Survey of Santa Monica Beaches in 1942," 6; "General Population by City, L.A. County, 1910–1950," ⟨http://www.laalmanac.com/⟩.

72. "$21,000,000 Sewage Treatment Plant and Ocean Outfall Recommended," *Western City*, May 1944, 20–21.

73. Geoffrey F. Morgan, "Now See What Has Happened to the Beaches!" *LAT*, 19 Apr. 1943; California, Department of Public Health, Bureau of Sanitary Engineering, "Report on a Pollution Survey of Santa Monica Beaches in 1942," 7.

74. "Beach Road Stirs Fight," *LAT*, 1 May 1935; "Ocean-Front Highway Opposed

by Santa Monica City Council," *LAT*, 18 May 1935; "Beach Road Route Fixed," *LAT*, 14 June 1935; "Beach Land Deed Aired," *LAT*, 18 Apr. 1935. Ryles's organization, the Save the Beach Association, should not be confused with the 1931 Save the Beach League.

75. "League Formed to Fight against Beach Pollution," *LAT*, 22 Nov. 1931; "Beach Units Join Hands," *LAT*, 31 Jan. 1936.

76. "Redondo Veterans Elect New Officer," *LAT*, 20 Dec. 1925; "Redondo Airs Civic Plans," *LAT*, 20 Jan. 1938; "Backers of Pension Plan Demand Ouster of Chamber Secretary" 19 Oct. 1938, *LAT*; "Hermosa Clears City Employee Who Fought 'Funny Money' Plan," *LAT*, 16 Nov. 1938; "Marked Gain in Attendance at Golden Gate Fair Reported," *LAT*, 18 June 1940; "Shortridge for High Dam," *LAT*, 16 July 1926; "Memorials Will Honor Peninsula Civic Leader," *LAT*, 16 May 1965.

77. Testimony of George Hjelte, Beach Study Conference: Proceedings of a Meeting of Representatives of Governmental and Private Agencies called by Board of Supervisors to Consider Beach and Shoreline Problems, 12 Apr. 1940, box 17, JAFP.

78. Young, *Our First Century*, 120–24, 140–44; on the Deauville Club, see "Santa Monica Beach Unit Sold by LAAC," *LAT*, 10 Sept. 1949.

79. "Act to Buy Film Beaches," *LAHE*, 17 Jan. 1945; "Seek Beach Strip," *Hollywood Citizen News*, 17 Jan. 1945, box 79, FBC. The *Herald Express* reported that these properties originally cost more than $500,000. Willing sellers included Louis B. Mayer, James M. Schenck, Mary Pickford, the Douglas Fairbanks estate, the Irving Thalberg estate, Bernie Hyman, J. W. Considine, Harry Rapf, and Mike Levy.

80. "City to Be Given Beach Park," *LAT*, 10 May 1930.

81. "Board Votes for Beaches," *LAT*, 30 Aug. 1936.

82. Charles S. Lamb, Playground and Recreation Commission, to Los Angeles City Council, "Subject: Acquisition of Certain Beach Properties at Venice," 9 Nov. 1937, box A660, attachment to "Communication from Shoreline Planning Assn," commun. 4309, LACA.

83. Gordon Whitnall, "Saving Private Recreation Areas for Permanent Public Use," *American City*, Mar. 1942, 66.

84. "SB 509—Appropriating $1,560,000 for Acquisition and Reforestation of Cutover Lands," Steno Reports, 25 Mar. 1943, 4.

85. "County Beach Plans Bared," *LAE*, 17 Jan. 1945; "Public Beach Plan Passed," *Hollywood Citizen News*, 16 Jan. 1945; "State Acquisition of Shore Line Urged," *LAT*, 17 Jan. 1945, all in box 79, FBC.

86. "County to Seek State Beach Fund," *LAT*, 22 Dec. 1944.

87. "Commission Plans to Get Beach Land," *Pico Post*, 30 Aug. 1945; "Beaches: Shoreline Group Meets on L.A. Program," *LAHE*, 30 Aug. 1945, box 79, FBC. Planning commissions and civic groups in other states issued similar reports calling for more public beach acquisition and development. See, for example, "Massachusetts Wants More Public Beaches and Town Forests," *American City*, Aug. 1941, 91.

88. "Bring Back Beaches for Public Use," *LAHE*, 29 Aug. 1945, box 79, FBC.

89. "Public Beach Plan Passed."

90. George P. Larson and Neil C. Cunningham, Shoreline Planning Assoc. of California, Inc., "Program of Activities," 27 Aug. 1946, 4, box 17, JAFP.

91. Ibid.

92. "County Beach Plans Bared."

93. Larsen, "Beaches Must Belong to the People," 67.

94. City Planning Commission (Edith S. Jameson), Resolution, 13 Nov. 1952, box A1159, commun. 56035, LACA.

95. "Move Hints End of Long Beach Dispute," *LAT*, 24 June 1948.

96. "Central Newport Group Turns 'Thumbs Down' on State China Cove Matching Land Proposal; List Five Reasons," *Newport Balboa Press*, 8 June 1950; "Ocean Front Property Owners Form Beach Protective Association," *Newport Balboa Press*, 6 July 1950.

97. "Beach Plan Opposition Stalls Action," *LAT*, 15 July 1955; "Ventura County Beach Master Plan Opposed," *LAT*, 13 Jan. 1956.

98. "Central Newport Group Turns 'Thumbs Down' on State China Cove Matching Land Proposal; List Five Reasons," and "Ocean Front Property Owners Form Beach Protective Association." Similarly, property owners in Long Beach helped defeat beach bonds in 1925. See "Beach Bonds Fail at Election," *Long Beach Press Telegram*, 13 Mar. 1925.

99. "Countywide Shoreline Plan Sharply Debated at Hearing," *LAT*, 30 Mar. 1961; "Property Owners Protest: Supervisors Decide to Think Again about Plan for Beaches," *LAT*, 14 July 1961. Ironically, during this same period of time elsewhere in Southern California, voters came to see urban development along the shore as an increasing threat to public access. This trend not only reinforced the public ownership but in 1972 yielded the California Coastal Commission, which has restricted development in the coastal zone ever since. See Davidson, "Beach versus 'Blade Runner.'"

100. "Countywide Shoreline Plan Sharply Debated at Hearing"; "Property Owners Protest: Supervisors Decide to Think Again about Plan for Beaches." The Redondo Beach City Council joined the opposition, petitioning to have a private yacht harbor in their community omitted from a revised master plan.

101. Douglas Flamming attributes the 1920s segregation movement, as did black Angelenos themselves, to increasing immigration of southern whites to Los Angeles. See Flamming, *Bound for Freedom*. See also Sides, *L.A. City Limits*, and Boyle, *Arc of Justice*.

102. Flamming, *Bound for Freedom*, 271–72.

103. Ibid., 271–75.

104. Similar tactics were used to block black subdivisions as well. In one particularly notable case, a group of wealthy white landowners in southwestern Los Angeles County convinced the county to condemn land slated for a black subdivision. The land eventually became Alondra Park. See ibid., 240–43.

105. Sylvester Weaver in "Restriction of Use of Beaches by Public," Steno Reports, 17 Aug. 1922, 4; Flamming, *Bound for Freedom*, 271–73.
106. Flamming, *Bound for Freedom*, 271–72.
107. "Beach Leases Fought," *LAT*, 17 Jan. 1925; "Beach 'Gift' Is Restrained," *LAT*, 8 Jan. 1924; "Sewer Tilt Delayed," *LAT*, 16 Jan. 1924; "Beach Suit Depending on Voters," *LAT*, 30 Jan. 1925.
108. Box A236, "Communication from City Clerk," commun. 638, LACA.
109. "Beach Suit Depending on Voters."
110. "Beach Leases Fought."
111. "Inquiry Begun in Club Blaze," *LAT*, 22 Jan. 1926.
112. "Beach Club Is Proposed by Negroes," *LAT*, 2 Apr. 1925.
113. "Negro Club Wins Fight for Entry," *LAT*, 22 May 1925.
114. "Inquiry Begun in Club Blaze," *LAT*, 22 Jan. 1926; "To Oppose Proposed Negro Club," *LAT*, 22 Nov. 1926.
115. "Inquiry Begun in Club Blaze"; "Arson Arrests Expected," *LAT*, 23 Jan. 1926.
116. "Inquiry Begun in Club Blaze."
117. "Negroes Appeal for Funds to Buy Tideland," *LAT*, 18 Nov. 1926.
118. "Ocean Front Site Is Purchased for New Clubhouse Project."
119. "Redondo Veterans Elect New Officer"; "Redondo Airs Civic Plans"; "Backers of Pension Plan Demand Ouster of Chamber Secretary"; "Hermosa Clears City Employee Who Fought 'Funny Money' Plan"; "Marked Gain in Attendance at Golden Gate Fair Reported"; "Shortridge for High Dam"; "Memorials Will Honor Peninsula Civic Leader."

CHAPTER TWO

1. H. O. Swartout to Board of Supervisors, 21 Sept. 1943, box 25, JAFP. Swartout was the Los Angeles County health officer. In his capacity as county health officer, he reported an increase in the number of traffic accidents downtown, "some of which are quite definitely due to eye irritation and consequent poor vision."
2. Elbert D. Owen to Los Angeles City Council, 17 Aug. 1943, and Emily K. Krug to Mayor Bowron, Sept. 1944, both attached to Fletcher Bowron to J. W. Livingston, 11 Aug. 1943, box A832, commun. 15399, LACA; Sherrie M. Rossen to Los Angeles City Council, 17 Sept. 1944, box A851, commun. 18283, LACA; Fletcher Bowron to William L. Stewart, 16 Oct. 1943, box 1, FBC; Frederic A. Kane to Los Angeles City Council, 8 Sept. 1944, box A851, commun. 18283, LACA. Not all workers criticized industrial smoke. The CIO Local 132, representing utility workers at the butadiene plant, opposed the city's efforts to close down their plant. See "Butadiene Plant Closed," *LAE*, 24 Oct. 1943.
3. Rosen, in "Businessmen against Pollution in Late Nineteenth Century Chicago," considers the economic incentives that underlay the Chicago business community's cooperation with antismoke efforts. In many cities, smoke control efforts pitted women reformers, who focused on public health and municipal housekeep-

ing, against businessmen's organizations, which focused on productivity. See, for example, Platt, "Invisible Gases," and Stradling, *Smokestacks and Progressives*, 52–55, 154. On women's distinctive approaches to urban problems more generally, see Flanagan, *Seeing with Their Hearts*, and Hoy, "'Municipal Housekeeping.'"

4. Krier and Ursin, *Pollution and Policy*, 46–49.

5. Stradling explains the importance of coal in American factories and homes and the ways that smoke regulators learned that expensive anthracite coals produced less soot and smoke than cheaper bituminous coal. He also describes how industrial regulations could cost employees more than their employers, as when the antismoke campaigns resulted in prosecution of locomotive firemen rather than railroad corporations themselves. See Stradling, "Dirty Work and Clean Air" and *Smokestacks and Progressives*, 6–20, 163–67.

6. I. A. Deutch, "Various Aspects of Air Pollution Control," delivered before the American Society of Heating and Ventilating Engineers, 6 May 1946, 1, box 25, JAFP. A similar low temperature inversion brought the dangers of air pollution to national attention when twenty people died in Donora, Pennsylvania, in 1948.

7. "Mystery Fumes Irritate Eyes," *LAT*, 10 July 1940.

8. Charles L. Senn to George M. Uhl, 30 July 1943, box A851, commun. 18283, LACA. For newspaper coverage of the original report, see "Cause of Gases Sought by City," *LAT*, 22 Sept. 1942.

9. Charles L. Senn to George M. Uhl, 22 Oct. 1943, box 25, JAFP. Fumes were recorded on 26 July, 21 September, 5 October, 12 October, and 25 October 1943. In 1939, aviation authorities called Los Angeles's haze "a serious menace to safe flying." See Deutch, "Various Aspects of Air Pollution Control." As early as 1940, the city health department blamed industrial "smokes, gases and fumes" for bouts of eye irritation in the Los Angeles area. See Senn to Uhl, 30 July 1943, LACA.

10. Kane to Los Angeles City Council, 8 Sept. 1944, LACA.

11. Sherrie M. Rossen to Los Angeles City Council, 17 Sept. 1944, LACA (emphasis in original). The city council received additional letters from a real estate agent who protested the invasion of Echo Park by noxious fumes, and it received several complaints from individuals who felt that the industrial fumes exacerbated breathing problems or endangered their health. See, for example, Owen to Los Angeles City Council, 17 Aug 1943, LACA. Health-related complaints include General Hospital Ward 400 to Los Angeles City Council, 4 Oct. 1943, and Emily Krug to Los Angeles City Council, Sept. 1944, both in box A832, commun. 15399, LACA. This one city council file contains five letters from constituents complaining about industrial fumes. Many others are found in the Fletcher Bowron Collection at the Huntington Library.

12. "Fumes Bring Plant Halt," *LAT*, 5 Oct. 1943.

13. "Fumes Storm Spurs Quest for Remedy," *LAT*, 6 Oct. 1943.

14. F. S. Wade to Los Angeles City Council, 24 Aug. 1943, box A832, commun. 15399, LACA. One article that quotes Southern California Gas as accepting respon-

sibility for the fumes problem is "Find Cause of Eye-Smarting Here," *LAHE*, 28 July 1943. See also "Grand Jury Checking Up on Fumes," *LAT*, 7 Oct. 1943.

15. Senn to Uhl, 22 Oct. 1943, JAFP; "End Ordered for Gas Fume Annoyances," *LAT*, 19 Sept. 1943; "Move to Shut Down Gas Plant," *LAHE*, n.d., box 74, FBC; Fletcher Bowron to City Council, 20 Sept. 1943, box A832, commun. 15399. LACA. Even the county grand jury supported Bowron's efforts to close the plant. See "Resolution Adopted by the Grand Jury of the County of Los Angeles," 20 Sept. 1943, box A832, commun. 15399, supplement 3, LACA.

16. "Grand Jury Questions City Officials about Gas Fumes," *LAT*, 8 Oct. 1943; "Council Acts on Fumes," *LAT*, 14 Oct. 1943.

17. "Councilmen Persuaded to Drop Gas Suit," *Los Angeles Daily News*, 27 Oct. 1943; "War Fumes and War Rubber," *LAT*, *LAE*, *LAHE*, *Los Angeles Daily News*, and *Hollywood Citizen News*, 18 Oct. 1943, all in box 74, FBC; Bradley Dewey to Los Angeles City Council, 22 Oct. 1943, box A835, commun. 16028, LACA; "U.S. Rebukes City's Suit on Gas Fumes," *Los Angeles Daily News*, 26 Oct. 1943; "Council Halts Suit to Close Butadiene Plant," *LAT*, 28 Oct. 43; "Butadiene Gas Suit Dropped," *LAE*, 28 Oct. 1943, all in box 74, FBC.

18. Quoted in "Fumes Bring Plant Halt." Charles Senn, head of the city health department's Sanitation Bureau, also began directing attention to other sources of pollution at this time. For example, on 6 October 1943, he reported heavy smoke from fourteen "heavy industrial plants" in Vernon and from the Standard Oil refinery in El Segundo. See "Fume Storm Spurs Quest for Remedy," *LAT*, 6 Oct. 1943.

19. "Fume Storm Spurs Quest for Remedy."

20. Joseph B. Ficklen III to H. O. Swartout, "Preliminary Outline of the Part an Enlarged Division of Industrial Hygiene Could Play in the Evaluation and Elimination and/or Control of Smoke and Fume Problem in Los Angeles County," 5 Sept. 1944, 3, box 25. JAFP.

21. "Action Taken to Halt Fumes," *LAE*, 31 Aug. 1944, box 76, FBC.

22. "Fumes Cited as Community Jag Cause," *Los Angeles Daily News*, 22 Sept. 1944, box 76, FBC.

23. "County Acts to Curb Smoke," *LAT*, 9 Aug. 1944.

24. Ibid.; H. O. Swartout, Los Angeles County health officer, to Board of Supervisors, 1 Aug. 1944, "Subject: The Fumes and Smoke Problem—Progress Report," 2–4, box 25, JAFP.

25. Morris Pendleton speech before LAACC Board of Directors, Steno Reports, 12 Oct. 1944, 8.

26. "D. A. Plans Test Suit in City's Smoke Fumes War," *Los Angeles Daily News*, 31 Aug. 1944, box 74, FBC.

27. Fletcher Bowron to Morris B. Pendleton, 2 Nov. 1944, box 1, FBC; "Morris B. Pendleton, Civic Leader, Industrialist, Dies," *LAT*, 24 Feb. 1985. The chair of the Citizens' Manpower Committee was the president of the LAACC; the balance of the eighty-five-member committee was drawn from labor unions, manufacturing

organizations, women's clubs, churches, veterans organizations, government agencies, newspapers, and businesspeople.

28. LAACC Minutes, 14 Sept. 1944, 3–4.
29. Pendleton speech before LAACC Board of Directors, 12 Oct. 1944, 8.
30. Ibid.
31. Ibid.
32. "Smoking Out Fumes Again," *Los Angeles Daily News*, 20 Sept. 1944; "County Fumes Czar Proposed," *LAT*, 20 Sept. 44, both in box 76, FBC.
33. Steno Reports, 14 Sept. 1944, 11; Steno Reports, 22 Sept. 1944, 12.
34. "Law Ordered Drafted to Curb Fumes Nuisance," *LAT*, 16 Sept. 1944; "County Acts to Curb Smoke"; "County Board Acts to Ban Smoke Fumes," *Los Angeles Daily News*, 8 Aug. 1944; "'Smoke Czar' Indorsed by 16 City Officials," *LAT*, 21 Sept. 1944, all in box 76, FBC.
35. "Complaint in Fumes Case Filed," *LAHE*, 15 Sept. 1944, box 76, FBC.
36. Steno Reports, 14 Sept. 1944, 11–13.
37. "Smoking Out Fumes Again"; "County Fumes Czar Proposed."
38. Los Angeles County Smoke and Fumes Commission, "First Annual Report to Los Angeles Board of Supervisors," 24 Oct. 1944, 2, box 25, JAFP; "Fume Fighters Try to See Past Butadiene Fog," *Los Angeles Daily News*, 20 Oct. 1943, box 74, FBC.
39. Los Angeles County Smoke and Fumes Commission, "First Annual Report to Los Angeles Board of Supervisors."
40. "Complaint in Fumes Case Filed."
41. Report to the Los Angeles County Board of Supervisors by the Los Angeles County Smoke and Fumes Commission, 13 Mar. 1944, attachment to A. H. Campion to Board of Supervisors, 11 May 1944, 1, box 25, JAFP.
42. Ibid.
43. Swartout to Board of Supervisors, 1 Aug. 1944, "Subject: The Fumes and Smoke Problem—Progress Report," 2; Report to the Los Angeles County Board of Supervisors by the Los Angeles County Smoke and Fumes Commission, 13 Mar. 1944, 3, 5; Los Angeles County Smoke and Fumes Commission, "First Annual Report to Los Angeles Board of Supervisors," 3.
44. Morris Pendleton speech before LAACC Board of Directors, Steno Reports, 14 Sept. 1944, 11–13.
45. LAACC Minutes, 14 Sept. 1944, 3–4.
46. For the Altadena Property Owners League critiques of county smoke ordinances, see "Work on 'Smoke Czar' Ordinances Started," *LAT*, 26 Sept. 1944, box 76, FBC.
47. Krier and Ursin, *Pollution and Policy*, 46–51. The standard way that American air pollution engineers measured smoke density during this period was the Ringelmann Smoke Chart.
48. Morris Pendleton speech before LAACC Board of Directors, Steno Reports, 19 Oct. 1944, 2–3.

49. "Fumes Curb Plan Altered," *LAT*, 30 Sept. 1944; "Conflict with State Code Seen in Smoke Ban," *LAT*, 13 Nov. 1944.

50. "The Shame of Smog," *LAT*, 26 Sept. 1946, box 81A, FBC.

51. Bowron to Pendleton, 2 Nov. 44, FBC.

52. "Brief of Meeting Held in Pasadena City Hall, October 19, 1945, at 2 p.m. by the Action Committee on Smog," 2–4, E. E. East Collection, Automobile Club of Southern California Archives, Los Angeles, California. The Action Committee on Smog included Pasadena's mayor and city manager, city managers from Glendale and South Pasadena, representatives from the Temple City and the Pasadena chambers of commerce, and from the Southern California Auto Club. See H. F. Holley, "Memo for files," 22 Oct. 1945, E. E. East Collection. The communities that did not even respond to invitations to participate in a countywide conference on smog control in 1946 included Bell, Claremont, Compton, El Monte, Glendora, Hawthorn, Manhattan Beach, Monrovia, Palos Verdes Estates, Pomona, Redondo Beach, San Gabriel, Santa Monica, Sierra Madre, Signal Hill, Torrance, Vernon, and West Covina. Of these, Vernon was perhaps the most industrial in the 1940s. El Segundo, home to Standard Oil's second-largest oil refinery, promised only qualified support for county smoke control efforts. See Mayors' Conference on Control of Smoke and Fumes, 8 May 1946, reporter's transcript, Los Angeles, box 25, JAFP.

53. H. O. Swartout to Board of Supervisors, "Subject: The Smoke and Fumes Nuisances—Second Progress Report," 27 Sept. 1944, 2–3, box 25, JAFP. As Swartout reported to the supervisors, factory owners seized on the logic of vital military production to protect themselves from smoke regulations. Standard Oil officials at the El Segundo refinery, for example, argued that "government pressure to increase the production of 100 octane gasoline for war purposes was largely to blame for their inability to operate their plant in a way that would avoid all the nuisances that could be avoided under normal conditions." Executives at General Chemical Company in Manhattan Beach "frankly admitted that new processes put into operation to meet wartime needs had resulted in the emission of noxious oxides of sulfur." Swartout also reported that the American Cyanamid Company in Azusa was "busy on orders from the Chemical Warfare Division of the Army . . . of such secret and urgent nature that entrance to the main part of the plant was not permitted."

54. H. O. Swartout to Board of Supervisors, "Recommendation: That Your Honorable Board Give Consideration to the Advisability of Passing a 'Smoke and Fumes' Ordinance Embodying Substantially the Following Provisions," 18 June 1945, 3, box 25, JAFP. See also H. O. Swartout to Board of Supervisors, "Subject: The Smoke and Fumes Nuisances—Second Progress Report," 1 Aug. 1944, 3, box 25, JAFP.

55. Steno Reports, 12 Oct. 1944, 8; Harold Kennedy, "The History, Legal and Administrative Aspects of Air Pollution Control in the County of Los Angeles," report submitted to the Board of Supervisors of the County of Los Angeles, 9 May 1954, box 59, FBC. For more information on the industrial community's reactions to the APCD, see Dewey, *Don't Breathe the Air*, 43–45.

56. "Air Pollution Control May Bog Down, 41 Cities Apathetic," *LAHE*, 7 Aug. 1946; "Smog Program Gets Lost in a Fog," *Los Angeles Daily News*, 8 Aug 1946; "Smog Control Drive Periled," *LAE*, 8 Aug. 1946, all in box 78, FBC.

57. Beach Vasey to Earl Warren, "Assembly Bill 1," 10 June 1947, in Governors Ch. Bill File, Ch. 632 (AB 1), 1947, California State Archives, Sacramento, California.

58. Ibid.; Harold Kennedy to Earl Warren, 9 June 1947, 3, in Governors Ch. Bill File, Ch. 632 (AB 1), 1947, California State Archives. The Automobile Club of Southern California was quite proud of its contributions to the passage of AB 1. The Auto Club sent representatives to meet with the mayors of the foothill cities, the Los Angeles City Council, and the county supervisors to argue for the model ordinance and then for greater regional coordination of air pollution regulation. The club also participated in the aerial surveys of Los Angeles County and in public education campaigns. See Engineering Department, Automobile Club of Southern California, "Summary of the Activities of the Automobile Club of Southern California in Connection with the Smog Problem in the Los Angeles Metropolitan Area," 1 Dec. 1950, E. E. East Collection.

59. Dewey, *Don't Breathe the Air*, 43. For Harold Kennedy's recollections, see Kennedy, "History, Legal and Administrative Aspects of Air Pollution Control in the County of Los Angeles," 10–13.

60. Dewey, *Don't Breathe the Air*, 45–46; "Threat of Disaster from Smog Hanging over Los Angeles," *LAT*, 16 Oct. 1948; "Smog Blanket Kills 15 in Eastern Mill Town," *LAT*, 31 Oct. 1948.

61. Kennedy, "History, Legal and Administrative Aspects of Air Pollution Control in the County of Los Angeles"; "Glendale Will Ask Permit to Build Incinerator," *LAHE*, 8 Sept. 48, box 90, FBC.

62. "Glendale Will Ask Permit to Build Incinerator"; J. F. Hamilton to Board of Supervisors, 8 June 55, box 26, JAFP. For more on McCabe's years at the APCD, see Krier and Ursin, *Pollution and Policy*, 65, 73–74.

63. Louis McCabe to Raymond V. Darby, 9 Jan. 1948, box 25, JAFP; "Bonfires Blamed," *Hollywood Citizen News*, 1 Mar. 45, box 77A, FBC. See also Crouch et al., *Sanitation and Health*, 80–84.

64. Mrs. J. C. Schutte to Raymond V Darby, 20 Oct. 1948, box 25, JAFP.

65. "Smog-Control Plan for Industry Gains Supervisors Full Support," *LAT*, 11 Feb. 1948; "New Smog Proposal Hit," *LAT*, 27 Apr. 1948.

66. "L.A. Kills Smog with Kindness," *Businessweek*, 24 Feb. 1951, 60–65.

67. On calls for a cooperative approach to air pollution regulation in Los Angeles, see, for example, George J. Murray Jr. to Preston Kline Caye, 5 Dec. 1945, attachment to H. F. Holley to George J. Murray, 21 Dec. 1945, E. E. East Collection; Bowron to Wilton L. Halverson, 2 Nov. 1944, box 1, FBC; R. L. Daugherty to J. A. Ford, 18 Jan. 1954, box 26, JAFP; and H. O. Swartout and I. A. Deutch, "The 'Smog' Problem," Sept. 1945, 6, box 25, JAFP.

68. See, for example, George L. Schuler to Los Angeles County Grand Jury, 22 Nov. 1948, box A986, commun. 35599, LACA.

69. Dewey, *Don't Breathe the Air*, 45.

70. "'Not So,' Oil Industry Replies to Smog Detectives' Findings," *LAT*, 28 Sept. 1948; Ed Ainsworth, "Oil Leaders Enter Smog Fight Talks," *LAT*, 12 Aug. 1948.

71. Earl Wayland Bowman, "Strike Closed Refineries Ending Smog, Writes Critic," *LAT*, 16 Sept. 1948; Ed Ainsworth, "Refineries Held Smog Leaders," *LAT*, 15 Sept. 1948.

72. Minutes of Dinner Meeting of the Citizens Smog Advisory Committee, 10 June 1947, 3, box 25, JAFP.

73. William Jeffers to Harold A. Henry, 23 Nov. 1948, box A987, commun. 35661, LACA.

74. C. H. Matheny and Frank L. Alexander, "History of Los Angeles Smog: War Chemical Used on Battlefields Responsible," 20 Oct. 1954 (typescript), box 26, JAFP.

75. Norman Chandler, the owner of the *Los Angeles Times*, and Ed Ainsworth, the *Los Angeles Times* editor, also attended public and private meetings to hammer out various industries' objections to smog control. For more information on these meetings, see the account of the crucial meeting at the Huntington Hotel in 1948 in Kennedy, "History, Legal and Administrative Aspects of Air Pollution Control in the County of Los Angeles," 14–16, and "Oil Leaders Enter Smog Fight Talks."

76. E. S. to J. A. Ford, "Re your penned notes on my memo of 5 Apr 1948," box 25, JAFP.

77. This was the second set of hearings convened in Los Angeles in 1950. The first, held in February, attracted almost no attention from the press or those groups most active in smog control. One of the few articles mentioning these hearings is "Women Marshaled in Battle on Smog," *LAT*, 19 Mar. 1950.

78. Dickey's position is outlined in "Smog Cut 25% in 22 Months; Relief Next Fall, Larson Says," *LAT*, 23 Feb. 1950. For information on the first of Dickey's bills, see "Survey on Smog Menace to Public Health Advocated," *LAT*, 25 Feb. 1950; "The Truth about the Smog," *LAT*, 12 Nov. 1950; and "Sensational Smog Stories Never Told," *LAT*, 30 Nov. 1950. The *Los Angeles Times* reacted to Dickey's health research proposal in "Smog Research Group Proposed in Assembly Bill," *LAT*, 18 Mar. 1950; "Let's Not Wreck Smog Control," *LAT*, 28 Mar. 1950; "Council to Oppose Dickey Bill as Hindering Smog Controls," *LAT*, 29 Mar. 1950; and "Assembly Group Kills Dickey Bill for State Study of Smog Problem," *LAT*, 30 Mar. 1950. For more on Dickey's committee, see also Krier and Ursin, *Pollution and Policy*.

79. Randall F. Dickey, "The Dismal Future of Smog Control," 12 Apr. 1955, 9, box 26, JAFP.

80. Dewey, *Don't Breathe the Air*, 45.

81. "Proper Perspective for Smog Inquiry Today," *LAT*, 22 Feb. 1950; "Smog Cut 25% in 22 Months; Relief Next Fall, Larson Says"; "Assembly Group Kills Dickey Bill for State Study of Smog Problem."

82. According to the *Los Angeles Times*, Los Angeles County officials "vigorously opposed" Dickey's proposals to change the Air Pollution Control District Act. See Ed Ainsworth, "S. F. Pledges Hands Off Smog Controls," *LAT*, 15 Dec. 1950. In June, the *Los Angeles Times* reported optimistically that Air Pollution Control District had corrected "perhaps 30 to 35% of the sources of smog" in Los Angeles County and that "the rest of the program should move along with much greater smoothness." See "Let's Not Dodge the Smog Issue," *LAT*, 11 June 1950.

83. "Smog Control Failing, Says State Law Foe," *LAT*, 27 Oct. 1950.

84. Ainsworth, "S. F. Pledges Hands Off Smog Controls." A representative from San Francisco testified during the Assembly Interim Committee hearings in Los Angeles that, although the existing state law did not provide San Francisco with adequate means for smog control, the mayor of San Francisco desired changes in the state pollution law that would address San Francisco's needs without interfering with Los Angeles air pollution control administration. See Ainsworth, "Sensational Smog Stories Never Told."

85. The Los Angeles County supervisors had invited Dickey to visit Los Angeles so he could see the APCD's accomplishments firsthand. Dickey scheduled the public hearings after refusing this invitation. "County Invites Inspection of Smog Curbs," *LAT*, 15 Nov. 1950.

86. "L.A. Smog Scandal Hinted as Assembly Probe Opens," *Los Angeles Mirror*, 27 Nov. 1950; similar coverage and identical quotes from Dickey in "L.A. Smog Sensation Looms, " *LAHE*, 27 Nov. 1950, both in box 78, FBC.

87. "L.A. Smog Scandal Hinted as Assembly Probe Opens." Similar coverage and identical quotes from Dickey in "Smog Officials Get Raking Over by Assembly Probers," *Los Angeles Daily News*, 27 Nov. 1950, box 78, FBC.

88. "Inspection Tour Rejected by Smog Control Attacker," *LAT*, 28 Nov. 1950.

89. "L.A. Smog Sensation Looms."

90. "Inspection Tour Rejected by Smog Control Attacker."

91. Ibid.

92. Two of the industrial plant owners who testified were Frank L. Alexander, who owned a dry kiln in San Pedro, and Alvin H. Renfrow, who owned a gray iron foundry. For accounts of their testimony before Dickey's committee, see "Little Is Done on Smog," *LAHE*, 29 Nov. 1950; "Smog Killing People, Probers Told," *LAE*, 29 Nov. 1950; "Present Smog Law Adequate, Larson Tells Assemblymen," *LAT*, 29 Nov. 1950; Ainsworth, "Sensational Smog Stories Never Told"; "Rip Larson on Stand in Smog Hearing," *Los Angeles Daily News*, 29 Nov, 1950; "City Council Orders Prosecution of Smog Violators," *LAE*, 30 Nov. 1950; "Director Defends Efforts to Rid Air of Pollution," *Wilmington Press Journal*, 29 Nov. 1950; Magner White, "City Council Orders Prosecution of Smog Violators; Prober Calls Control Here 'Absolute Failure,'" *LAE*, 30 Nov. 1950, box 78, FBC.

93. Magner White, "Dr. Krick Warns Death Lurking in Increasing Smog," *LAE*, 4 Dec. 1950. See also "Smog Chief Denies 'Deception' Charge," *Los Angeles*

Mirror, 29 Nov. 1950, box 78, FBC; "Present Smog Law Adequate, Larson Tells Assemblymen."

94. For the testimony on the public health dangers of smog, see "Intense Smog Speeds Death, Quiz to Hear," *LAE*, 27 Nov. 1950; "L.A. Smog Sensation Looms"; "Study Hints Smog Raises Respiratory Death Rate," *LAT*, 27 Nov. 1950; Harry Goldblatt, as quoted in "Doctor Warns Hearing L.A. Smog Could Cause Cancer," *LAHE*, 28 Nov. 1950; "Smog Problem Unsolved as State Closes Inquiry," *Hollywood Citizen News*, 30 Nov. 1950; "Doctors Urge Research in Air Pollution," *Los Angeles Mirror*, 28 Nov. 1950, box 78, FBC. Caltech chemist A. J. Haagen-Smit exposed combustion gases to ultraviolet light and thus created a "laboratory-made smog" that caused the same kind of damage to spinach observed throughout the Los Angeles area. As Haagen-Smit himself explained to the Assembly Interim Committee, a complex series of chemical reactions among combustion gases and a wide variety of industrial and domestic emissions exposed to sunlight together created Los Angeles's distinctive haze. Haagen-Smit explained that this research did not identify a single, discrete cause of either crop damage or eye irritation; he insisted, however, that sulfur dioxide, one of the key oil refinery emissions controlled by APCD regulations, did contribute to smog. Larson and Haagen-Smit both concluded that Haagen-Smit's research suggested that any and all hydrocarbon emissions, be they from automobile engines, furnaces, backyard incinerators, oil refineries, or foundries, added to air quality problems. Larson, however, still considered the role of sunlight in smog "only a theory so far." See "Puzzle of Smog Production Solved by Caltech Scientist," *LAT*, 20 Nov. 1950; Ainsworth, "Sensational Smog Stories Never Told"; "Present Smog Law Adequate, Larson Tells Assemblymen"; "Smog Official Hits Back at Critics," *Los Angeles Daily News*, 28 Nov. 1950, box 78, FBC. See also "Eye Irritating Agent in Smog Said Still a Puzzle," *Hollywood Citizen News*, 28 Nov. 1950; "Solon Probers Claim L.A. Hides Smog Cause," *Los Angeles Mirror*, 28 Nov. 1950, all in box 78, FBC.

95. "Shocking Smog Facts Charged by Probers," *LAE*, 28 Nov. 1950, box 78, FBC.

96. Quoted in "Hearing Told No Medical Research Done on Smog," *LAHE*, 28 Nov. 1950.

97. "Puzzle of Smog Production Solved by Caltech Scientist"; "Smog Official Hits Back at Critics." See also "Eye Irritating Agent in Smog Said Still a Puzzle" and "Solon Probers Claim L.A. Hides Smog Cause."

98. "Little Is Done on Smog" (emphasis in original).

99. Ibid.

100. Kenneth Hahn, as quoted in "Smog Tears Stir Wrath of Council," *Los Angeles Mirror*, 29 Nov. 1950, and in "Councilmen 'Can't See' Smog Report, Order Crackdown," *People's World*, 30 Nov. 1950, both in box 78, FBC. See also "Smog Bad Word, City Dads Told," *Los Angeles Mirror*, 5 Dec. 1950, box 78, FBC.

101. "Council Seeks Remedy for Smog Eye," *Los Angeles Daily News*, 28 Nov. 1950; "Little Is Done on Smog."

102. "Demand Drastic New Steps to Abate L.A. Smog," *LAHE*, 30 Nov. 1950, box 78, FBC.

103. "Smog Mystery—Could It Be All That Glue?" *People's World*, 30 Nov. 1950, box 78, FBC.

104. "Smog Problem Unsolved As State Closes Inquiry."

105. "Stupid Politics Seen in Failure of Smog Elimination," *LAHE*, 30 Nov. 1950.

106. Ibid.

107. Ibid.

108. "Supervisors Invite Smog Critics to Join Inspection," *Los Angeles Daily News*, 5 Dec. 1950; "Councilmen Asked to See Smog Control," *Los Angeles Daily News*, 1 Dec, 1950; "Council Plans Tour of Smog Curb Areas," *Hollywood Citizen News*, 2 Dec. 1950; "Don Masks, Tour L.A., Council Asked," *North Hollywood Valley Times*, 2 Dec. 1950, box 78, FBC.

109. "Checkup on Fumes Curbs to Be Made," *LAT*, 15 Dec. 1950, box 78, FBC. The panel of experts included County Counsel Harold W. Kennedy; Herbert Walker, the chair of the APCD hearing board; Roger Truesdail, a member of the Citizens' Smog Advisory Committee, from which Jeffers now distanced himself; Louis McCabe, the APCD's first director; meteorologists; physicians; and the APCD's main smog researcher, A. J. Haagen-Smit.

110. "Solons Tour Smog District," *Los Angeles Mirror*, 28 Dec. 1950, box 78, FBC.

111. Gordon Larson before the LAACC Board of Directors, Steno Reports, 7 Dec. 1950, 13. For the chamber's position on health research, see "Research to Determine Possible Influence of Smog on the Public Health" Steno Reports, 8 June 1950, 4.

112. "New Developments in Smog Control," Steno Reports, 29 Oct. 1953, 5–8; "Executive Session," Steno Reports, 20 Jan. 1955, 8–9.

113. "New Developments in Smog Control," 5–8.

114. Chester G. Hanson, "Smog-Health Study Proposal Hits Snag," *LAT*, 19 June 1951.

115. "Resolution," 31 Oct. 1952, box 26, JAFP; Roger H. Jessup and Herbert C. Legg to Board of Supervisors, "Subject: Citizen Participation in Solution of Air Pollution Problems," 31 Oct. 1952, box 26, JAFP; "New Developments in Smog Control," 5–8.

116. "New Developments in Smog Control," 6. By 1950, the LAACC had changed the name of its Smoke and Fumes Committee to the Air Pollution Control Committee. Other civic groups, including the Pasadena Council of Women's Clubs, made similar changes at this time to keep up with changes in the scientific understanding of smog.

117. Ibid.

118. Arnold O. Beckman to Board of Supervisors, 17 Jan. 1955, LAACC Board of Directors Minutes, 20 Jan. 1955, LAACC Collection.

119. Ibid.; Arnold Beckman before LAACC Committee, Steno Reports, 20 Jan. 1955, 10.

120. Beckman before LAACC Committee, Steno Reports, 20 Jan. 1955, 10.

121. Beckman to Board of Supervisors, 17 Jan. 1955.

122. "Fumes Cited as Community Jag Cause." On the Altadena Property Owners League and uniform countywide smoke ordinances, see "Fumes County Control Urged by Engineer," *LAHE*, 20 Sept. 1944; "Hearing Today on Fume Issue," *LAE*, 20 Sept. 1944; "County Fumes 'Czar' Proposed," *LAT*, 20 Sept. 1944; "County Officials Agree on Joint Fumes Action," *LAT*, 22 Sept. 1944; "Board Backs Smoke Fight," *LAE*, 27 Sept. 1944; and "County Ordinance Drafted for Creating Fumes 'Czar,'" *LAT*, 28 Sept. 1944, all in box 76, FBC.

123. "New War on Fumes Launched," *LAHE*, 20 Nov. 1945, box 78, FBC.

124. Jeffers to Henry, 23 Nov. 1948, LACA.

125. "Women Marshaled in Battle on Smog"; "Doctor Warns Hearing L.A. Smog Could Cause Cancer."

126. Monterey Park Smog Committee, "Report to City Council," 6 Dec. 1954, box 26, JAFP.

127. Arthur J. Will to Los Angeles County Supervisors, "Subject: Study and Recommendations on Implementing the Operations of the Air Pollution Control District in the County of Los Angeles," 11 Oct. 1954, 10, box 26, JAFP. The Pure Air Committee advocated more aggressive air pollution regulations, and challenged the close relationship between the APCD and a coalition of heavy industries, petroleum processors, and utilities that funded air pollution research and called itself the Air Pollution Foundation. See J. Gustav White to J. A. Ford, 21 Dec. 1953; Pure Air Committee, "Statement from Board of Directors," 15 Nov. 1954; Will to Los Angeles County Supervisors, "Subject: Study and Recommendations on Implementing the Operations of the Air Pollution Control District in the County of Los Angeles," all in box 26, JAFP.

128. "Smoggy Nightmare," *Time*, Nov. 1954, 63–64; "Blight on the Land of Sunshine," *Life*, 1 Nov. 1954, 17–19.

129. Francis H. Packard and E. James Lee to J. A. Ford, 24 Jan. 55; Arthur J. Will to J. A. Ford, "Subject: Organization of Enforcement Division—Air Pollution Control District," 1 Feb. 1955, both in box 26, JAFP. The Air Pollution Foundation received contributions from construction firms such as Bechtel; auto and aircraft manufacturers ranging from American Motors and Mack Trucks to Lockheed and Northrop; ceramic kiln companies; rubber manufacturers, including Goodrich and Firestone; and a few major retailers, newspapers, and transportation firms. What marred the public image of the group the most, however, was the involvement of the Western Oil and Gas Association, private utility companies, and chemical processors such as DuPont and Ethyl Corporation.

130. "'Smoke Czar' Indorsed by 16 City Officials."

131. For more on the Automobile Club's position that the APCD ought to do more to control industrial smog, see, for example, "New War on Fumes Launched."

132. Mayors' Conference on Control of Smoke and Fumes, 8 May 1946, reporter's transcript, box 25, JAFP.
133. Kennedy, "History, Legal and Administrative Aspects of Air Pollution Control in the County of Los Angeles," 8, 14.
134. Ibid., 15.
135. Beckman to Board of Supervisors, 17 Jan. 1955.
136. "L.A. Kills Smog with Kindness," 60–65.

CHAPTER THREE

1. By the 1930s, the Army Corps had constructed the Port of Los Angeles and built flood control channels to protect the harbor, but the Army Corps' approach to flood control was controversial. The Los Angeles Chamber of Commerce, for one, disapproved with the Army Corps' decision to channelize the Los Angeles River, and, more generally, of the federal government's growing influence in local affairs. The chair of the LAACC's flood control committee simultaneously rejected the Army Corps' flood plans and urged the chamber to endorse those plans because of the benefits of federal spending. See, for example, LAACC Minutes, 19 Mar. 1931, 5; Steno Reports, 26 Mar. 1936, 5–7; Steno Reports, 2 Feb. 1939, 11; Steno Reports, 16 Mar. 1939, 8–10. In his authoritative *Hazardous Metropolis*, Orsi describes the flood control controversies and explains why Los Angeles came to rely on the Army Corps of Engineers. Other histories of Los Angeles flood control include Bigger, *Flood Control in Metropolitan Los Angeles*; Gumprecht, *Los Angeles River*; Hoult's master's thesis, "Whittier Narrows Dam"; and, to a lesser extent, Crouch, *Intergovernmental Relations*, vol. 15. Bigger and Crouch wrote while the flood projects were very much under way and provide important detail on the history of those projects in the service of understanding intergovernmental relations. Hoult, who lost property to Whittier Narrows Dam, completed his thesis in the months just before the compromise that ended the Whittier Narrows Dam stalemate; his work is valuable because his impressions of the conflict were formed during a multitude of interviews with El Monte residents and key actors. Gumprecht's beautifully written book places flood control in the context of Los Angeles's relationship with its rivers and recent efforts to make the river, frankly, more like a river.

2. Orsi, *Hazardous Metropolis*, 107–8; see also Bigger, *Flood Control in Metropolitan Los Angeles*, 14–18, 26–31.

3. Rufus Putnam, "The Proposed Civil Works Program of the Los Angeles Engineer District of the Corps of Engineers," address before the Construction Industries Committee of the Los Angeles Chamber of Commerce, 10 Jan. 1945, 3–4, Los Angeles District, Army Corps of Engineers, Los Angeles, California.

4. Crouch discusses the role of community groups in identifying projects for the Army Corps and then lobbying for appropriations in Congress in *Intergovernmental Relations*, 93. The role of unofficial groups like chambers of commerce in proposing

and securing funding for federal or state projects is not unique to flood control. See, for example, Seely, *Building the American Highway System*; Rose, "Getting the Interstate System Built"; and Stine, *Mixing the Waters*. Hirt examines ongoing relationships between interest groups, Congress, and federal agencies in *A Conspiracy of Optimism*.

5. The Army Corps of Engineers did hold a general public hearing on Los Angeles and San Gabriel River flood control in March 1936 "to ascertain the extent and character of flood-control improvement desired by local interests." This hearing "disclosed that local interests desire protection from floods in the drainage basins of Los Angeles and San Gabriel Rivers and Ballona Creek by the construction of adequate channel improvements, flood-control basins, and debris basins." See "'Los Angeles and San Gabriel Rivers and Their Tributaries, and Ballona Creek, Calif.' Letter from the Secretary of War transmitting a letter from the chief of engineers, United States Army, dated Apr 11 1940 . . ." U.S. Congress, House of Representatives, 3d sess., Document 838, 11 June 1940. Water Resources Center Archive, Berkeley, California.

6. LACFCD annual report as cited in Bigger, *Flood Control in Metropolitan Los Angeles*, 3.

7. Orsi, *Hazardous Metropolis*, 37–52; Bigger, *Flood Control in Metropolitan Los Angeles*, 12–14, 18–20. James W. Reagan was a controversial choice as chief engineer of the flood control district because he had fewer professional credentials than the rest of the board of experts and because when the rest of this board issued its report recommending reforestation and check dams in the mountains, spreading grounds in the foothills to reduce runoff and conserve water, and levees to keep rivers from flooding the plains of Los Angeles county, Reagan dissented. He advocated large-scale river channel improvements on the plains. Reagan generated additional controversy once in office by refusing to follow the plans laid out by the majority of the board; this all added to the deep divisions in the county over how flood control should be funded and what kinds of flood control structures worked best.

8. Crouch, *Intergovernmental Relations*, 92–93.

9. Orsi, *Hazardous Metropolis*, 55–74. The canyon wall collapsed in September 1929; the grand jury confirmed the bribery charge in January 1930. The matter was not settled until 1936.

10. Hoult, "Whittier Narrows Dam," 12.

11. Orsi, *Hazardous Metropolis*, 81; Hoult, "Whittier Narrows Dam," 12. For one early summary of the comprehensive plan, see "Detailed Flood-Control Plan Given to County Supervisors," *LAT*, 5 Oct. 1930.

12. "Map Visualizes How Proposed County Flood Control System Would Store Water Underground," *LAT*, 5 Oct. 1930; Hoult, "Whittier Narrows Dam," 12.

13. "Flood Control Need Detailed," *LAT*, 11 Oct. 1931; "Federal Flood Aid Sought," *LAT*, 27 Oct. 1931.

14. "Coastal Plain Water Sought," *LAT*, 29 June 1932.

15. Hoult, "Whittier Narrows Dam," 13.

16. Donald M. Baker to Herbert C. Legg, 13 Dec. 1934, box 10, JAFP.

17. Hoult, "Whittier Narrows Dam," 13. The prospect of Long Beach staking claims to water at the Narrows sparked vociferous protests from the San Gabriel Valley Protective Association; that group had initially endorsed Long Beach's proposals because its members thought Whittier Narrows Dam would increase the amount of water available to the irrigation companies that made up its membership.

18. Crouch, *Intergovernmental Relations*, 92–95. Los Angeles did not regain state flood control aid until 1945.

19. "Flood Curb Funds Asked," *LAT*, 6 Sept. 1933; "Capital Asks Flood Plan," *LAT*, 11 Oct. 1933; Hoult, "Whittier Narrows Dam," 15. In September 1933, the Los Angeles County Board of Supervisors noted that 87 percent of Los Angeles's total flood control bill, or $118,916,539, went directly to protecting the harbor; the county also expected to spend $30,553,627 on projects in the National Forest ("Flood Curb Funds Asked," *LAT*, 6 Sept. 1933). For more on the county's application to the PWA, see Los Angeles Engineering Council of Founder Societies, "Report of Committee," in Los Angeles Engineering Council of Founder Societies, "Report of the Special Engineering Committee on Flood Control," Feb. 1934, Water Resources Center Archive.

20. "Capital Asks Flood Plan."

21. "Project Delay Laid to Trask," *LAT*, 2 Nov. 1933.

22. Hoult, "Whittier Narrows Dam," 15–18.

23. "Project Delay Laid to Trask."

24. For more on the La Cañada flood and its aftermath, see Orsi, *Hazardous Metropolis*, 75–101; Los Angeles Engineering Council of Founder Societies, "Report of Committee," 9. For a description of a more recent debris flow in the San Gabriel Mountains, see McPhee, *Control of Nature*.

25. Los Angeles Engineering Council of Founder Societies, "Report of Committee," 3, 7–9; "Statement of President Baker, Los Angeles Engineering Council at Meeting with Board of Supervisors," Los Angeles Flood Control District, Los Angeles, 6 Mar. 1934, in Los Angeles Engineering Council of Founder Societies, "Report of the Special Engineering Committee on Flood Control," Feb. 1934. The Los Angeles Engineering Council represented two thousand engineers in the Los Angeles area who were also members of the American Society of Civil Engineers, American Institute of Mining and Metallurgical Engineers, American Society of Mechanical Engineers, and the American Institute of Electrical Engineers.

26. "Project Delay Laid to Trask"; "P.W.A. Aid Plea Dropped," *LAT*, 21 Mar. 1934; Crouch, *Intergovernmental Relations*, 93.

27. Hoult, "Whittier Narrows Dam," 15–18.

28. "Dam Fund Spending Held Legal," *LAT*, 15 June 1934.

29. Orsi, *Hazardous Metropolis*, 94–95; "Board Gets Work List," *LAT*, 22 Sept. 1934; S. M. Fisher, "Report . . . on Control and Conservation of Flood, Storm or

Other Waste Waters of the District," 27 Sept. 1934, Los Angeles County Flood Control District, Los Angeles, 1934, 1–3, Water Resources Center Archive. The 1934 bonds failed 350,500 to 324,500. Public confidence in the LACFCD remained very low for years. In June 1940, for example, the Property Owners League of California demanded that the county dissolve the flood control district because it had grown too fast, spent too much, and operated inefficiently. See "Statement of William A. Pixley, Managing Director, Property Owners' Assn of California in the Public Hearing on the 1940–41 Los Angeles County Budget, Before the Board of Supervisors on June 10, 1940," box 22, JAFP.

30. Hoult, "Whittier Narrows Dam," 15–18.

31. Los Angeles voters approved the Colorado River Aqueduct in 1931, and the Bureau of Reclamation completed Hoover Dam in 1935. In 1931, Eaton had told the Los Angeles Chamber of Commerce that water conservation would "go a long way toward paying for the cost" of flood control projects in greater Los Angeles. Hoover Dam dramatically reduced Los Angeles County's need to conserve local floodwaters for agricultural, industrial, or domestic use. Eaton's position in 1934 on Whittier Narrows Dam and on the importance of water conservation at the Narrows marked this dramatic change of circumstance. See Steno Reports, 1 Oct. 1931, 6.

32. James G. Jobes, "The United States Engineer Department—Its Organization and Work in Southern California," annual address before the City and County Engineers Association of Los Angeles, 1936?, 13–14, Los Angeles District, Army Corps of Engineers.

33. Los Angeles District of the Army Corps of Engineers, "History of Federal Flood Control Work in Southern California," Los Angeles, 1939, 1. Los Angeles District, Army Corps of Engineers.

34. Ibid.

35. Ibid.

36. For the LAACC's fears about the Army Corps, see Steno Reports, 1 Oct. 1931, 6.

37. Theodore Wyman, "Flood Control Progress in Los Angeles County," 7 June 1939, 1–3, Los Angeles District, Army Corps of Engineers. Los Angeles received Emergency Recovery Act appropriations for flood control in August 1935. By early 1936, the Army Corps had more than sixteen thousand unemployed Angelenos at work on flood control projects. The Army Corps eventually added the Lopez Flood Control Basin to the Los Angeles watershed projects. The Los Angeles Flood Control District had included both Hansen and Sepulveda dams in their 1931 Comprehensive Plan.

38. Wyman, "Flood Control Progress in Los Angeles County," 3.

39. Orsi, *Hazardous Metropolis*, 110–12.

40. Hoult, "Whittier Narrows Dam," 18–20.

41. "Dam Opposed at El Monte," *LAT*, 29 Mar. 1938; Hoult, "Whittier Narrows Dam," 37; F. J. Safley, "Army Engineers Plan for Flood Control on San Gabriel River:

An Adverse Report on Proposed Whittier Narrows Retarding Reservoir," 2 May 1939, 2, box 681, ACEC.

42. Jerry Voorhis to Julian L. Schley, 18 Mar. 1938, box 681, ACEC; see also Edwin C. Kelton to Office of Division Engineer, South Pacific Division, San Francisco, California, "Subject: Protest against Construction of Whittier Narrows Reservoir by Citizen's Flood Control Committee of El Monte," 7 Mar. 1940, box 681, ACEC.

43. "Dam Opposed at El Monte." See also Hoult, "Whittier Narrows Dam," 18–20, 32–33.

44. H. E. Collins to Franklin D. Roosevelt, 24 Mar. 1939, box 681, ACEC.

45. El Monte Community Chamber of Commerce to Edwin C. Kelton, "Protest by Citizens Flood Control Committee," 8 Feb. 1940, box 681, ACEC.

46. Hoult, "Whittier Narrows Dam," 18.

47. In 1936, the Los Angeles Chamber of Commerce specifically objected to the Army Corps' preference for concrete river channels over flood control works that enhanced water conservation and "question[ed] the advisability of . . . asking Federal Government to become so intimate in our affairs." See Steno Reports 26 Mar. 1936, 7.

48. Hoult, "Whittier Narrows Dam," 19.

49. F. J. Safley, "Proposed Whittier Narrows Reservoir Project," attachment to Safley to Herbert C. Legg, 20 Apr. 1938, box 681, ACEC. Safley addressed much of his correspondence to Herbert C. Legg because Legg opposed Whittier Narrows Dam from the beginning. See Herman L. Perry to Richard M. Nixon, 17 Jan. 1948, PE 351, June–Mar. 1948, Nixon Presidential Library, Yorba Linda, California.

50. Hoult, "Whittier Narrows Dam," 15–18.

51. Theodore Wyman to Herbert C. Legg, 25 May 1938, 2, box 680, ACEC; see also Edwin C. Kelton, "A Review of the Report on 'Flood Discharge Data Los Angeles County, California,' Accompanying Letter by Messers. Safley, Bell, & Reagan to the House of Representatives, Washington, D. C., Dated 14 Sept 1940," 25 Nov. 1940, 11–12, box 680, ACEC.

52. Christopher P. Konrad, "Effects of Urban Development on Floods," U.S. Geological Survey, Fact Sheet 076–03, Nov. 2003, ⟨http://pubs.water.usgs.gov/fs07603⟩.

53. Safley, "Army Engineers Plan for Flood Control on San Gabriel River," 3–4, and "Addendum" dated 1 Feb. 1940; see also "Engineers Attack County's Flood Control Plans," *Pasadena Star News*, 20 Sept 1940, both in box 681, ACEC. A research hydrologist who reviewed the Army Corps of Engineers' and Safley's plans in light of current practices in flood control noted that Safley probably overstated the need to use larger floods as the basis for designing flood control in the San Gabriel River. The Army Corps of Engineers' design had more than enough capacity. Moreover, because flood controls based on river channel designs function in large part by moving floodwaters through the channels very quickly, river channels such as Safley, Bell, and Reagan proposed require maintenance to keep vegetation and debris from slowing water. Their plan would also have required the reconstruction of bridges all

along the river to make sure that these did not obstruct flood flows. The dam-based flood control promoted by the Army Corps involved less ongoing maintenance and less reengineering of downstream structures. Currently, the Los Angeles Flood Control District uses the Whittier Narrows Dam to divert some floodwaters from the San Gabriel–Rio Hondo into the Los Angeles River; at the time it designed the Whittier Narrows Dam, however, the Army Corps of Engineers intended the dam to help keep floods on the San Gabriel and Rio Hondo out of the Los Angeles River. This may account for some of differences between Safley's and the Army Corps' analysis of flood control needs on the San Gabriel River. Christopher P. Konrad, pers. commun., 13 Sept. 2006.

54. Safley, Bell, and Reagan to Speaker of the House of Representatives, 14 Sept. 1940, cover letter to F. J. Safley, "Flood Discharge Data—Los Angeles County, California"; F. J. Safley, "Addendum," 1 Feb. 1940, to Safley, "Army Engineers Plan for Flood Control on San Gabriel River"; "Engineers Attack County's Flood Control Plans," all in box 681, ACEC.

55. F. J. Safley to Board of Supervisors, 18 Sept, 1940, box 681, ACEC.

56. "Engineers Attack County's Flood Control Plans."

57. Kelton to Office of Division Engineer, South Pacific Division, San Francisco, California, "Subject: Protest against Construction of Whittier Narrows Reservoir by Citizen's Flood Control Committee of El Monte," 7 Mar 1940, 8. According to Thomas Hoult, a staff member of the Army Corps of Engineers' Los Angeles District office wrote notes in the margin of a letter from the Temple School District calling Safley, Bell, and Reagan "hotdoggers" who had no business determining flood control designs. See note on margin of letter, Temple School District to Los Angeles District, Army Corps of Engineers, 15 Mar, 1938, cited in Hoult, "Whittier Narrows Dam."

58. H. E. Hedger to F. J. Safley, "Federal Projects—Report of September 14, 1940 by Messers. F. J. Safley, J. A. Bell and Jas. W. Reagan. Request for Data," 18 Nov. 1940, box 681, ACEC.

59. M. C. Tyler to Jerry Voorhis, 25 Apr. 1938, box 680, ACEC.

60. Long Beach Board of Water Commissioners, "Resolution No. 114: A Resolution Urging Construction of Proposed Whittier Narrows Dam," 21 Apr. 1938, box 680, ACEC.

61. John Butzmann to Army Corps of Engineers, 15 Feb. 1939; Butzmann to Army Corps of Engineers, 23 June 1940; Mrs. Rex C. DeLamar to Army Corps of Engineers, 24 Feb. 1940; AAG Krichhoff, Army Corps of Engineers, to DeLamar, 12 July 1939; Mrs. Rex C. DeLamar to Army Corps of Engineers, 24 Feb. 1940; Mrs. Joseph Neelands to Army Corps of Engineers, 8 Dec. 1939; Martin A. Smith to Army Corps of Engineers, 22 Aug. 1939; John R. Kirkpatrick to Theodore Wyman, 12 Oct. 38; John R. Kirkpatrick (of El Monte) to Theodore Wyman, 20 Apr. 1939; Lelah Fowler to Army Corps of Engineers, 28 Dec. 1938; Helen M. Jensen to Jerry Voorhis, 12 Dec. 38, all in box 680, ACEC.

62. Collins to Roosevelt, 24 Mar. 1939, ACEC. City engineers in Azusa and Duarte, upstream from El Monte, began to publicly protest the other major San Gabriel River project, the Santa Fe retarding basin, using arguments similar to those coming from El Monte. See "Cities Flood Fear Allayed," *LAT*, 30 Mar. 1938.

63. Theodore Wyman to Jerry Voorhis, 10 Aug. 1938, "Whittier Narrows Dam, Los Angeles County, California," box 681, ACEC.

64. Long Beach Board of Water Commissioners, "Resolution No. 114." See also Fred S. Porter to E. C. Kelton, 7 Mar. 1940, box 680, ACEC.

65. Tyler to Voorhis, 25 Apr. 1938, ACEC.

66. Norwalk Chamber of Commerce to Theodore Wyman, 10 Oct. 1938, box 680, ACEC.

67. Long Beach Board of Water Commissioners, "Resolution No. 114."

68. "Californians to Seek Much from Congress," *LAT*, 3 Jan. 1937. The *Los Angeles Times*' consistent support for flood control is based on a comprehensive survey of articles in the *Los Angeles Times* clippings file under floods and flood control, 1915–50, and on searches of the Proquest Historical *Los Angeles Times* database for articles on Whittier Narrow Dam and on San Gabriel River flood control, 1925–50.

69. Hoult, "Whittier Narrows Dam," 75–76.

70. "County Seeks Flood Funds," *LAT*, 24 Mar. 1940; Warren B. Francis, "Los Angeles Flood Funds Plea Pushed at Washington," *LAT*, 4 Apr. 1940.

71. See, for example, V. E. O'Neil to Los Angeles District, 27 Dec. 1945, and attachments, box 680; Alvin K. Maddy to Los Angeles District, 2 Jan. 1946, and attachments, box 681, ACEC.

72. Edwin C. Kelton, "Flood Control Program of Army Engineers in Los Angeles District," American Society of Civil Engineers, 23 Apr. 1940, 3, Los Angeles District, Army Corps of Engineers.

73. H. E. Hedger to Edwin C. Kelton, 22 Apr. 1940, cover letter to P. F. Cogswell, "Flood Data Present by the El Monte California Flood Committee in Support of Their Protest against the Construction of the Proposed Whittier Narrows Reservoir on the San Gabriel River," 20 Mar. 1940, box 680, ACEC.

74. Hoult, "Whittier Narrows Dam," 39.

75. Cogswell, "Flood Data Present by the El Monte California Flood Committee."

76. Charles W. Cook to Board of Supervisors, 22 Feb. 1940; John Butzmann et al. to Board of Supervisors, 20 Feb. 1940; Sylvia E. Houghton to Board of Supervisors, 26 Feb. 1940, all in box 680, ACEC. Garvey Acres was named for an early El Monte pioneer, Richard Garvey, a Pony Express rider who also helped found Monterey Park. He raised stock and farmed some six thousand acres of land in eastern Los Angeles County, built a small, spring-fed irrigation network, and starting in 1906 began subdividing and selling his land. See Burdett, *Greater Los Angeles and Southern California Portraits and Personal Memoranda*, 187.

77. "Mayor Denies Recall Charge," *LAT*, 29 Oct. 1938. The instigators of the El Monte recall charged the mayor and the two city councilors of voting to license

poker rooms in El Monte, and they wanted to remove the city clerk for failing to keep accurate records of city council proceedings. This was an unsettled time in suburban municipal politics in the Los Angeles region. In the first successful mayoral recall in the country, city of Los Angeles voters recalled Mayor Frank Shaw in 1938. Frustrated with municipal corruption, disappointed with mayoral policies, or inspired by the campaign against Shaw, three other communities, Arcadia, Hermosa Beach, and South Pasadena, joined El Monte in recalling or attempting to recall mayors in 1939 and 1940. See "Arcadia to Vote on Recall Today," *LAT*, 10 May 1939; "Southland Elections Marked by Record Voter Turnout," *LAT*, 10 Apr. 1940; "Entire Hermosa City Council Recalled; Two Mayors Ousted, One Defeats Move," *LAT*, 11 Apr. 1940.

78. J. C. Ells to Edwin C. Kelton, 12 Sept. 1941; Edwin C. Kelton to Chief of Engineers, 23 Sept. 1941, both in box 680, ACEC.

79. "Statement of William A. Pixley, Managing Director, Property Owners' Assn of California in the Public Hearing on the 1943–44 Los Angeles County Budget, Before the Board of Supervisors on June 15, 1943," 9, JAFP. Los Angeles County kept flood control construction in the budget during the war, even though shortages made construction impossible. The Property Owners' Association believed the county supervisors did so simply to accumulate a surplus to fund postwar construction.

80. Part of Los Angeles's preparations included electing William Smith chair of the board of supervisors. He had long promoted federal flood control projects and was widely credited with securing federal flood appropriations before the war. See "Supervisor Smith New County Government Chairman" *LAT*, 6 Dec. 1944; "County Seeks Flood Funds."

81. "More Flood Control," editorial in *LAT*, 15 Feb. 1945.

82. Jerry Voorhis to E. Reybold, 16 May 1945, box 680, ACEC; Frank Rogers, "Whittier Narrows Dam and Reservoir Fund Turned Down," unidentified newspaper clipping, in box 30, Voorhis Papers, Honnold Library, Claremont, California.

83. "Dam Project Hit at Mass Meeting," *LAT*, 1 Sept. 1945.

84. Ralph D. Becker to Harry S. Truman, 30 Apr. 1945, box 681, ACEC.

85. "Competition," editorial in *Hollywood Citizen News*, 23 May 1945; "Fighting Cement Trust," *NYT*, 23 Nov. 1903.

86. As many as 40 percent of the signatures on petitions against the quarry were later found to be fraudulent or forged. Three men were prosecuted for forging signatures on the opposition's petitions with the intent of rendering those petitions void. The *Los Angeles Times* ultimately defended Bell's character, but only after accusing Bell of framing his referenda petitions to deliberately confuse the voters. See "Trick Indicated in Bell Battle," *LAT*, 19 Feb. 1930; "Bell Vote Due in April," *LAT*, 28 Feb. 1930; "Trickery Charged to Bell," *LAT*, 1 Mar. 1930; "Shabby Trickery," *LAT*, 20 Feb. 1930; "Petitions Show Many Mistakes," *LAT*, 22 Mar. 1930; "Bell Petitions' Quiz Launched," *LAT*, 26 Mar. 1930; and "Three Held as Forgery Suspects," *LAT*, 30 Mar 1930.

87. "Preliminary Report of Revised General Plan for Whittier Narrows Flood Control Basin and the Improvement of San Gabriel River and Rio Hondo Channels, Downstream of Whittier Narrows Dam," enclosure to Rufus W. Putnam to Los Angeles District Chief Engineer, 1 Aug. 1944, 1, 14; Los Angeles County Board of Supervisors of the Los Angeles County Flood Control District, "Resolution Approving Revisions Proposed by U.S. District Engineer in Comprehensive Plan for Flood Control and Conservation Relating to the Whittier Narrows Flood Control Dam and Basin and the Rio Hondo and San Gabriel River Channels," 27 Mar. 1945, 2; Rufus W. Putnam to Chief of Engineers, "Subject: Definite Project for Whittier Narrows Flood-Control Basin, San Gabriel River, Los Angeles County Drainage Area, California, Flood Control," 14 Sept. 1945, 4, all in box 681, ACEC.

88. "Questions of Anti–Whittier Narrows Dam Association of San Gabriel Valley Regarding Plan 'A,' Whittier Narrows Dam and Basin, and Alternate Plans, with Answers by Los Angeles District, Corps of Engineers, War Department," undated typescript, 3, box 681, ACEC.

89. In 1945, E. Reybold, the lieutenant general of the Army Corps of Engineers, wrote to Congress member William M. Whittington describing "the abundance of home sites on high ground and in the immediate vicinity" of the flood control basin that displaced residents could move to. See Reybold to Whittington, 9 May 1945, 4, box 681, ACEC.

90. Rufus W. Putnam, "Project Summary and Historical Sketch: Whittier Narrows Flood-Control Basin Near El Monte, California," 28 Feb. 1945, 12, box 681, ACEC.

91. Jerry Voorhis to William M. Whittington, 12 Mar. 1945, box 681, ACEC. Whittington was chair of the House Flood Control Committee in 1945.

92. Rufus W. Putnam to Chief of Engineers, "Proposed Construction of Whittier Narrows Dam," 2 July 1945, box 681, ACEC.

93. "Projects for Harbors and Flood Control Set," *LAT*, 1 Oct. 1945; "House Votes Funds for Projects in California," *LAT*, 1 Dec. 1945. See also Hoult, "Whittier Narrows Dam," 23–24. Additional California projects authorized by Congress in the fall of 1945: Big Dry Creek Reservoir and diversion, Kings River and Tulare Lake basin projects, Folsom Dam, Table Mountain Reservoir, San Joaquin River flood control levees, and Isabel Reservoir. Harbor improvements authorized included LA-Long Beach, San Diego, Newport Beach, San Francisco, and Monterey.

94. Compton Chamber of Commerce, "Resolution Supporting the Construction of the Whittier Narrows Flood Control Dam, Los Angeles County, California," 3 Jan. 1946; Gardena Valley Chamber of Commerce, "A Resolution Urging Congress to Appropriate Funds Necessary to the Construction of the Whittier Narrows Dam in Los Angeles County, California," 7 Jan. 1946; Hawthorne Chamber of Commerce, "A Resolution Urging Congress to Appropriate Funds Necessary to the Construction of the Whittier Narrows Dam in Los Angeles County, California," 27 Dec. 1945, all in box 680, ACEC. The Gardena and Hawthorne resolutions are identical.

The Los Angeles Chamber of Commerce also registered its support for Whittier Narrows Dam. See LAACC Minutes, 5 Dec. 1946, 129.

95. Robert Shoemaker, "Brief on Behalf of the City of Long Beach Harbor Board to Be Presented to the Appropriations Committee of the House of Representatives at Its Hearing on the Subject of Appropriations for Preliminary Construction in the Whittier Narrows Dam in Los Angeles County, California," 10 Jan. 1946, 1–4, box 681, ACEC.

96. Ibid., 3.

97. Ibid., 6.

98. Ibid.

99. John B. Mann to U.S. Engineers Office, 7 Jan. 1946, box 680; Robert S. Lewis to Jerry Voorhis, 12 Jan. 1946, box 681, both in ACEC. On the formation of the Anti–Whittier Narrows Dam Association, see Hoult, "Whittier Narrows Dam," 24.

100. "Voorhis Wins Dam Restudy," *LAT*, 17 Apr. 1946.

101. "List of Parties to Whom Public Notice Dated 12 Nov 1946 Was Sent, Alternative Plans for Whittier Narrows Project," undated typescript, box 680, ACEC.

102. E. H. Marks to Chief of Engineers, teletype, 16 June 1946, and attachments, box 681, ACEC.

103. "Whittier Dam Hearing Stirs Heated Arguments," *LAT*, 13 Dec. 1946.

104. Ross Shafer to R. C. Hunter, 15 Oct. 1946, box 681, ACEC.

105. Ibid.

106. Kelvin C. Vanderlip to Joseph O. Killian, 22 Jan. 1947, box 681, ACEC. The Palos Verdes Corporation, the real estate development company operating at some distance from both Whittier Narrows and Long Beach Harbor, endorsed Whittier Narrows Dam because it would protect industrial development and improve water conservation.

107. El Monte Chamber of Commerce and Anti–Whittier Narrows Dam Association, "Do you want to lose your property at low condemnation prices" postcard, attachment to Joseph O. Killian to Chief of Engineers, 30 Jan. 1947, box 681, ACEC.

108. Robert S. Hicks to Anti–Whittier Narrows Dam Association, 11 Dec 1946, Box 680, ACEC.

109. Ibid.

110. Ibid.

111. R. M. Nixon, "Whittier Narrows," handwritten notes for campaign speech, in Speech File, Whittier Narrows Dam Notes, 1946–47, PPS 208.33, Nixon Presidential Library. Later commentators explained Voorhis's defeat variously as a product of overconfidence, Nixon's deep connections with powerful special interests, and widespread newspaper support for the challenger. For more on Nixon's 1946 congressional campaign, see Gellman, *Contender*.

112. Gale O. Kenyon to County Board of Supervisors, 18 Apr. 1946, box 681, ACEC.

113. Robert S. Lewis to R. C. Hunter, "Re: Your 'Public Notice,' dated 26 Sept.

1946, concerning 'Alternative Plans for Whittier Narrows Project,' 21 Oct. 1946; Zelfa Hammond de Bolt to U.S. Engineers, care of San Gabriel Flood Control Project, 6 Oct. 1946; both in box 681, ACEC.

114. Olin S. Proctor to U.S. Engineers Office, 6 Dec. 1947, box 681, ACEC.

115. The Anti–Whittier Narrows Dam Association accused the Army Corps of coming up with the idea for the dam before receiving instructions to do so from local government agencies or from Congress. The Army Corps denied this, pointing out that E. C. Eaton of the Los Angeles County Flood Control District first proposed a dam at the Narrows. "Questions of Anti–Whittier Narrows Dam Association of San Gabriel Valley Regarding Plan 'A,' Whittier Narrows Dam and Basin, and Alternate Plans, with Answers by Los Angeles District, Corps of Engineers, War Department," 4, ACEC. On the Anti–Whittier Narrows Dam Association's analysis of Army Corps cost estimates, see ibid., 4, 6–8, 10.

116. "Whittier Dam Hearing Stirs Heated Arguments."

117. E. H. Marks to Chief of Engineers, "Subject: Public Hearing on Alternative Plans and Restudy of Whittier Narrows Project," 28 Jan. 1947, box 681, ACEC.

118. P. A. Ferlinga to Los Angeles District, "Subject: Restudy of Alternative Plans, Whittier Narrows, Los Angeles County Drainage Area, California," 14 Mar. 1947, box 681, ACEC.

119. A. T. W. Moore to Chief of Engineers, 17 Apr. 1947, box 681, ACEC. Plan B land condemnation would have cost $40 million to Plan A's $39 million and would have affected 350 fewer residences than Plan A.

120. Quenda Schindler to Harry Truman, 20 Feb. 1948, box 681, ACEC. For additional letters clearly protesting the dam rather than fatalistically querying about the fate of specific properties, see Robert S. Lewis to Jerry Voorhis, 29 Jan. 1945; Ralph D. Decker to Harry S. Truman, 30 Apr. 1945, box 680, ACEC.

121. Lois C. Hoult to *El Monte Herald*, letter to the editor, 15 Dec. 1946; see also Thomas F. Hoult to R. C. Hunter, 15 Dec. 1946, both in box 680, ACEC (emphasis in original).

122. Marks to Chief of Engineers, "Subject: Public Hearing on Alternative Plans and Restudy of Whittier Narrows Project," 28 Jan. 1947, ACEC.

123. Killian to Chief of Engineers, 30 Jan. 1947, ACEC.

124. M. E. Salsbury to District Engineer, Los Angeles District, 9 Jan. 1947, attachment to Killian to Chief of Engineers, 30 Jan. 1947, ACEC.

125. Unsigned letter to James Forrestal, 10 June 1947; James Forrestal to Secretary of War, "Attention: Chief of Engineers," 16 June 1947, both in box 681, ACEC. Attachments to the unsigned letter addressed to Forrestal make clear that it was eventually signed by Los Angeles County Flood Control District engineer Harold Hedger and Whittier City engineer Marshall Bowen, along with two others. Hedger and Bowen were both committed proponents of the dam.

126. Killian to Chief of Engineers, 30 Jan. 1947, ACEC.

127. Moore to Chief of Engineers, 17 Apr. 1947, box 681, ACEC.

128. Herman L. Perry to R. M. Nixon, 18 Nov. 1947, PE 330, Oct.–Dec. 1947, Nixon Presidential Library.

129. Orsi, *Hazardous Metropolis*, 127; "Draft: Details of the Project, 6 Oct 1949," attachment to H. W. Thompson, "Memorandum for Files, Subject: Whittier Narrows Flood Control Basin," 21 Oct. 1949, box 681, ACEC.

130. E. J. DeGroff to Harry S. Truman, 22 Apr. 1949, and DeGroff to Truman, 27 June 1949, both in box 681, ACEC. DeGroff simply argues that alternative flood control strategies would be cheaper. On water level problems possibly caused by Army Corps test boring, see San Gabriel River Conservancy to J. M. Carter, 13 June 1949, and W. D. Luplow to San Gabriel River Conservancy, 28 July 1949, both in box 681, ACEC.

131. "Group Loses Plea against Whittier Dam," *LAT*, 10 Aug. 1949; San Gabriel River Conservancy to Harry S. Truman, 10 June 1949; San Gabriel Valley Conservancy to Harry Truman, 14 July 1949; San Gabriel Valley Conservancy to Bess Truman, 28 July 1949, all in box 681, ACEC. See also "Questions of Anti–Whittier Narrows Dam Association of San Gabriel Valley Regarding Plan 'A,' Whittier Narrows Dam and Basin, and Alternate Plans, with Answers by Los Angeles District, Corps of Engineers, War Department," 11, ACEC. A 5.9-magnitude earthquake centered around Whittier Narrows killed eight people and did some $20 million in damage in 1987. For more information, see Stover and Coffman, *Seismicity of the United States, 1568–1989*.

132. Orsi, *Hazardous Metropolis*, 127.

133. E. E. Wallace to Earl Warren, 15 Sept. 1945, box 680, ACEC.

134. Perry to Nixon, 17 Jan. 1948, Nixon Presidential Library.

135. Ibid. See also Perry to Nixon, 18 Nov. 1947, Nixon Presidential Library.

136. J. G. Gallagher to William Smith, 19 Dec. 1946, attachment to Killian to Chief of Engineers, 30 Jan. 1947, ACEC.

137. Christopher P. Konrad, pers. commun., 13 Sept. 2006.

138. Long Beach Board of Water Commissioners, "Resolution No. 346: A Resolution Urging Congress to Appropriate Funds to Initiate the Construction of the Whittier Narrows Dam in Los Angeles County, California," 27 Dec. 1945, Los Angeles District, Army Corps of Engineers. Identical or nearly identical resolutions were also submitted by the Long Beach Board of Harbor Commissioners, the Compton, Gardena Valley, and Hawthorne chambers of commerce.

139. Nothing symbolized the gap between Long Beach and El Monte as clearly as the other major federal enterprise in El Monte undertaken in the 1930s. In 1935, as the Los Angeles County Flood Control District waited to see whether Congress would approve Los Angeles's flood control plans, the Federal Subsistence Homesteads Corporation (FSHC) selected El Monte for a national demonstration housing project. The subsistence homesteads in the El Monte development consisted of 140 small houses, each on an acre plot planted with fruit and nut trees located north of the embattled Whittier Narrows basin. The FSHC designed the development to

give working-class families an agricultural income to supplement industrial wages and selected families who could not otherwise afford it either a house or retirement. The El Monte project was part of a larger national campaign by the FSHC to encourage industry to locate away from overcrowded cities and to improve the housing and economic prospects of industrial workers. The FSHC eventually built or planned a hundred such homestead communities, including one in Van Nuys, California.

The *Los Angeles Times* heralded the FSHC project in El Monte as the realization of "an ideal in semi-rural living" that the *Times* itself had promoted for more than a decade. But the entire Federal Subsistence Homesteads program reflected an ongoing effort to resolve the tension between America's industrial present and its agrarian roots. The program, with its goal of decentralized industry and its expectation that industrial workers would benefit from agriculture and landownership, reflected long-standing anxieties about the social costs of urban growth, industry, social and economic centralization, and the existence of a permanent working class. It offered a solution: an industrial workforce rooted in the land, and diversified enterprise to provide security for both individuals and the nation as a whole. This dream of an agricultural-industrial nation did not survive the Great Depression. After the war, homeownership in the suburb supplanted the "semi-rural farm home" as the twentieth century's manifestation of the agrarian ideal. See Ross H. Gast, "Farm Homes for City Workers," *LAT*, 2 Jan. 1935.

CHAPTER FOUR

1. See Nye, *American Technological Sublime*, 137–40. Before it was built, the dam was usually called Boulder Dam or Boulder Canyon Dam, although it was actually built in Black Canyon. In 1930, Secretary of the Interior Ray Lyman Wilbur gave it the name Hoover Dam, in honor of Herbert Hoover's role in getting the dam built, but it was renamed Boulder Dam by Secretary of the Interior Harold Ickes. In 1947, the name Hoover Dam was restored by Congress. I refer to the dam most often as Boulder Dam because that was its usual designation during the 1920s.

The legal and political conflicts over the Colorado River have generated some of the best scholarship on the environment and the American West. Hundley has written several books examining California's water development in legal and political terms. Two of these, *Water and the West* and the comprehensive *Great Thirst*, explore the Colorado River and Hoover Dam in terms of American domestic politics. *Water and the West* is particularly authoritative on the Colorado River Compact. In a third volume, *Dividing the Waters*, Hundley examines the conflicts between Mexico and the United States over four rivers, including the Colorado. Pisani uses the Colorado River controversies to explain American law, politics, and federalism in *Water and American Government*. Worster incorporated Hoover Dam into his discussion of hydraulic society in *Rivers of Empire*. For Arizona's perspective on Colorado River development, see Johnson, *Central Arizona Project*. Additional works of interest include Moeller, *Phil Swing and Boulder Dam*, and, of course, Stegner, *Beyond the Hundredth Meridian*, and Reisner, *Cadillac Desert*. While some of the more recent of these works, namely those by Hundley and Pisani, have commented on power development at Hoover Dam, the history of joint public-private hydroelectric power generation has not been a major feature of these works.

2. The methods developed to refine designs for Hoover Dam, specifically the balance between the dam's horizontal arches, which resist the weight of water pressing downhill, and the dam's vertical cantilever strength, which resists the pressure of water to push the foot of the dam out from under the rest of the structure, are still used today by the Bureau of Reclamation and other engineers. Larry Nuss, Bureau of Reclamation, pers. comm., 30 July 2004. Tables of trail load tests made in the Hoover Dam model lab studies were published in the widely consulted "Blue Books" and detailed in the *Hoover Dam Bulletins on Trial Load Methods*. The concrete cooling methods developed for Hoover Dam are also widely used. Only the advent of computer modeling reduced the centrality of Hoover Dam to modern dam design.

3. Hundley, *Water and the West*, 20–22, and *Great Thirst*, 206–7. After less than ten years of construction, the Imperial Valley boasted 400 miles of canals, 160,000 acres of cultivated farmland and a population of 15,000. Average annual rainfall in Imperial County is 2.9 inches per year. Temperatures range from winter lows in the 30s to summer highs in the 110s.

4. Hundley, *Water and the West*, 20–29, and *Great Thirst*, 207–8. For a detailed discussion of the conflicts between the Imperial Irrigation District and Mexican authorities, see Hundley, *Dividing the Waters*, 41–48.

5. Moeller, *Phil Swing and Boulder Dam*, 12–14; Hundley, *Water and the West*, 30–33.

6. Hundley, *Water and the West*, 206–11; Worster, *Rivers of Empire*, 191–212.

7. "Annual Report to the Shareholders of Southern California Edison for the year 1919," Los Angeles, 1919, 10–11, Corporate Communications Department, Edison International, Rosemead, California. Southern California Edison even offered to purchase power from the aqueduct to allow the city to offset its water system costs without competing with the private utilities. See "Offer to Buy Power Officially Recorded," *LAT*, 6 May 1914. The power bonds paid for construction of the Saint Francis Dam, which collapsed in 1928, killing some four hundred people in the Santa Clara Valley of Ventura County. For more on the Saint Francis Dam disaster, see Jackson and Hundley, "Privilege and Responsibility."

8. Los Angeles tried to condemn the power plant in order to increase municipal power supply. In 1922, the U.S. Court of Appeals reversed a lower court's decision to permit Los Angeles to condemn the Southern Sierras Owens Gorge plant on the grounds that the decision would have allowed California's major cities to "demolish, piece meal, the great hydro-electric systems of the state" and to steal water and power away from the communities that relied on private water and power services.

"Owens Gorge Case Decision Is Reversed," *Sierras Service Bulletin*, Nov. 1922, 4; E. B. Criddle, "What the L. A. Litigation Means," *Sierras Service Bulletin*, June–July 1921, 1, Corporate Communications Department, Edison International. Statement of Mr. Ralph L. Criswell, president of the Los Angeles City Council, in U.S. Congress, House Committee on Irrigation of Arid Lands, "Hearings on H.R. 11449." At least in theory, the Los Angeles Department of Water and Power could have decided to base municipal power supplies on oil-burning generators, but until the Signal Hill oil strike of 1921, Los Angeles's oil reserves were widely regarded as more or less tapped out.

9. Criswell's statement in U.S. Congress, House Committee on Irrigation of Arid Lands, "Hearings on H.R. 11449."

10. "Boulder Dam Six-State Pact Effective Today," *LAT*, 21 June 1929.

11. U.S. Congress, House, Committee on Irrigation of Arid Lands, *Hearings before the Committee on Irrigation of Arid Lands . . . on H.R. 11449*, pt. 1, 82–97. The communities that passed the uniform resolution in favor of HR 11449 included San Diego, Los Angeles, Orange, Upland, San Bernardino, San Fernando, Fullerton, Long Beach, Alhambra, Riverside, Santa Ana, Santa Barbara, Pasadena, San Gabriel, and Coronado. Berkeley and the League of Southern California Municipalities also supported the dam. Santa Monica endorsed the dam but emphasized its value for flood control and irrigation. Imperial County Irrigation District and other Southern California farm bureaus and farming communities also sent the Committee on the Irrigation of Arid Lands resolutions in favor of the dam.

12. Testimony of Horace Porter, mayor of Riverside, quoted in "Problems of the Imperial Valley and Vicinity," U.S. Senate, *Correspondence from the Secretary of the Interior . . . together with the proceedings of the conference on the construction of the Boulder Canyon Dam*, 284.

13. "Few Faddists Deceive Them," *LAT*, 4 Aug. 1921; "Council Falls for Joke Film," *LAT*, 4 Nov. 1921; "Sh! City Film Plot Thickens," *LAT*, 6 Nov. 1921. They hired silent film star and director Earnest C. Warde to direct this film.

14. In 1925, in *Wyoming v. Colorado* and *Kansas v. Colorado*, the U.S. Supreme Court applied prior appropriation to interstate streams. See Hundley, *Water and the West*, 74–76, 177–80.

15. Hundley, *Water and the West*, 253–57; Pisani, *Water and American Government*, 227.

16. Hundley, *Water and the West*, 253–57; Pisani, *Water and American Government*, 227.

17. Quoted in *New York Times* editorial, reprinted in "East Shies at Boulder Plan," *LAT*, 4 Feb. 1927.

18. U.S. Congress, Senate, Committee on Irrigation and Reclamation, "Report on Boulder Canyon Reclamation Project, 69th Cong., 1st sess., Report 654, pt. 1, in *Colorado River Hearings*, 13; Speech of Phil D. Swing of California in the House of Representatives, 11 Mar. 1926, in *Colorado River Hearings*, 14.

19. "Compact Sole Arizona Issue," *LAT*, 29 Mar. 1924.

20. Bisbee Chamber of Commerce to A. B. Fall, 22 June 1922, box 49, Albert Fall Papers, Huntington Library, San Marino, California.

21. "Question of Right of Power Plans," *LAT*, 3 Aug. 1921.

22. Ibid.

23. "Power Bond Issue Fought," *LAT*, 21 May 1923.

24. "Speech of Honorable Charles H. Rutherford on the Colorado River Compact," delivered in the Arizona State Senate, 20 Feb. 1923, in "Statements by Citizens of Arizona relative to the Colorado River Problem. . . ," Protection and Development of the Lower Colorado River Basin: Information Presented to the Committee on Irrigation and Reclamation, in Connection with H.R. 2903, in *Colorado River Hearings*, 73–84. On Southern California Edison's permit applications, see R. H. Ballard, in "Boulder Canyon Project: Excerpts from the Hearings before the Committees on Irrigation and Reclamation . . . of the 68th, 69th, and 70th Congresses on the Swing-Johnson Bill . . . ," in *Colorado River Hearings*, 16, and Pisani, *Water and American Government*, 227. In testimony before Congress, Edison's general manager declared the utility ready to build a hydropower dam on the Colorado independent of federal efforts. Southern California's need for power, and the dearth of undeveloped power sites closer to Los Angeles, not only justified the expense of developing the Colorado but made the project quite necessary.

25. "Report of the Colorado River Committee of Arizona State Assembly of the American Association of Engineers," in "Statements by Citizens of Arizona relative to the Colorado River Problem . . . ," in *Colorado River Hearings*, 21.

26. Kiwanis Club of Phoenix, "History of the Ownership of the Power Sties on the Colorado River," 19 Jan. 1923, in "Statements by Citizens of Arizona relative to the Colorado River Problem. . . ," in *Colorado River Hearings*, 39–41.

27. "Arizonan Hits Boulder Plan," *LAT*, 1 Jan. 1925. Glen Canyon advocates were quick to point out that the High Line Canal would not require pumping; water deliveries from Boulder Canyon did. Arizona Congress member Carl Hayden received numerous letters in support of the Glen Canyon–High Line Canal project. See, for example, R. B. Hovland to Carl Hayden, "Colorado River Development," 31 Mar. 1924, in "Statements by Citizens of Arizona relative to the Colorado River Problem . . . ," in *Colorado River Hearings*, 59. See also Ralph L. Criswell's testimony for Los Angeles, "Protection and Development of Lower Colorado River Basin . . . Hearings before the Federal Power Commission and Other Matters Relating to the Development of the Colorado River," Washington, 1924, 78–79.

28. "Work Backs River Bill," *LAT*, 5 Jan. 1928.

29. Hundley, *Water and the West*, 171–74. In the 1940s, California did attempt to limit upper basin development in order to preserve its access to unappropriated surplus water.

30. Pisani, *Water and American Government*, 210–13.

31. Ibid., 205–10.

32. Ibid., 202–5.

33. Ibid., 213–15.

34. "Public Power First," *New Republic*, 17 Feb. 1926, 346.

35. American Public Works Association, *History of Public Works in the United States*, 249.

36. Hubbard, *Origins of the TVA*, 1–2, 4–5; "Henry Ford Goes Bargain Hunting," *The Nation*, 20 Dec. 1922, 683; George Norris, "Shall We Give Muscle Shoals to Henry Ford?" *Saturday Evening Post*, 24 May 1924, 30–31, 56, 60; "Muscle Shoals in Crisis," *New Republic*, 30 May 1928, 33–34. Henry Ford wanted to lease the Muscle Shoals complex for a hundred years—both power plants, Wilson Dam, the Cyanamid plant, the two towns, and four thousand acres of land. He offered to pay $5 million, plus $219 million in rent and maintenance over the term of the lease. The federal government spent $150 million to build these facilities; Wilson Dam alone was expected to generate $48 million a year worth of electricity. When the Alabama Power Company purchased the Muscle Shoals steam power plant, Ford insisted that the federal government replace that power plant. Ford's plan included the sale of forty thousand tons of nitrate fertilizer a year at an 8 percent profit. On the stalemate at Muscle Shoals, see American Public Works Association, *History of Public Works in the United States*, 249. Presidents Coolidge and Hoover vetoed bills for public development in 1928 and 1930. Coolidge was sharply criticized for his defense of private enterprise. In 1926, Nebraska Democrat Edgar Howard denounced Coolidge for "murdering every piece of legislation which does not have advanced approval of the Morgan Mellon group." Edgar Howard to *Los Angeles Examiner*, 4 June 1926, box 141, Philip Swing Papers, Special Collections, University of California, Los Angeles.

37. On the Muscle Shoals debates, see Hubbard, *Origins of the TVA*. To woo farmers, the public power side suggested in 1927 that the federal government complete Wilson Dam, build distribution lines, sell electricity to public utilities, and use the proceeds to fund research on fertilizers.

38. The forces for public ownership were joined by periodicals like *The Nation* and the *New Republic*, which made allusions to the Progressives' earlier campaigns to regulate railroads and control monopolies. *The Nation* condemned state utility regulations because "all those whose purpose it is to defeat genuine efforts at adequate regulation and this precisely because they recognize the demonstrated inability of the individual States to cope with the problem" supported state oversight. See Guido H. Marx; "How to Control Public Utilities," *The Nation*, 1 Apr. 1931, 348; "The Utilities as an Issue," *New Republic*, 7 May 1930, 311–12.

39. Hubbard, *Origins of the TVA*, 1–2; William Kent to Committee on Irrigation of Arid Lands, telegram, 16 Feb. 1924, box 144, Swing Papers; "How Muscle Shoals Stands," *New Republic*, 18 Apr. 1928, 260.

40. For example, "Southwest League Convention," *Sierra Service Bulletin*, Dec. 1921, 2, Corporate Communications Department, Edison International.

41. Franklin Hichborn to John E. Raker (judge, Washington D.C.), 16 Feb. 1924,

box 144, Swing Papers. Hichborn sent an identical letter to Swing on California's Water and Power Act State Campaign Committee letterhead.

42. "Would Lease Muscle Shoals; Hint of Another Oil Scandal," *Labor News*, 14 May 1926.

43. William J. Schaefle, "The People of the United States Do Not Want Another Tea Pot Dome Scandal," *American Globe*, Apr. 1928, 5–6, box 43, Swing Papers.

44. American Public Works Association, *History of Public Works in the United States*, 249.

45. Hundley, *Water and the West*, 12–14. The Reclamation Service's partner in the first survey was Southern California Edison's antecedent, Edison Electric Company.

46. Myers, *River of Controversy*, 16,; Pisani, *Water and American Government*, 227.

47. Pisani, *Water and American Government*, 227.

48. "Political Engineering," *Sierras Service Bulletin*, Feb. 1931, 2, Corporate Communications Department, Edison International.

49. "Utility Companies United to Oppose U.S. Projects," transcribed from *Washington News*, 17 Oct. 1927, box 144, Swing Papers. For use of Red Scare rhetoric in the Muscle Shoals debate, see also Hubbard, *Origins of the TVA*, 288.

50. Frank B. McMillin and George B. Chandler, "Why Ohio Is Interested," undated typescript, box 144, Swing Papers.

51. Albert Fall to Warren G. Harding, 24 Sept. 1921, "3rd Enclosure. Subject: Colorado River Power Project and Appointment of Commissioner," box 47, Fall Papers; "Mr. Swing Has Feelings Hurt," *LAT*, 2 Apr. 1924.

52. Franklin Hichborn to Committee on Irrigation of Arid Lands, telegram, 16 Feb. 1924, box 144, Swing Papers. Hichborn cited a 1923 investigation that revealed that California utilities had contributed $500,000 to the campaign to defeat the Water Power Act.

53. "Furious Charge of the Edison Brigade of Six Hundred Agents," unidentified newspaper, 10 Apr. 1924, Scrapbook 1A, 45, box 157, Swing Papers; "'Trust' Scored as Foe of Dam," *LAT*, 13 Apr. 1927.

54. Hundley, *Water and the West*, 273.

55. "Work Plans River Aid," *LAT*, 12 Mar. 1927.

56. Ibid. In his State of the Union speech in 1927, President Coolidge endorsed a flood control and irrigation dam on the Colorado that only secondarily provided power and water to urban Southern California. He blamed Philip Swing for letting his personal ambitions interfere with the dam. See "Congress and the Colorado," *LAT*, 22 Dec. 1927.

57. "Hoover Urges Boulder Dam Be Built at Once," *LAT*, 22 Aug. 1926.

58. "Flood Control Imposed Duty," *LAT*, 19 Nov. 1927.

59. Kyle D. Palmer, "New Swing-Johnson Bill Fails to End Opposition," *LAT*, 6 Feb. 1926.

60. Kyle D. Palmer, "Coolidge Advances New Colorado River Plan," *LAT*, 11 Jan. 1926.

61. Charles L. Underhill to *Los Angeles Examiner*, 2 June 1926, box 141, Swing Papers. Underhill was a Republican representative from Massachusetts's Ninth District. See also attachments to M. Thomson to Philip Swing, 24 July 1926, box 141, Swing Papers.

62. Edgar Howard to *Los Angeles Examiner*, 4 June 1926, box 141, Swing Papers. Howard was Democrat from Nebraska's Third District. For a progressive critique of Mellon and private exploitation of Niagara Falls, see "Public Power First," 346.

63. John C. Shafer to *Los Angeles Examiner*, 3 June 1926, box 141, Swing Papers.

64. Grant H. Hudson to *Los Angeles Examiner*, 2 June 1926, box 141, Swing Papers.

65. "Aid on River Besought," *LAT*, 29 June 1926; "Governor Calls Special Session on River Pact," *LAT*, 13 Oct. 1926. For the *Los Angeles Times* position on the Special Session and support for unqualified ratification of the six-state compact, see "Responsibility," *LAT*, 15 Oct. 1926.

66. "Wyoming Asks California to Approve River Pact," *LAT*, 19 Oct. 1926.

67. "Utah Seeks New Pact," *LAT*, 14 Oct. 1926. For similar statements from the governors of New Mexico, Colorado, and Utah, see "Governor Asserts Fate of River Pact at Stake," *LAT*, 20 Oct. 1926, and "Governors Give Warning on River Compact Issue," *LAT*, 21 Oct. 1926.

68. Hiram Johnson to Philip Swing, 13 Oct. 1926, box 141, Swing Papers; see also "Utah Seeks New Pact."

69. Philip Swing to Herbert C. Jones, 18 Oct. 1926; Philip Swing to L. Ward Bannister, 14 Oct. 1926, both in box 141, Swing Papers.

70. "Flays River Pact Foes," *LAT*, 15 Oct. 1926; Johnson to Swing, 13 Oct. 1926, Swing Papers; "Governor Asserts Fate of River Pact at Stake."

71. "Arizona to Advance Own Plan on River Project," *LAT*, 5 Dec. 1926.

72. "House Committee Sends River Pact Ultimatum," *LAT*, 12 Dec. 1926; Kyle D. Palmer, "River Bill Riders Up," *LAT*, 16 Dec. 1926; "Division of Revenues River Issue," *LAT*, 22 Jan. 1927. For negotiations in the Colorado River Commission, see Hundley, *Water and the West*, 264–66.

73. "Arizona Submits Offer for River Agreement," *LAT*, 10 Dec. 1926.

74. Quoted in Kyle D. Palmer, "Coolidge Again Indorses Plea for River Action," *LAT*, 13 Jan. 1927.

75. Ibid.

76. Kyle D. Palmer, "River Bill Battle Ends in Committee Approval," *LAT*, 23 Dec. 1926.

77. Harry A. Slattery to Philip Swing, 13 Dec. 1927, box 134, Swing Papers.

78. Richard V. Oulahan, "Senate Filibuster on Boulder Dam Goes on All Night," *NYT*, 29 May 1928; "All Night Dam Filibuster Grinds Away in Senate," *LAT*, 29 May 1928.

79. Elmer O. Leatherwood, "A National Legislator's View on Colorado River Development," *Tax Digest*, Dec. 1926, 203–6, box 17, Swing Papers.

80. "Will Urge Coolidge to Push Boulder Dam," *NYT*, 11 Jan. 1927.

81. Quoted in Palmer, "River Bill Riders Up."
82. Palmer, "Coolidge Again Indorses Plea for River Action."
83. "Boulder Dam," *NYT*, 31 Jan. 1927.
84. David S. Law, La Crosse, to James D. Beck, 17 Jan. 1927; Henry Soltau, Hussa Canning and Pickle, Bangor, Wis., to J. D. Beck, 17 Jan. 1927; A. J. Wash, Lange Grocery, Sparta, Wis., to Joseph D. Beck, 17 Jan. 1927; V. F. Shereda, Owen State Bank, Owen, Wis., to Joseph D. Beck, 17 Jan. 1927, all attachments to unsigned letter to Philip Swing, "I find that every one connected with the deluge of power telegrams is willing to say they have received them," n.d., Swing Papers. See also Frank J. Quinn to W. E. Hull, 17 Jan. 1927; James Douglas Ayers to Charlotte W. Preston, 24 Jan. 1927; and "Telegram from president of power concern in Texas to his congressman," n.d., all in box 145, Swing Papers.
85. "Flood Crest Strains Dam," *LAT*, 22 Feb. 1927; "Urges Canyon Dam to Prevent Floods," *NYT*, 4 Feb. 1927. The flood danger to the Imperial Valley was caused by an unusually deep snow pack and heavy rains, which swelled the spring runoff. For more on the Mississippi Valley Flood of 1927, see Daniel, *Deep As It Come*, or Barry, *Rising Tide*.
86. "'Trust' Scored as Foe of Dam."
87. "Congress Fight Near over Boulder Canyon," *NYT*, 18 Jan. 1927. Johnson also routinely called opponents of the bill "tools of the power trust." See, for example, "Senate Debate on Dam Starts," *LAT*, 27 Apr. 1928, and "Boulder Dam Plot Charged to Hearst," *NYT*, 23 May 1928.
88. Philip Swing to W. E. Hull, 2 Feb. 1927, box 145, Swing Papers. In his letter Swing states, "This is not a government ownership project at all, but is the recommendation of the government after the United States engineers had made four or five years of study ... this bill contains their recommendations for the steps necessary to ... solve the flood control problem on the Lower Colorado River." Norris Hundley noted that the Mississippi Valley floods of April 1927 increased sympathy for these flood control arguments. See Hundley, *Water and the West*, 272.
89. Kyle D. Palmer, "River Legislation Faces New Danger of Defeat," *LAT*, 16 Jan. 1927.
90. "River Bill Must Wait on State Conferences," *LAT*, 27 Jan. 1927.
91. "Cloture Is Asked on Boulder Dam," *NYT*, 25 Feb. 1927; "Senate Tied in Knots," *LAT*, 27 Feb. 1927.
92. John R. Haynes to E. A. Dickson, 25 Feb. 1927, John R. Haynes Papers, Special Collections, University of California, Los Angeles.
93. Ibid.
94. *Sunday Dispatch*, 4 Dec. 1927, retyped by and attached to Harry A. Slattery to Philip Swing, 13 Dec. 1927, box 134, Swing Papers; "A Substitute for Regulation," *New Republic*, 30 Mar. 1927, 157–58.
95. Ibid.; "Substitute for Regulation," 157–58.
96. Hundley, *Water and the West*, 270–72.

97. "Engineers Flay Boulder Plans," *LAT*, 19 Apr. 1928.
98. "Lines Formed for Dam Fight," *LAT*, 22 May 1928.
99. "Dam Storm Thunders," *LAT*, 23 May 1928; "Boulder Dam Plot Charged to Hearst."
100. "Boulder Dam Fight Will Open in Senate Today," 26 Apr. 1928; Leslie Saunders to Philip Swing, 21 Apr. 1923, box 141, Swing Papers; C. W. Koiner, George E. Cryer, et al. to Addison T. Smith, n.d., box 138, Swing Papers.
101. "Johnson Emits Thunderbolts," *LAT*, 21 Feb. 1928; "Senate Debate on Dam Starts."
102. "Johnson Emits Thunderbolts"; Statements by Citizens of Arizona relative to the Colorado River Problem . . . ," in *Colorado River Hearings*, 43–44; "Insurance Interests Help Defeat Boulder Canyon Dam Legislation," *Western Progressive*, Mar. 1927, 1–2, box 17, Swing Papers. See also Hundley, *Great Thirst*, 220–23.
103. "River Bill Runs into New Snag," *LAT*, 7 Apr. 1928; "Senate Bills Swamp House," *LAT*, 16 Apr. 1928.
104. "River Bill Runs into New Snag"; "Senate Bills Swamp House." The Senate passed the McNary-Haugen farm relief bill several times between 1924 and 1928, but President Coolidge vetoed it each time. The bills would have supported farm incomes by creating a federal corporation to purchase surplus farm products for future resale on the domestic or foreign markets. See Johnson, "Part-Time Leader," and Winters, "Ambiguity and Agricultural Policy," *Agricultural History*.
105. "Senate Filibuster Lasts for 20 Hours," *NYT*, 26 May 1928; "Filibuster Threat Bars Tax Bill Vote," *NYT*, 21 May 1928.
106. Quoted in "Threat Made of Filibuster," *LAT*, 31 Mar. 1928.
107. "Boulder Bill Up Next Week," *LAT*, 3 Apr. 1928.
108. "Boulder Dam Fight Will Open in Senate Today." The House of Representatives also tried to force California and Arizona to compromise. In 1928, for example, a House committee gave the two states until 15 March to meet to settle their differences. See "Dams and Politicians," *NYT*, 18 Mar. 1928.
109. "Boulder Bill Up Next Week."
110. For King's alternative flood control plans, see "Californians Weigh Dam Compromise," *NYT*, 29 Apr. 1928; Kyle D. Palmer, "River Foes Open Fire," *LAT*, 22 Feb. 1927. For one reaction, see William M. Entenman, "Danger to Imperial Valley Viewed as a Very Real One," *NYT*, 1 Apr. 1928.
111. "Boulder Dam Measure Revised for Senate," *NYT*, 17 Mar. 1928; "Boulder Bill Up Next Week"; "Senate Debate on Dam Starts."
112. Kyle D. Palmer, "Coolidge Asks Parley with Mexico on Colorado Water," *LAT*, 3 Feb. 1927; "Data on Water Treaty Sought," *LAT*, 4 May 1928; "Oratory Flows over Dam Site," *LAT*, 24 May 1928. For more on U.S.-Mexico water rights disputes on the Colorado, see Hundley, *Dividing the Waters*.
113. Richard V. Oulahan, "Four-Billion Mark Looms in Congress," *NYT*, 13 May 1928.

114. "Senate Debate on Dam Starts"; "Urges Federal Aid for Boulder Dam," *LAT*, 6 Dec. 1927; "Dams and Politicians." See also Richard V. Oulahan, "Public Ownership in Two Measures Issue for Coolidge," *NYT*, 21 May 1928.

115. "Boulder Dam Weathers Day's Battle in House," *LAT*, 25 May 1928. For coverage of the progress of Swing-Johnson through the House, see "Boulder Dam Battle Holds House Interest," *NYT*, 24 May 1928, and "Boulder Dam Bill Passed by House," *NYT*, 26 May 1928.

116. "Boulder Dam Weathers Day's Battle in House."

117. Oulahan, "Senate Filibuster on Boulder Dam Goes on All Night"; "Senators Battle over Boulder Dam," *NYT*, 30 May 1928; Richard V. Oulahan, "Congress Ends Session with Senate in Uproar over Boulder Dam Bill," *NYT*, 30 May 1928.

118. Richard V. Oulahan, "Coolidge Speech Backed by Aides," *NYT*, 19 Nov. 1928; "Stormy Session Awaits Congress," *NYT*, 2 Dec. 1928.

119. "Debate Renewed on Boulder Dam," *NYT*, 6 Dec. 1928; "Dam Battle Resumed," *LAT*, 6 Dec. 1928.

120. "Johnson Balks at Concession," *LAT*, 9 Dec. 1928; "Boulder Dam Flow Divided by Senate," *NYT*, 12 Dec. 1928; "Boulder Dam Bill Signed by President Coolidge," *LAT*, 22 Dec. 1928. See also Hundley, *Water and the West*, 268–70. According to Norris Hundley, the water allocation agreements in the Boulder Canyon Act were intended as a recommendation, but they have been misread as absolute rights. Before the final vote on the Swing-Johnson bill, the Senate rejected several additional amendments, including one that would have allowed the Bureau of Reclamation to build a power plant only if it could not lease power rights to municipal or state governments or to private utilities.

121. "Boulder Dam Flow Divided by Senate"; "Boulder Dam Bill Passes the Senate," *NYT*, 15 Dec. 1928; "President Signs Boulder Dam Bill," *NYT*, 22 Dec. 1928. The bill passed the Senate 65 to 11; Ashurst and Hayden voted against the bill. Arizona did not give up even after Congress approved Hoover Dam. In June 1930, Senator Hayden tried to withhold funds for dam construction, arguing that this would give California and Arizona time to settle their remaining differences (Laurence M. Benedict, "Brakes Urged on Dam Funds," *LAT*, 24 June 1930). Then, Arizona filed five separate permits to develop hydropower at Boulder Canyon ("Boulder Plant Pleas Rejected," *LAT*, 12 July 1930). Three months later Arizona filed suit, challenging the legality of the Swing-Johnson bill. Arizona argued that the Colorado River Compact, the Swing-Johnson bill, and the water and power contracts entered into under the bill were all unconstitutional (Laurence M. Benedict, "Arizona Files Dam Suit," *LAT*, 7 Oct. 1930).

122. California, Colorado River Commission, *Colorado River and the Boulder Canyon Project*, 160.

123. Ibid., 116.

124. Pisani, *Water and American Government*, 229.

125. Benedict, "Brakes Urged on Dam Funds."

126. "Hoover Urges Boulder Dam Be Built at Once"; Pisani argues persuasively that Hoover regarded flood control, irrigation, and domestic water supply as more important features of a Boulder Canyon dam than hydropower. See Pisani, *Water and American Government*, 228–29.

127. J. R. Haynes, "While it is a logical deduction from the text of the Swing-Johnson Bill . . . ," 25 Mar. 1930, box 11, Haynes Papers.

128. Philip Swing to Chas. L. Childers, 21 Feb. 1930, box 136, Swing Papers.

129. "Boulder Dam Power," *Sierras Service Bulletin*, Aug. 1929, 2, Corporate Communications Department, Edison International.

130. Judson King, "Uncle Sam and His Water Supply: Some Notes on the Report of the President's Water Resources Policy Commission," National Popular Government League, *Bulletin* 241, 27 Jan. 1951, 5, box 54, Samuel B. Morris Papers, Huntington Library.

131. "Insurance Interests Help Defeat Boulder Canyon Dam Legislation"; "Address by William Green, President, American Federation of Labor, Atlantic City, June 8, 1927," *Water Resources*, Jan. 1928, 15, both in box 43, Swing Papers. See also Bisbee Chamber of Commerce to A. B. Fall, 22 June 1922, Fall Papers. Banks opposed to the Swing-Johnson bill are mentioned in "Telegram from Houston, Texas, Banker Whose Bank Handles Accounts of Stone and Webber to a Congressman in Interior State outside Houston District," n.d., box 145; and James Douglas Ayers to Charlotte W. Preston, 24 Jan. 1927, box 141, both in Swing Papers. According to Donald Pisani, the U.S. Chamber of Commerce and the American Society of Civil Engineers opposed almost all Bureau of Reclamation dams in 1928. See Pisani, *Water and American Government*, 148–49. See also Olson, "Colorado River Compact," app. 2: Activities of Private Power Companies in Colorado River Development.

132. Frank B. McMillin, George B. Chandler, Ohio Chamber of Commerce, "Why Ohio Is Interested," n.d., box 144, Swing Papers. The U.S. Chamber of Commerce publicized similar positions. Given the connection between the U.S. Chamber of Commerce and the utility industry, this is hardly surprising. Lewis E. Pierson, president of the U.S. Chamber of Commerce in 1927 and 1928, sat on the boards of directors of several power companies; a number of utility executives served on the governing board of the U.S. Chamber of Commerce's house magazine, *Nation's Business*. See Judson King, "Who's Who in the Super-Power Lobby," National Popular Government League, *Bulletin* 115, 10 Feb. 1928), 15, box 145, Swing Papers.

CHAPTER FIVE

1. "Boulder Dam," *NYT*, 17 Dec. 1928.

2. "Stanford University Group Report on Water Resources Policy to the President's Water Resources Policy Commission," Stanford University Food Research Institute, Palo Alto, California, 3, box 42, Samuel B. Morris Papers, Huntington Library, San Marino, California.

3. On water development conflicts before and after World War II, see Hundley, *Great Thirst*, 221; Reisner, *Cadillac Desert*, 260–61; and Worster, *Rivers of Empire*, 274–75.

4. "Stanford University Group Report on Water Resources Policy to the President's Water Resources Policy Commission," 3, Morris Papers.

5. Harry S. Truman, Executive Order 10095, "Establishment of the President's Water Resources Policy Commission," in *PWRPC Report*, 309.

6. For a good summary of the causes of and reactions to this interagency rivalry, see Rogers, *America's Water*, 50–54.

7. Maass, *Muddy Waters*, 23, 28, 101. Both the 1949 and the 1955 Hoover Commissions on the Reorganization of the Executive Branch of the Government proposed to change federal river planning. These repeated failures demonstrate how entrenched these agencies and their competition had become. For further explanations of the ways congressional committee structures undermined comprehensive planning, see Rogers, *America's Water*, 53–54, and Maass, *Muddy Waters*, 115–17.

8. Reuss, "Pick Sloan Plan."

9. Reisner, *Cadillac Desert*, 182–86.

10. Ibid.

11. Edward. A. Ackerman, "Memorandum of Fifth Meeting, Committee on River Program Analysis, President's Water Resources Policy Commission," 19 May 1950, 2, box 45; Everett T. Winter to Miss Anderson, 14 June 1950, box 41, both in Morris Papers.

12. Maass, *Muddy Waters*, 119, 121, 123.

13. E. W. Rising, "President's Message Criticizing H.R. 5472," *National Water Conservation Conference Newsletter*, no. 78, 24 May 1950; "Approval of H.R. 5472; Message from the President of the United States," House of Representatives Document 597, 81st Cong., 2d sess., 22 May 1950, box 44, Morris Papers.

14. Dewey Anderson to Samuel B. Morris, 4 Jan. 1950. box 42, Morris Papers.

15. Department of Interior, Bureau of Reclamation, "Conservation and Utilization of Water," box 45, Morris Papers.

16. Rising, "President's Message Criticizing H.R. 5472"; "Approval of H.R. 5472; Message from the President of the United States," Morris Papers.

17. In the 1920s, Robert Bradford Marshall proposed comprehensive, statewide water development to eliminate bitter water rights disputes between California's industrial and agricultural communities. This plan, while not a direct influence on the PWRPC, embodied the Progressive planning impulse that became river basin planning in the 1950s. On the "Marshall Plan," see Pisani, *From the Family Farm to Agribusiness*, 394–98. For more on the urban-rural water conflicts that spawned calls for comprehensive water planning for California, see works on Los Angeles's Owens Valley project, San Francisco's Hetch Hetchy project, and the East Bay public waterworks, including Worster, *Rivers of Empire*; Hundley, *Great Thirst*; Kahrl, *Water and*

Power; Walton, *Western Times and Water Wars*; Righter, *Battle over Hetch Hetchy*; and Sarah S. Elkind, *Bay Cities and Water Politics*.

18. M. L. Cooke, "Taking the Sense of the Meeting," 27 Jan. 1951, box 45, Morris Papers.

19. United States, National Resources Committee, Water Resources Committee, *Drainage Basin Problems and Programs*; Samuel B. Morris to Roy F. Bessey, 9 Nov. 1940, box 25, Morris Papers.

20. Gilbert F. White, "Water Limits to Human Activity in the United States," attachment to G. F. White to Samuel B. Morris, 17 Apr. 1950, box 42, Morris Papers.

21. Attachment to Abel Wolman to H. S. Morse, 11 Jan. 1939, box 118, Morris Papers; Samuel B. Morris to V. T. Boughton, 7 Dec. 1951, box 54, Morris Papers. Abel Wolman was the most prominent member of the American Water Works Association's policy committee.

22. "Water Utopia in 2023 Pages," *San Francisco Chronicle*, 9 Apr. 1951, box 54, Morris Papers.

23. Ibid.; "WRPC Report Echoes Radical Public Ownership Policies," *Electric Light and Power*, Jan. 1951, 96, box 45, Morris Papers.

24. LWJ [Lewis Webster Jones], "Prologue," 5 Aug. 1950, box 42, Morris Papers.

25. "Comments of Roland R. Renne to Leland Olds concerning first draft of manuscript on water resources policy," 8 July 1950, enclosure to R. R. Renne to Leland Olds, 8 July 1950, box 42, Morris Papers.

26. *Arizona Republic*, 18 Dec. 1950, as quoted in Morris L. Cooke to Members of the PWRPC, "News Bulletin #9," 26 Jan. 1951, box 45, Morris Papers.

27. *PWRPC Report*, 307; "Stanford University Group Report on Water Resources Policy to the President's Water Resources Policy Commission," Morris Papers.

28. Testimony of Arthur Powell Davis, in U.S. Congress, House, Committee on Irrigation of Arid Lands, 67th Cong., 2d sess., *Hearings before the Committee on Irrigation of Arid Lands . . . on H.R. 11449*, Pt. 1, 15, 16, 22 June 1922, 27.

29. Maass, *Muddy Waters*, 118–22; "Index: Official Memorandums—NRC," Aug. 1936, box 18, Morris Papers.

30. Leland Olds, "Recommendations of the President's Water Resources Policy Commission with Emphasis on Planning Conceptions and Procedure," 28 Aug. 1951, 2, box 55, Morris Papers; *PWRPC Report*, 52.

31. *PWRPC Report*, 43–53. Only in New England, where dense development and compact watersheds dictated that planners treat multiple rivers as a single unit, did the PWRPC abandon the notion that water planning should take place within watershed boundaries.

32. "Statement of the Secretary of the Interior Oscar L. Chapman before the President's Water Resources Policy Commission," 2 May 1950, 1, box 44, Morris Papers.

33. Maass, *Muddy Waters*, 90, 98.

34. Judson King, "Do We Want More TVAs?," 30 Mar. 1946, 17, Box 42, Morris Pa-

pers; "Excerpt from a letter from J. T. Sanders, Legislative Counsel of the National Grange," box 45, Morris Papers.

35. CIO, "Magnificent Columbia."

36. Ibid., 3.

37. Ibid., 17–18, 20.

38. Samuel P. Hays has written extensively on the role that changing values played in American recreation and environmental politics. See Hays, *Beauty, Health and Permanence* and *Explorations in Environmental History*.

39. CIO, "Magnificent Columbia," 17–18.

40. Ibid., 17–18, 20.

41. Don Sterling, "Interstate Pacts Backed by Utah in Water Hearing," *Denver Post*, 28 June 1950, box 44, Morris Papers. Sterling's article included a lengthy account of AFL and International Brotherhood of Electrical Workers member Alfred Shackelford's testimony at the public hearing held by the PWRPC in Denver in June 1950.

42. CIO, "Magnificent Columbia," 20.

43. Ibid., 16.

44. Isaak Walton League, "Crisis Spots in Conservation," Chicago, 1949, 9, box 43, Morris Papers.

45. Ibid., 7–9.

46. Sterling, "Interstate Pacts Backed by Utah in Water Hearing," Morris Papers; "Suggestions of the U.S. Department of Agriculture Relating to National Water Resources Policies," box 43, Morris Papers.

47. John Geoffrey Will to Morris L. Cooke, 13 July 1950, 1–3, box 43, Morris Papers.

48. Isaak Walton League, "Crisis Spots in Conservation," 7–15, Morris Papers; *PWRPC Report*, 17.

49. Samuel B. Morris, "President's Address," American Public Power Association, 28 Mar. 1950; Felix S. Cohen to Morris L. Cooke, 8 Mar. 1950, 1–3, both in box 42, Morris Papers. Parker Dam on the Colorado River, the Garrison Dam on the Rio Grande, and proposed dams on the Grand, Columbia, Colorado. and Missouri rivers were all expected to flood large segments of Indian reservations.

50. Chamber of Commerce of the United States, Natural Resources Department, "Government by Authorities," 1950, box 43, Morris Papers; "Statement of the Oxford Paper Company to the President's Water Resources Policy Commission in Re Development of Water Resources in the United States and Federal Participation Therein," submitted at Commission Hearing, Springfield, Massachusetts, 25 July 1950, box 41, Morris Papers; W. W. Horner, "National Water Resources Viewpoint of Engineers Joint Council," 23 Oct. 1951, box 42, Morris Papers. The Engineers Joint Council included representatives of the American Society of Civil Engineers, American Institute of Mining and Metallurgical Engineers, the American Society

of Mechanical Engineers, the American Institute of Electrical Engineers, and the American Institute of Chemical Engineers. Horner, one of the PWRPC's most vocal critics in the Engineers Joint Council, also served on the U.S. Chamber of Commerce's Natural Resources Committee.

51. Chamber of Commerce of the United States, Natural Resources Department, "Government by Authorities," 1–3, 14, Morris Papers.

52. National Water Policy Panel, Engineers Joint Council, "A Water Policy for the United States: A Critique of the Report of the President's Water Resources Policy Commission," July 1951, box 42, Morris Papers.

53. "Basin Development Committee Report to National Reclamation Association," Spokane, Washington, 15–17 Nov. 1950, ii, box 54, Morris Papers.

54. "Abel Analyzes Proposed Legislation: Water Resources Act Called 'Dismal Disappointment,'" *Western Water News*, June 1952, box 53, Morris Papers.

55. "More Supergovernment," *San Diego Union*, 24 Oct. 1951, box 55, Morris Papers. The *Denver Post* took a similar line in comments on the PWRPC's proposal in Sterling, "Interstate Pacts Backed by Utah in Water Hearing," Morris Papers.

56. "They Say to Columbia Basin, 'Hurry,'" *Oregon Journal*, editorial, 19 Dec. 1950, quoted in Cooke to Members of the PWRPC, "News Bulletin #9," Morris Papers.

57. "Comments of Roland R. Renne to Leland Olds Concerning First Draft of Manuscript on Water Resources Policy," Morris Papers.

58. Howard Miller to Stuart Salisbury, "Subject: Report of President's Water Resources Policy Commission," 16 Jan. 1951, box 45, Morris Papers.

59. Ibid.; Daniel B. Neble, "Policy Statement—Pacific Northwest Development Association," 11 May 1950, box 41, Morris Papers.

60. "A New System of Government," *Electrical World*, 5 Nov. 1951, box 55, Morris Papers.

61. "More Supergovernment," Morris Papers.

62. "The Same Old Story," editorial in the *Idaho Statesman*, 19 Dec. 1950, as quoted in Cooke to Members of the PWRPC, "News Bulletin #9," Morris Papers.

63. "Proposed Resolutions for Consideration of the California Caucus at the National Water Conservation Conference," Chicago, 21 Sept. 1949, attachment to Howard A. Miller to Samuel B. Morris, 11 Jan. 1950, box 42, Morris Papers.

64. Chamber of Commerce of the United States, Natural Resources Department, "Government by Authorities," 10–11, Morris Papers; "They Say to Columbia Basin, 'Hurry,'" Morris Papers; National Water Policy Panel, Engineers Joint Council, "A Water Policy for the United States: A Critique of the Report of the President's Water Resources Policy Commission," Morris Papers.

65. Samuel B. Morris to Bernard A. Foster Jr., 25 May 1951, 2, box 55, Morris Papers.

66. *PWRPC Report*, 151.

67. P. S. Burgess, "Points of Difference," 18 June 1950, 1, box 42, Morris Papers.

68. *PWRPC Report*, 151. The Bureau of Reclamation's first ancillary power plant

was constructed in 1909 at the Roosevelt Dam on Salt River in Arizona. By 1950, Reclamation operated plants with a total capacity of 3,294,000 kilowatts capacity and expected its new plants to add 3,136,650 kilowatts more. Senators Carl Hayden (Arizona) and O'Mahoney (Wyoming) cosponsored the amendment to the appropriations bill that directed these revenues to the reclamation fund.

69. *PWRPC Report*, 246.

70. Samuel B. Morris to Leland Olds, 23 Aug. 1950, "Re: Policy Formulation," 3; Morris, "President's Address," 17–19, 24–25, both in box 42, Morris Papers.

71. Jane Perry to Leland Olds, "Subject: Summary of Responses to 3/17 Letter, Question 3: Use of Surpluses to Pay Subsidies," box 42, Morris Papers. No one on the PWRPC saw federal water policy through narrowly regional eyes, but the Central Arizona Project may have informed their positions on the power issues. Certainly Morris's proposals for low power rates and industrial water supply echoed Los Angeles's own position on Colorado River development.

72. Elmer B. Staats to Morris L. Cooke, "Policy Issues in the Field of Land and Water Resources Development Requiring the Attention of the President's Water Resources Policy Commission," 8 Feb. 1950, 23, box 42, Morris Papers; Charles McKinley to Morris L. Cooke, 6 Feb. 1950, 3, box 43, Morris Papers.

73. McKinley to Cooke, 6 Feb. 1950, 3, Morris Papers.

74. Burgess, "Points of Difference," Morris Papers.

75. Morris to Olds, 23 Aug. 1950, "Re: Policy Formulation," 5, Morris Papers.

76. P. S. Burgess, "Reclamation's Part in Western Development," 15 July 1950, attachment to P. S. Burgess to Samuel B. Morris, 17 July 1950, box 42, Morris Papers.

77. *PWRPC Report*, 151. The original repayment deadline was extended to twenty years in 1914, to forty years in 1926. In 1939, Congress authorized the bureau to extend repayment ten years at a time.

78. Samuel B. Morris to Joseph S. Davis, 1 Feb. 1950, box 42, Morris Papers.

79. For more on the battles over acreage limitations on Reclamation projects, see Hundley, *Great Thirst*, 262–72.

80. Kneese, "Economics and Water Resources," 23–35; "Statement of the Secretary of the Interior Oscar L. Chapman before the President's Water Resources Policy Commission, May 2, 1950," 4–5, 9, Morris Papers.

81. Staats to Cooke, "Policy Issues in the Field of Land and Water Resources Development Requiring the Attention of the President's Water Resources Policy Commission," Morris Papers.

82. *PWRPC Report*, 65.

83. William Voight Jr., "Comment on 'A Water Policy for the American People,'" 8 Jan. 1951, box 45, Morris Papers.

84. Isaak Walton League, "Crisis Spots in Conservation," 7–8.

85. James H. Allen to Melvin E. Scheidt, 15 Nov. 1951, 1, box 54, Morris Papers.

86. "Comments of Roland R. Renne to Leland Olds concerning first draft of manuscript on water resources policy," Morris Papers.

87. Morris to Olds, 23 Aug. 1950, "Re: Policy Formulation," 3; Morris, "President's Address," 17–19, 24–25, both in box 42, Morris Papers.
88. *PWRPC Report*, 168.
89. Ibid., 12–14, 168.
90. Robert McKinney (chair, New Mexico Economic Development Commission) to Morris L. Cooke, 1 Mar. 1950, box 42, Morris Papers.
91. Quotation from *PWRPC Report*, 15.
92. Ibid., 14, 170.
93. Ibid., 14–15.
94. Ibid., 227–28.
95. Morris, "President's Address," 17–19, Morris Papers; *PWRPC Report*, 39.
96. *PWRPC Report*, 227.
97. Ibid., 245.
98. Ibid., 227, 244; Edison Electric Institute, "Principles for Sound Water Resources Development," 14 Apr. 1950, box 54, Morris Papers.
99. "Private Power Came First," *Electrical World*, 29 Jan. 1951, 114, box 53, Morris Papers.
100. Ibid.
101. James W. Parker, president of Detroit Edison, as quoted in "Presidential Commission Urges Nationwide Water Development," *Riverside Enterprise*, 19 Dec. 1950, box 54, Morris Papers.
102. "Unsound and Unfair Policy," *Electrical West* 106:1, 92, box 45, Morris Papers.
103. "WRPC Report Echos Radical Public Ownership Policies," *Electric Light and Power*, Jan. 1951, 96, box 45, Morris Papers.
104. "Statement of the Oxford Paper Company to the President's Water Resources Policy Commission in Re Development of Water Resources in the United States and Federal Participation Therein," Morris Papers.
105. Jane Perry to Leland Olds, "Subject: Summary of Responses to 3/17 Letter; Question 8. Hydroelectric Power Policy," 6, box 42, Morris Papers.
106. Edison Electric Institute, "Principles for Sound Water Resources Development," Morris Papers; Charles L. Kaupke, "To Members of the Kings River Water Association," undated addendum to Kings River Water Association, "Digest and Analysis of the President's Water Resources Policy Commission Report of Dec. 1950," both in box 54, Morris Papers.
107. "Water Report Aids Arizona River Project," *Phoenix Gazette*, 18 Dec. 1950, box 54, Morris Papers.
108. Ibid.
109. "Confusing the Water Question," *Santa Monica Evening Outlook*, 25 Sept. 1950, box 54, Morris Papers.
110. Ibid.
111. "Presidential Commission Urges Nationwide Water Development," Morris Papers.

112. "Confusing the Water Question," Morris Papers.

113. Judson King, "Uncle Sam and His Water Supply: Some Notes on the Report of the President's Water Resources Policy Commission," National Popular Government League, *Bulletin* 241, 27 Jan. 1951, 5, box 54, Morris Papers.

114. "Abel Analyzes Proposed Legislation," *Western Water News*, June 1952, box 54, Morris Papers.

115. Ibid.

116. Morris to Gilmore Tillman, 11 July 1952, box 54, Morris Papers.

117. "Proposed Resolutions for Consideration of the California Caucus at the National Water Conservation Conference," Morris Papers.

118. Miller to Morris, 11 Jan. 1950, Morris Papers.

119. Washington State University as quoted in Jane Perry to Leland Olds, "Subject: Summary of Responses to 3/17 Letter, Question 4. National vs. Regional Interests," 7, box 42, Morris Papers.

120. Ibid.

121. LWJ [Lewis Webster Jones], "Prologue," Morris Papers.

122. "Confusing the Water Question," Morris Papers.

123. F. R. Schank, testimony at Water Resources Policy Commission, Spokane, Washington, 16–17 June 1950, box 41, Morris Papers.

124. H. H. Mobley, "Water Fiasco," attachment to Samuel B. Morris to Leland Olds, 16 Aug. 1950, box 42, Morris Papers; Jane Perry to Leland Olds, "Subject: Summary of Responses to 3/17 Letter," 9–10, box 42, Morris Papers.

125. H. H. Mobley, "Water Fiasco," Morris Papers.

CONCLUSION

1. "County Works List Complete," *LAT*, 24 July 1933; "More Idle Men Will Get Work," *LAT*, 16 Dec. 1933; "Federal Fund of $8,000,000 Asked for Sewers," *LAT*, 19 May 1942.

2. "Acquisition of Beach Frontage for Public Use," Steno Reports, 24 July 1924, 10; Los Angeles Chamber of Commerce, "Chronological Record of Accomplishments, 1927–1935," 96, LAACC Collection.

3. "Long Beach Chamber Ok's Whipstocking," *Huntington Beach News*, 23 July 1936. For a list of other business and civic organizations that supported this legislation, see "Civic Leader Urges Vote for Proposition No. 4," *LAT*, 17 Oct. 1936; "Drilling Issue Boon to Parks; Garland Sees No Need of Bond Proposals If Proposition No. 4 Passes," *LAT*, 21 Oct. 1936; and "New Revenue for State Cited; Proposition 4 Will in Effect Cut Taxes, Says Garland, Urging 'Yes,'" *LAT*, 27 Oct. 1936.

4. For more on the Shoreline Planning Association's activism on tidelands oil drilling, see "Inland Residents Declared against Tideland Drilling," *LAT*, 2 Nov. 1938.

5. These are Koppes's terms for the Progressive Era emphasis on regulations for the public good and the later procorporate policies of the New Deal, World

War II, and Cold War periods. See Koppes, "Environmental Policy and American Liberalism."

6. Laurence Todd, "Power Control Breaks Down," *The Nation*, 12 Mar. 1930, 289–90; Hundley, *Water and the West*, 273. See also "Power Propaganda—Correspondence" folder in Philip Swing Papers, Special Collections, University of California, Los Angeles.

7. A. A. Imberman, "A Public Relations Policy for Private Utilities," *Public Opinion Quarterly* 13:1 (1949): 23–30; "The Quarter's Polls," *Public Opinion Quarterly* 11:2 (1947): 289. In 1945, the *New York Herald Tribune* asked Americans if they thought it would be a good idea to have less government regulation of business after the war. Fifty-four percent of respondents answered that less regulation was a good idea; only among the poorest respondents did fewer than half approve of less regulation. See Cantril, *Public Opinion*, 350.

In January 1947, the American Institute of Public Opinion asked, "Do you think the United States Government should own the following things in this country—Banks? Railroads? Coal Mines? Electric power companies?" *Public Opinion* compared the 1947 responses with similar questions asked in 1936 and 1945. The results:

ELECTRIC POWER COMPANIES			
	Yes	No	Undecided
1936	40%	52%	8%
1945	29	50	21
1947	28	64	8

RAILROADS			
	Yes	No	Undecided
1936	30%	60%	10%
1945	19	64	17
1947	26	67	7

BANKS			
	Yes	No	Undecided
1936	36%	56%	8%
1945	27	61	21
1947	26	66	8

COAL MINES			
	Yes	No	Undecided
1936	27%	64%	9%
1945	29	59	12
1947	33	61	6

Source: "The Quarter's Polls," *Public Opinion Quarterly* 11:2 (1947): 289.

8. Broesamle, *Reform and Reaction in Twentieth Century American Politics*; Link, "What Happened to the Progressive Movement in the 1920s?"; Brinkley, *End of Reform*; Brinkley, *Liberalism and Its Discontents*; Galambos and Pratt, *Rise of the Corporate Commonwealth*.

9. On consumer culture, see Cohen, *Consumers' Republic*.

10. George L. Hoxie, "The Fictitious 'Surplus' of the Los Angeles Municipal Electric Power Department," Nov. 1930, LAACC Collection.

11. "Standard of California's War Program," *Petroleum World*, Aug. 1943, 22; Carrington Kind, "Washington Summary and Forecast," *Petroleum World*, Aug. 1943, 19.

12. "Petitions Hit City's Fumes," *LAT*, 9 Sept. 1944; "County Grand Jury Acts on Smoke-Fumes Issue," *LAT*, 14 Sept. 1944; "Law Ordered Drafted to Curb Fumes Nuisance," *LAT*, 16 Sept. 1944, all in box 76, FBC.

13. On the conflicts between large and small oil companies, see Ickes, *Secret Diary of Harold L. Ickes*, 3:34, 696. See also Nash, *United States Oil Policy*; Engler, *Politics of Oil*; and Freudenberg and. Gramling, *Oil in Troubled Waters*.

BIBLIOGRAPHY

ARCHIVAL COLLECTIONS
Berkeley, California
  Bancroft Library
    Abstracts of Articles of Incorporation for California Oil Companies on File in Alameda
  Water Resources Center Archive
    Los Angeles Engineering Council of Founder Societies, "Report of Committee," in Los Angeles Engineering Council of Founder Societies, "Report of the Special Engineering Committee on Flood Control," Feb. 1934.
Claremont, California
  Honnold Library
    H. Jerry Voorhis Papers
Laguna Niguel, California
  National Archives and Records Administration
    Army Corps of Engineers Collection
Los Angeles, California
  Automobile Club of Southern California Archives
    E. E. East Collection
  Los Angeles City Archives
  University of California, Special Collections
    John R. Haynes Papers
    Philip Swing Papers
  University of Southern California, Regional History Center
    Los Angeles Area Chamber of Commerce Collection
    Los Angeles Herald Clippings and Photograph Collection
Rosemead, California
  Corporate Communications Department, Edison International
Sacramento, California
  California State Archives

San Marino, California
  Huntington Library
    Fletcher Bowron Collection
    Albert Fall Papers
    John Anson Ford Papers
    Samuel Morris Papers
Yorba Linda, California
  Nixon Presidential Library
    Whittier Narrows Dam Notes, Speech File

GOVERNMENT DOCUMENTS

California. Colorado River Commission. *Colorado River and the Boulder Canyon Project.* Sacramento: 1930.

———. Department of Public Health, Bureau of Sanitary Engineering. "Report on a Pollution Survey of Santa Monica Beaches in 1942." 26 June 1943, Sacramento.

Los Angeles District of the Army Corps of Engineers. "History of Federal Flood Control Work in Southern California." Los Angeles, 1939. Los Angeles District of the Army Corps of Engineers, Los Angeles, California.

U.S. Congress. House. Committee on Irrigation of Arid Lands. *Hearings before the Committee on Irrigation of Arid Lands . . . on H.R. 11449.* Pt. 1. 67th Cong., 2d sess., 15, 16, and 22 June 1922.

———. *Hearings on H.R. 11449.* Pt. 3. 67th Cong., 2d sess., 22–24 June 1922, in "Development of the Colorado River Basin," pamphlet, Huntington Library, San Marino, California.

U.S. Congress. Senate. Committee on Irrigation and Reclamation. *Colorado River Hearings and Miscellaneous Documents.* Vol. 1. 68th Cong., 1st sess., 1924.

U.S. Congress. Senate. *Correspondence from the Secretary of the Interior . . . together with the proceedings of the conference on the construction of the Boulder Canyon Dam held at San Diego, Calif.* Senate Document 142. 67th Cong., 2d sess., 1922.

U.S. National Resources Committee. Water Resources Committee. *Drainage Basin Problems and Programs.* Washington: GPO, 1937.

NEWSPAPERS AND MAGAZINES

American City
American Home
Architectural Record
Atlantic Monthly
Bulletin of the Municipal League of Los Angeles
Businessweek
Commonweal
Electrical World
Electrical West
Electric Light and Power
Fortnight
Good Housekeeping
House and Garden
Huntington Beach News
Hygeia

Labor News
Life
Long Beach Press Telegram
Los Angeles Times
The Nation
National Geographic
Newport Balboa Press
New Republic
New York Times
Oil Age
Pasadena Star News
Petroleum World
Playground and Recreation
Public Opinion Quarterly

Redondo Reflex
San Francisco Chronicle
Santa Monica Evening Outlook
Saturday Evening Post
Scientific Monthly
Shore and Beach
Sierras Service Bulletin
Sunday Dispatch
Tax Digest
Time
Venice Evening Vanguard
Western City
Western Progressive
Western Water News

OTHER PRIMARY SOURCES

Downey, Sheridan. *Truth about the Tidelands*. San Francisco: N.p., 1948.
Griffin, Donald F. *Coastline Plans and Action: For the Development of the Los Angeles Metropolitan Coastline*. Los Angeles: Haynes Foundation, 1944.
Ickes, Harold. *The Secret Diary of Harold L. Ickes*. 3 vols. New York: Simon and Schuster, 1951.
Olmsted Brothers and Bartholomew and Assoc. *Parks, Playgrounds and Beaches for the Los Angeles Region: A Report Submitted to the Citizens' Committee on Parks, Playgrounds and Beaches*. Los Angeles: Citizens' Committee on Parks, Playgrounds and Beaches, 1930.
President's Water Resources Policy Commission. *A Water Policy for the American People*. Vol. 1. Washington, D.C.: GPO, 1951.
Robbins, George W., and L. Deming Tilton, eds. *Los Angeles: Preface to a Master Plan*. Publication No. 19. Los Angeles: Pacific Southwest Academy, 1941.

SECONDARY WORKS

American Public Works Association. *History of Public Works in the United States, 1776–1976*. Edited by Ellis L. Armstrong. Chicago: American Public Works Association, 1976.
Barry, John. *Rising Tide: The Great Mississippi Flood of 1927 and How It Changed America*. New York: Simon and Schuster, 1997.
Bartley, Ernest R. *The Tidelands Oil Controversy: A Legal and Historical Analysis*. Austin: University of Texas Press, 1953.
Beierle, Thomas C., and Jerry Cayford, *Democracy in Practice: Public Participation in Environmental Decisions*. Washington, D.C.: Resources for the Future, 2002.
Bigger, Richard. *Flood Control in Metropolitan Los Angeles*. Berkeley: University of California Press, 1959.

Black, Brian. *Petrolia: The Landscape of America's First Oil Boom.* Baltimore: Johns Hopkins University Press, 2000.
Boyle, Kevin. *Arc of Justice: A Saga of Race, Civil Rights, and Murder in the Jazz Age.* New York: Henry Holt and Co., 2004.
Branch, Melville C. "Oil Extraction, Urban Environment and City Planning." *Journal of the American Institute of Planners* 38:3 (1972): 140–54.
Brinkley, Alan. *The End of Reform: New Deal Liberalism in Recession and War.* New York: Alfred A. Knopf, 1995.
———. *Liberalism and Its Discontents.* Cambridge: Harvard University Press, 1998.
Brock, Clifton. *Americans for Democratic Action.* Westport, Conn.: Greenwood Press, 1985.
Broesamle, John L. *Reform and Reaction in Twentieth Century American Politics.* Westport, Conn.: Greenwood Press, 1990.
Burdett, Robert J., ed. *Greater Los Angeles and Southern California Portraits and Personal Memoranda.* Chicago: Lewis Publishing Co., 1910.
Cantril, Hadley, ed., *Public Opinion, 1935–1946.* Princeton, N.J.: Princeton University Press, 1951.
Clark, J. G. *Energy and the Federal Government: Fossil Fuel Policies, 1900–1946.* Urbana: University of Illinois Press, 1987.
Clark, Thomas R. *Defending Rights: Law, Labor Politics, and the State in California, 1890–1925.* Detroit: Wayne State University Press, 2002.
Cobb, Roger W., and Marc Howard Ross. *Cultural Strategies of Agenda Denial: Avoidance, Attack, and Redefinition.* Lawrence: University Press of Kansas, 1997.
Cochran, Clark E. "Political Science and 'The Public Interest.'" *Journal of Politics* 36:2 (1974): 327–55.
Cohen, Lizbeth. *A Consumers' Republic: The Politics of Mass Consumption in America.* New York: Knopf, 2003.
Collins, Robert M. *The Business Response to Keynes, 1929–1964.* New York: Columbia University Press, 1981.
"Conflicting State and Federal Claims of Title in Submerged Lands of the Continental Shelf." *Yale Law Review* 56 (1947): 356–70.
Cranz, Galen. *The Politics of Park Design: The History of Urban Parks in America.* Cambridge, Mass.: MIT Press, 1982.
Crouch, Winston W. *Intergovernmental Relations: Metropolitan Los Angeles. A Study in Integration.* Vol. 15. Los Angeles: Haynes Foundation, 1953.
Crouch, Winston W., Wendell Maccoby, Margaret G. Morden, and Richard Bigger. *Sanitation and Health.* Los Angeles: Haynes Foundation, 1952.
Cumbler, John T. *Reasonable Use: The People, the Environment and the State, New England 1790–1930.* New York: Oxford University Press, 2001.
Dahl, Robert. *Who Governs?* New Haven: Yale University Press, 1961.
Daniel, Pete. *Deep As It Come: The 1927 Mississippi River Flood.* New York: Oxford University Press, 1977.

Davidson, Ronald A. "The Beach versus 'Blade Runner': Recasting Los Angeles' Relationship to Modernity." *Historical Geography* 35 (2007): 45–79.

———. "Before 'Surfurbia': The Development of the South Bay Beach Cities through the 1930s." *Yearbook of the Association of Pacific Coast Geographers* 66 (2004): 80–94.

Davis, Mike. *Ecology of Fear: Los Angeles and the Imagination of Disaster.* New York: Metropolitan Books, Henry Holt and Co., 1998.

Dean, Cornelia. *Against the Tide: The Battle for America's Beaches.* New York: Columbia University Press, 1999.

Deverell, William. *Whitewashed Adobe: The Rise of Los Angeles and the Remaking of Its Mexican Past.* Berkeley: University of California Press, 2004.

Dewey, Scott Hamilton. *Don't Breathe the Air: Air Pollution and U.S. Environmental Politics, 1945–1970.* College Station: Texas A&M University Press, 2000.

Diamond, Adam. "What a Waste: Municipal Refuse Reform and a Century of Solid-Waste Management in Los Angeles." *Southern California Quarterly* 88:3 (2006): 336–65.

Einhorn, Robin. *Property Rules: Political Economy in Chicago, 1830–1872.* Chicago: University of Chicago Press, 1991.

Elkind, Sarah S. *Bay Cities and Water Politics: The Battle for Resources in Boston and Oakland, 1880–1930.* Lawrence: University Press of Kansas, 1998.

———. "Public Oil, Private Oil: The Tidelands Oil Controversy, World War II and the Control of the Environment." In *The Way We Really Were: The Golden State in the Second Great War,* edited by Roger Lotchin, 120–42. Chicago: University of Illinois Press, 2000.

Engler, Robert. *The Politics of Oil: A Study of Private Power and Democratic Directions.* New York: Macmillan, 1961.

Erie, Steven P. "How the Urban West Was Won: The Local State and Economic Growth in Los Angeles, 1880–1932." *Urban Affairs Quarterly* 47:4 (1992): 519–55.

Ethington, Philip J. *The Public City: The Political Construction of Urban Life in San Francisco, 1850–1900.* Berkeley: University of California Press, 1994.

Flamming, Douglas. *Bound for Freedom: Black Los Angeles in Jim Crow America.* Berkeley: University of California Press, 2005.

Flanagan, Maureen A. *Seeing with Their Hearts: Chicago Women and the Vision of the Good City, 1871–1933.* Princeton, N.J.: Princeton University Press, 2002.

Fogelson, Robert M. *The Fragmented Metropolis: Los Angeles, 1850–1930.* Cambridge: Harvard University Press, 1967.

Franks, Kenny A., and Paul F. Lambert, *Early California Oil: A Photographic History, 1865–1940.* College Station: Texas A&M University Press, 1985.

Freudenberg, William R., and Robert Gramling. *Oil in Troubled Waters: Perceptions, Politics and the Battle over Offshore Drilling.* Albany: State University of New York Press, 1994.

Galambos, Louis, and Joseph Pratt, *The Rise of the Corporate Commonwealth: U.S. Business and Public Policy in the Twentieth Century*. New York: Basic Books, 1988.

Galston, William A. "An Old Debate Renewed: The Politics of the Public Interest." *Daedalus* 136:4 (2007): 10–19.

Gandy, Oscar H., Jr. *Beyond Agenda-Setting: Information Subsidies and Public Policy*. Norwood, N.J.: Ablex Publishing, 1982.

Gellman, Irwin F. *The Contender: Richard Nixon, the Congress Years, 1946–1952*. New York: Free Press, 1999.

Gish, Todd. "Growing and Selling Los Angeles: The All-Year Club of Southern California, 1921–1941." *Southern California Quarterly* 89:4 (2007): 391–415.

Goldstein, Joan. *The Politics of Offshore Oil*. New York: Praeger, 1982.

Gottlieb, Robert, and Irene Wolt. *Thinking Big: The Story of the Los Angeles Times and Its Publishers and Their Influence on Southern California*. New York: G. P. Putnam's Sons, 1977.

Gumprecht, Blake. *The Los Angeles River: Its Life, Death and Possible Rebirth*. Baltimore: Johns Hopkins University Press, 1999.

Hayden, Dolores. *The Power of Place: Urban Landscapes as Public History*. Cambridge, Mass.: MIT Press, 1995.

Hays, Samuel P. *Beauty, Health and Permanence: Environmental Politics in the United States, 1955–1985*. New York: Cambridge University Press, 1987.

———. *Conservation and the Gospel of Efficiency: The Progressive Conservation Movement, 1890–1920*. Cambridge: Harvard University Press, 1959.

———. *Explorations in Environmental History: Essays by Samuel P. Hays*. Edited by Joel A. Tarr. Pittsburgh: University of Pittsburgh Press, 1998.

Hirt, Paul W. *A Conspiracy of Optimism: Management of the National Forests since World War Two*. Lincoln: University of Nebraska Press, 1994.

Hise, Greg. *Magnetic Los Angeles: Planning the Twentieth-Century Metropolis*. Baltimore: Johns Hopkins University Press, 1997.

———. "'Nature's Workshop': Industry and Urban Expansion in Southern California, 1900–1950." *Journal of Historical Geography*, 27:1 (2001): 74–92.

Hoult, Thomas. "The Whittier Narrows Dam: A Study in Community Competition and Conflict." M.A. thesis, Whittier College, 1948.

Hoy, Suellen M. "'Municipal Housekeeping': The Role of Women in Improving Urban Sanitation Practices, 1880–1917." In *Pollution and Reform in American Cities, 1870–1930*, edited by Martin V. Melosi, 173–98. Austin: University of Texas Press, 1980.

Hubbard, Preston John. *Origins of the TVA: The Muscle Shoals Controversy, 1920–1932*. Nashville, Tenn.: Vanderbilt University Press, 1961.

Hundley, Norris. *Dividing the Waters: A Century of Controversy between the United States and Mexico*. Berkeley: University of California Press, 1966.

———. *The Great Thirst: Californians and Water. A History*. Rev. ed. Berkeley: University of California Press: 2001.

———. *Water and the West: The Colorado River Compact and the Politics of Water in the American West*. Berkeley: University of California Press, 1975.

Issel, William. "Business Power and Political Culture in San Francisco, 1900–1940." *Journal of Urban History* 16:1 (1989): 52–77.

———. "'Citizens Outside the Government': Business and Urban Policy in San Francisco and Los Angeles, 1890–1932." *Pacific Historical Review* 57:2 (1988): 117–45.

———. "Liberalism and Urban Policy in San Francisco from the 1930s to the 1960s." *Western Historical Quarterly* 22:4 (1991): 431–50.

Issel, William, and Robert Cherney. *San Francisco, 1865–1932: Politics, Power, and Urban Development*. Berkeley: University of California Press, 1986.

Jackson, Donald C., and Norris Hundley Jr., "Privilege and Responsibility: William Mulholland and the St. Francis Dam Disaster." *California History* 82:3 (2004): 8–47, 72–78.

Jacoby, Karl. *Crimes against Nature: Squatters, Poachers, Thieves, and the Hidden History of American Conservation*. Berkeley: University of California Press, 2003.

Johnson, Marilynn S. *The Second Gold Rush: Oakland and the East Bay in World War II*. Berkeley: University of California Press, 1994.

Johnson, Rich. *The Central Arizona Project, 1918–1968*. Tucson: University of Arizona Press, 1977.

Johnson, Roger T. "Part-Time Leader: Senator Charles L. McNary and the McNary-Haugen Bill." *Agricultural History* 54:4 (1980): 527–41.

Judd, Richard W. *Common Lands, Common People: The Origins of Conservation in Northern New England*. Cambridge: Harvard University Press, 1997.

Kahrl, William. *Water and Power: The Conflict over Los Angeles' Water Supply in the Owens Valley*. Los Angeles: University of California Press, 1982.

Kennamer, J. David. *Public Opinion: The Press and Public Policy*. Westport, Conn.: Praeger, 1992.

Klyza, Christopher McGrory. *Who Controls Public Lands: Mining, Forestry and Grazing Policies, 1870–1990*. Chapel Hill: University of North Carolina Press, 1996.

Kneese, Allen V. "Economics and Water Resources." In *Water Resources Administration in the United States: Policy, Practice, and Emerging Issues*, edited by Martin Reuss, 23–35. East Lansing: Michigan State University Press, 1993.

Koppes, Clayton. "Environmental Policy and American Liberalism: The Department of the Interior, 1933–1953." *Environmental Review* 7 (1983): 17–41.

Krier, James E., and Edmund Ursin. *Pollution and Policy: A Case Study on California and Federal Experience with Motor Vehicle Air Pollution, 1940–1975*. Berkeley: University of California Press, 1977.

Krutilla, John V. "Some Environmental Effects of Economic Development." *Daedalus*, Special Issue: "America's Changing Environment," 96:4 (1967): 1058–70.

Langton, Stuart. *Citizen Participation Perspectives: Proceedings of the National Conference on Citizen Participation*. Lincoln Filene Center for Citizenship and Public Affairs. Medford, Mass.: Tufts University, 1979.

Link, Arthur S. "What Happened to the Progressive Movement in the 1920s?" *American Historical Review* 64:4 (1959): 833–51.

Lipset, Seymour Martin, and William Schneider. *The Confidence Gap: Business, Labor and Government in the Public Mind*. New York: Free Press, 1983.

Lotchin, Roger. *The Bad City in the Good War: San Francisco, Los Angeles, Oakland and San Diego*. Bloomington: Indiana University Press, 2003.

———. "The City and the Sword: San Francisco and the Rise of the Metropolitan-Military Complex, 1919–1941." *Journal of American History* 65:4 (1979): 996–1020.

Lowi, Theodore J. *The End of Liberalism*. New York: Norton, 1979.

Lyons, William E., David Lowery, and Ruth Hoogland DeHoog. *The Politics of Dissatisfaction: Citizens, Services and Urban Institutions*. Armonk, New York: M. E. Sharpe, 1992.

Maass, Arthur. *Muddy Waters: The Army Engineers and the Nation's Rivers*. Cambridge: Harvard University Press, 1951.

McClain, Paula Denice. *Minority Group Influence: Agenda Setting, Formulation, and Public Policy*. Westport, Conn.: Greenwood Press, 1993.

McPhee, John. *The Control of Nature*. New York: Farrar, Straus, Giroux, 1989.

Moe, Terry M. *The Organization of Interests*. Chicago: University of Chicago Press, 1980.

Moeller, Beverly. *Phil Swing and Boulder Dam*. Berkeley: University of California Press, 1971.

Munkirs, John R. *The Transformation of American Capitalism: From Competitive Market Structures to Centralized Private Sector Planning*. Armonk, New York: M. E. Sharpe, 1985.

Myers, William A. *River of Controversy: A Review of the Involvement of the Southern California Edison Co. and Its Predecessors in the Development of the Colorado River, 1902–1942*. [Rosemead, Calif.]: Southern California Edison, 1982.

Nadeau, Remi A. *City Makers: The Story of Southern California's First Boom, 1868–1876*. Costa Mesa, Calif.: Trans-Anglo Books, 1965.

Nash, Gerald D. *The American West in the Twentieth Century: A Short History of an Urban Oasis*. Albuquerque: University of New Mexico Press, 1977.

———. *The American West Transformed: The Impact of the Second World War*. Bloomington: Indiana University Press, 1985.

———. *The Crucial Era: The Great Depression and World War II, 1929–1945*. New York: St. Martin's Press, 1992.

———. *The Federal Landscape: An Economic History of the Twentieth Century West*. Tucson: University of Arizona Press, 1999.

———. *United States Oil Policy, 1890–1964*. Pittsburgh: University of Pittsburgh Press, 1968.

———. *World War II and the West: Reshaping the Economy*. Lincoln: University of Nebraska Press, 1990.

Nash, Roderick. *Wilderness and the American Mind*. New Haven: Yale University Press, 1967.

Nicolaides, Becky. *My Blue Heaven: Life and Politics in Working-Class Suburbs of Los Angeles, 1920–1965*. Chicago: University of Chicago Press, 2002.

Niemi, Richard G., John E. Mueller, and Tom W. Smith. *Trends in Public Opinion: A Compendium of Survey Data*. New York: Greenwood Press, 1989.

Nye, David E. *American Technological Sublime*. Cambridge, Mass.: MIT Press, 1994.

Olien, Roger M., and Diana Davids Olien. *Oil and Ideology: The Cultural Creation of the American Petroleum Industry*. Chapel Hill: University of North Carolina Press, 1999.

Olson, Rueul Leslie. "The Colorado River Compact." Ph.D. diss., Harvard University, 1926.

Orsi, Jared. *Hazardous Metropolis: Flooding and Urban Ecology in Los Angeles*. Berkeley: University of California Press, 2004.

Ovnick, Merry. *Los Angeles: The End of the Rainbow*. Los Angeles: Balcony Press, 1994.

Pisani, Donald. *From Family Farm to Agribusiness: The Irrigation Crusade in California and the West, 1850–1931*. Berkeley: University of California Press, 1984.

———. *The Reclamation Bureau, National Water Policy, and the West, 1902–1935*. Berkeley: University of California Press, 2002.

———. *Water and American Government: The Reclamation Bureau, National Water Policy, and the West, 1902–1935*. Berkeley: University of California Press, 2002.

Platt, Harold L. "Invisible Gases: Smoke, Gender, and the Redefinition of Environmental Policy in Chicago, 1900–1920." *Planning Perspectives* 10:1 (1995): 67–97.

Pollock, Ivan L. *History of Economic Legislation in Iowa*. Iowa City: State Historical Society of Iowa, 1918.

Quam-Wickham, Nancy. "Cities Sacrificed on the Altar of Oil: Popular Opposition to Oil Development in 1920s Los Angeles." *Environmental History* 3:2 (1998): 189–209.

Radford, Gail. "From Municipal Socialism to Public Authorities: Institutional Factors in Shaping American Public Enterprise." *Journal of American History* 90:3 (2003): 863–90.

Raymond, Leigh. "Localism in Environmental Policy: New Insights from an Old Case." *Policy Science* 35 (2002): 179–201

Reisner, Marc. *Cadillac Desert: The American West and Its Disappearing Water*. New York: Viking Press, 1986.

Reuss, Martin "The Pick Sloan Plan." *Builders and Fighters: U.S. Army Engineers in World War II*. Publication EP 870-1-42. Washington: Army Corps of Engineers, 1992. ⟨http://www.usace.army.mil/publications/eng-pamphlets/ep870-1-42/⟩.

———, ed. *Water Resources Administration in the United States: Policy, Practice, and Emerging Issues*. East Lansing: Michigan State University Press, 1993.

Righter, Robert W. *The Battle over Hetch Hetchy: America's Most Controversial Dam and the Birth of Modern Environmentalism*. New York: Oxford University Press, 2005.

Rogers, Peter. *America's Water: Federal Roles and Responsibilities*. Cambridge, Mass.: MIT Press, 1993.

Rolle, Andrew F. *Los Angeles: From Pueblo to City of the Future*. San Francisco: MTL, 1995.

Rose, Mark. "Getting the Interstate System Built: Road Engineers and the Implementation of Public Policy, 1955–1985." *Journal of Policy History* 2:1 (1990): 23–55.

Rosen, Christine Miesner. "Businessmen against Pollution in Late Nineteenth Century Chicago." *Business History Review* 69 (1995): 351–97.

Sabin, Paul. *Crude Politics: The California Oil Market, 1900–1940*. Berkeley: University of California Press, 2005.

Schmitt, Peter. *Back to Nature: The Arcadian Myth in Urban America*. New York: Oxford University Press, 1969.

Seely, Bruce. *Building the American Highway System: Engineers as Policy Makers*. Philadelphia: Temple University Press, 1987.

Shaffer, Marguerite. "Seeing American First: The Search for Identity in the Tourist Landscape." In *Seeing and Being Seen: Tourism in the American West*, edited by David M. Wrobel and Patrick T. Long, 165–93. Lawrence: University Press of Kansas, 2001.

Sides, Josh. *L.A. City Limits: African American Los Angeles from the Great Depression to the Present*. Berkeley: University of California Press, 2003.

Simon, Rita J. *Public Opinion in America, 1936–1970*. Chicago: Rand McNally College Publishing Co., 1974.

Sitton, Tom. *John Randolph Haynes, California Progressive*. Stanford, Calif.: Stanford University Press, 1992).

———. *Los Angeles Transformed: Fletcher Bowron's Urban Reform Revival, 1938–1953*. Albuquerque: University of New Mexico Press, 2005.

Smith, Zacharay A. *Interest Group Interaction and Groundwater Policy Formation in the Southwest*. Lanham, Md.: University Press of America, 1985.

Starr, Kevin. *Embattled Dreams: California in War and Peace, 1940–1950*. New York: Oxford University Press, 2002.

Stegner, Wallace. *Beyond the Hundredth Meridian: John Wesley Powell and the Second Opening of the West*. Boston: Houghton Mifflin Co., 1954.

Still, Mark Sumner. "'Fighting Bob' Shuler: Fundamentalist and Reformer." Ph.D. diss., Claremont Graduate School, 1988.

Stine, Jeffrey K. *Mixing the Waters: Environment, Politics, and the Building of the Tennessee-Tombigbee Waterway*. Akron, Ohio: University of Akron Press, 1993.

Stover, Carl W., and Jerry L. Coffman. *Seismicity of the United States, 1568–1989.* U.S. Geological Survey Professional Paper 1527. Washington, D.C.: GPO, 1993.

Stradling, David. "Dirty Work and Clean Air: Locomotive Firemen, Environmental Activists, and Stories of Conflict." *Journal of Urban History* 28:1 (2001): 35–54.

———. *Smokestacks and Progressives: Environmentalists, Engineers, and Air Quality in America.* Baltimore: Johns Hopkins University Press, 1999.

Stradling, David, and Richard Stradling. "Perceptions of the Burning River: Deindustrialization and Cleveland's Cuyahoga River." *Environmental History* 13:3 (2008): 515–35.

Tygiel, Jules. *The Great Los Angeles Oil Swindle: Oil, Stocks and Scandal during the Roaring Twenties.* New York: Oxford University Press, 1994.

Verge, Arthur C. *Paradise Transformed: Los Angeles during the Second World War.* Dubuque, Iowa: Kendall/Hunt Publishing Co., 1993.

Vietor, Richard H. K. *Energy Policy in America since 1945: A Study of Business-Government Relations.* New York: Cambridge University Press, 1984.

Walter, Jack L. "A Critique of the Elitist Theory of Democracy." *American Political Science Review* 60 (1955): 285–95.

Walton, John. *Western Times and Water Wars: State, Culture and Rebellion in California.* Berkeley: University of California Press, 1992.

Warren, Louis S. *The Hunter's Game: Poachers and Conservationists in Twentieth Century America.* New Haven: Yale University Press, 1997.

Webb, LaVarr G. "How the West Hungers for Federal Land." *Business and Society Review* 37 (1980–81): 12–17.

Wild, H. Mark. *Street Meeting: Multiethnic Neighborhoods in Early Twentieth Century Los Angeles.* Berkeley: University of California Press, 2005.

Wille, Lois. *Forever Open, Clear, and Free: The Struggle for Chicago's Lakefront.* Chicago: University of Chicago Press, 1991.

Williams, James. *Energy and the Making of Modern California.* Akron, Ohio: University of Akron Press, 1997.

Winters, Donald L. "Ambiguity and Agricultural Policy: Henry Cantwell Wallace as Secretary of Agriculture." *Agricultural History* 64:2 (1990): 191–98.

Wolfson, Adam. "Public Interest Lost?" *Daedalus* 136:4 (2007): 20–29.

Worster, Donald. *Rivers of Empire: Water, Aridity, and the Growth of the American West.* New York: Oxford University Press, 1985.

Yergin, Daniel. *The Prize: The Epic Quest for Oil, Money, and Power.* New York: Simon and Schuster, 1991.

Young, Betty Lou. *Our First Century: the Los Angeles Athletic Club 1880–1980.* Los Angeles: Los Angeles Athletic Club Press, 1979.

Zimmerman, Tom. "Paradise Promoted: Boosterism and the Los Angeles Chamber of Commerce." *California History* 64:1 (1985): 22–33.

INDEX

AFL. *See* American Federation of Labor

African Americans, 10, 19–20, 46–49, 195 (n. 101)

Agenda setting, 2–3, 10, 13, 19, 30, 42–43, 49–50, 52–55, 58–66, 78, 85–90, 116, 144–47, 160–65

Agriculture, 7, 8, 104, 117, 120–22, 125, 128–30, 134, 136–37, 156–57, 160–62, 165–67, 170–72, 218 (n. 139); large-scale vs. small-scale/subsistence, 11, 83, 218 (n. 139); surpluses/overproduction, 134, 139, 151, 154–55, 158, 166. *See also* Farmers

Ainsworth, Ed, 202 (n. 75), 203 (nn. 82, 84)

Air pollution, 6, 8, 10–11, 74, 80, 86, 196 (n. 3); and agriculture, 64, 81; and automobiles and buses, 10–11, 55, 58, 64, 80, 201 (n. 58), 204 (n. 94); and backyard incinerators, 60, 64, 68–69, 75, 77, 80, 204 (n. 94); causes of, debates about, 10–11, 56–57, 61–63, 68, 71, 74–75; causes of, science of, 10–11, 71, 74–76, 204 (n. 94); communities affected by, 56–59, 66–67; complaints about, 10–11, 52, 58, 65, 70, 75–77, 80; crisis of 1943, 52, 55–58; and dumps and municipal incinerators, 62, 64, 68, 75, 77; and industry, 52, 54–60, 62–65, 67–70, 71–76, 79, 80, 200 (n. 53), 203 (n. 92), 204 (n. 94), 206 (n. 192); and oil refining, 59, 62, 67, 70, 206 (n. 192); and public health, 54, 69, 72, 73; and war production, 56–57, 61, 65, 200 (n. 53)

—reduction equipment: investments in, 57, 71, 73–74, 78; regulations requiring, 57, 63, 69–70, 73–74; technologies, 55, 57, 61, 69, 71, 72, 74, 76

—regulation of, 54–56, 61–66, 71–73, 197 (n. 5), 199 (n. 47), 201 (n. 58); barriers to, 68–69 (*see also* War production); business influence on, 52–54, 59–66, 180, 196 (n. 3); industry opposition to, 58, 67, 69, 73–74, 200 (n. 53), 203 (n. 92); public demand for, 59, 61, 67, 206 (n. 127); regional management of, 10, 57–70; voluntary, by business and industry, 10–11, 52–54, 71–72, 81–82, 196 (n. 3). *See also* Los Angeles Chamber of Commerce: Air Pollution Control Committee; Los Angeles Chamber of Commerce: Smoke and Fumes Committee; Los Angeles County, Calif.—Air Pollution Control District; Pendleton, Morris B.

Air Pollution Foundation, 80, 206 (n. 127), 206 (n. 129)

Alexander, Frank L., 202 (n. 74), 203 (n. 92)

Alexander, Titus, 47–48

All-American Canal, 118, 121, 125, 143. *See also* Imperial Irrigation District

Altadena, Calif., 56, 58–59, 60, 79

Altadena Property Owners League (APOL), 13, 58–64, 79–80

American Federation of Labor (AFL), 147, 161, 232 (n. 41)

American Legion, 139
American Public Power Association, 162
American Shore and Beach Preservation Association, 17
American Society of Civil Engineers, 163, 209 (n. 25), 229 (n. 131), 232–33 (n. 50)
American Water Works Association, 156, 231 (n. 21)
Angeles National Forest, 90–91, 209 (n. 19)
Anti-communism, 5, 174, 176, 183. *See also* Red-baiting
Anti-government politics, 8, 120, 171–74
Anti-government sentiment. *See* Political rhetoric
Anti-industry sentiment. *See* Political rhetoric
Anti-Whittier Narrows Dam Association, 102, 105, 107, 109–10, 115, 216 (n. 99), 217 (n. 115)
APCD. *See* Los Angeles County, Calif.—Air Pollution Control District
APOL. *See* Altadena Property Owners League
Aquifers. *See* Groundwater
Arcadia, Calif., 214 (n. 77)
Arizona, 11, 120, 122–25, 131, 133–38, 140–45, 157, 173, 182–84, 219 (n. 1), 227 (n. 108), 228 (n. 121), 234–35 (n. 68). *See also* Colorado River: water rights
Ashurst, Henry F., 124, 134, 140–43, 228 (n. 58)
Asian Americans, 46
Assembly Bill No. 1, 67, 70, 73, 201 (n. 58)
Audubon Society, 103–4, 110, 113
Automobile Club of Southern California, 67, 79, 200 (n. 52), 201 (n. 58), 206 (n. 131)

Automobiles, 7, 8, 10, 52, 55, 60, 80, 204 (n. 94)
Azusa, Calif., 200 (n. 53), 213 (n. 62)

Baker, Donald, 90
Beach clubs, 17, 19, 26, 29, 30–35, 42, 44, 46–49, 146, 181, 191 (nn. 44, 49); building projects and public access, 32–35, 48–49
Beach communities, 21, 26, 28, 31, 34, 38, 41, 42, 44–46, 47–49, 58, 107, 189 (n. 16), 190 (n. 35), 195 (n. 100), 200 (nn. 52, 53), 213 (n. 77), 215 (n. 93), 216 (n. 106)
Beaches: attitudes toward, 9–10, 17–20, 28–30, 35–37, 49–50, 192 (n. 60); commercial development of, 19, 28, 32–37, 180 (*see also* Oil drilling); erosion and erosion-prevention structures, 19, 33, 37–42, 91, 191, 193 (n. 65); facilities on, 19, 31, 36, 37–38; geologic and hydrologic processes on, 19, 38, 193 (n. 65); private, 8, 17, 20, 30–37, 42, 45, 50; and property values, 19, 35, 37–39, 42, 45, 49, 50; public, 9–10, 17–20, 40, 49, 151; public ownership and public beach movement, 10, 17, 19–20, 25, 28, 32–34, 37–46, 47–49, 181; racial segregation of, 10, 19, 46–49 (*see also* Segregation); and real estate interests, 10, 17, 19, 30–33, 34, 37, 40–46, 49, 50, 181 (*see also* Shoreline Planning Association); and water pollution, 19, 37, 39–41, 42, 50 (*see also* Oil drilling: dangers and nuisances from)
Beckman, Arnold O., 78, 81
Bell, Alphonzo, 103, 214 (n. 86)
Bell, Calif., 66, 200 (n. 52)
Bell, John A., 96–98, 100, 107, 113, 211–12 (n. 53), 212 (n. 57)
Beverly Hills, Calif., 66

Black Canyon of the Colorado River, 117, 219 (n. 1)
Bonds and bond funds, 35, 90, 92, 107, 195 (n. 98), 209–10 (n. 29), 220 (n. 7)
Booms (explosive growth), 8, 17, 88, 121; industrial, 8, 88; oil, 17, 22, 25, 26, 88, 189 (n. 13); population, 3, 8, 17, 37, 39, 46, 55, 88, 150; real estate, 17, 36, 40, 88, 120–21; World War II, 55, 102, 150. *See also* New residents; War production
Boosters, 7, 8, 19, 30, 46, 60, 70, 161, 172, 188 (n. 1)
Boulder Canyon Dam. *See* Boulder Dam
Boulder Canyon Dam Act, 120–28, 131–45, 146, 148, 183, 226 (n. 88), 228 (nn. 120, 121), 229 (n. 131); Senate filibusters of, 120, 133–34, 137–43
Boulder Dam, 7, 11–12, 83, 92, 117–47, 148, 150, 152, 158, 163, 165, 171, 182–84, 188 (n. 19), 210 (n. 31); and hydro-electric power, 11, 121, 123, 125, 126–27, 129, 130–33, 133–34, 144–47. *See also* Colorado River: water rights; Water Power Act of 1920
Bowron, Fletcher, 56–58, 60–61, 64–65, 69, 198 (n. 15)
Brinkley, Alan, 5, 186 (n. 6)
Bruce's Beach (Manhattan Beach, Calif.), 47
Burgess, Paul S., 156–57, 166–67, 170
Business groups, 10, 14, 17, 34, 69, 80–81, 110, 124, 140, 156, 162–64, 172–73, 191 (n. 42), 206 (nn. 127, 129), 231 (n. 21); affecting federal policy, 2, 4, 5–6, 11–12, 13, 85–87, 142, 146–47, 151, 178–84; drafting legislation, 2, 10, 38, 41–43, 50, 52, 55, 63–64, 78, 110, 180–81; influence in local politics, 1, 2, 4–8, 9–12, 12–14, 20, 41–44, 49–51, 52–53, 60–61, 70–71, 80–82, 119, 178–84; providing research reports and studies, 2, 10, 41–43, 52, 60, 61, 78, 80, 180 (*see also* Reports and studies); supporting local officials, 1, 2, 10, 52, 54, 65–66, 77–78, 80–83; underhanded tactics in politics, 120, 132, 214 (n. 86); undermining public confidence in government, 120, 128–29, 131–33, 142–44, 146–47, 150, 183 (*see also* Private enterprise); as voice of the public, 1–4, 12–13, 20, 30, 40–41, 49–51, 85–87, 119–20, 146, 151, 162–63, 174, 179–82, 184, 187 (n. 7) (*see also* Public opinion—voice or representative of). *See also* Agenda setting; Los Angeles Chamber of Commerce; Realty boards; Shoreline Planning Association
Butadiene, 56–57, 62, 196 (n. 2)

California, 2, 77; Board of Health, 19, 39–40; Coastal Commission, 195 (n. 99); Division of Water Resources, 89, 90, 108; northern, 8, 122; Park Commission, 28, 34, 43; Railroad Commission, 48; Southern, 6, 9, 11, 20, 32, 33, 41, 55, 60, 68, 80, 81, 100, 117, 119, 122, 125, 134, 142, 144, 173, 175, 183, 191 (n. 44), 195 (n. 99), 221 (n. 11), 222 (n. 24), 224 (n. 56); Supreme Court, 92. *See also* California Legislature
California Beaches Association, 41
California Development Company, 120–21, 123
California Institute of Technology. *See* Caltech
California Legislature, 24–25, 43, 67, 70, 77, 81, 134–35; Senate, 43
—Assembly, 41, 67, 72, 94 (*see also* Assembly Bill No. 1); Interim Committee on Water and Air Pollution, 71–76, 203 (n. 84), 204 (n. 94) (*see also* Dickey, Randall F.)
Caltech, 70, 74, 75–78, 204 (n. 94)

INDEX   253

Cameron, Ralph H., 134, 140
Capitalism, 127, 156, 173. *See also* Red-baiting
Case study method, 5, 9, 12–13, 20, 100, 119, 180
Central Arizona Project, 144, 173, 234 (n. 71)
Central Newport Beach Community Association, 45
Central Valley Project, 165
Chambers of commerce, 1–4, 7, 10, 28–31, 34, 40, 41, 48, 50, 67, 77, 81, 85, 99–100, 104, 124, 139–40, 147, 161, 200 (n. 52), 207 (n. 4), 218 (n. 138). *See also* El Monte Chamber of Commerce; Long Beach Chamber of Commerce; Los Angeles Chamber of Commerce; U.S. Chamber of Commerce, Natural Resouces Committee
Chandler, Harry, 135
Chandler, Norman, 81, 202 (n. 75)
Chapman, Oscar, 159
Check dams. *See* Flood control structures
Chicago, Ill., 32, 54, 63, 196 (n. 3)
Cincinnati, Ohio, 54
CIO. *See* Congress of Industrial Organizations
Citizen groups. *See* Interest groups
Citizens Anti-Smog Action Committee, 13, 18, 200 (n. 52)
Citizens' Manpower Committee, 60, 198–99 (n. 27)
Clark, Hal R., 48–49
Class conflicts and rhetoric, 5–6, 13, 30–31, 85, 95, 103, 109, 111, 188 (n. 2), 237 (n. 7). *See also* Farmers; Rural vs. urban; Unions
Clean Air Act of 1970, 55
Cleveland, Dan, 102–3
Cold War, 5, 20, 157, 164, 171–76, 182, 236–37 (n. 5). *See also* Red-baiting

Colorado, 123, 125, 139, 141, 143, 225 (n. 67)
Colorado Council of Sportsmen, 161, 164
Colorado River, 11, 117–47, 148, 157–58, 161–62, 164, 173, 182–83, 210 (n. 31), 232 (n. 49), 234 (n. 71); and hydroelectric power, 123, 136, 144–46 (*see also* Southern California Edison); and irrigation, 117, 120–22, 123, 125, 127–28, 135–37, 142, 145, 148; Lower Basin, 123–24, 134–35, 141 (*see also* Arizona; California; Nevada); Upper Basin, 123, 133, 134, 135 (*see also* Colorado; New Mexico; Upper Colorado River Commission; Utah; Wyoming); water rights, 122–25, 133–44, 145, 228 (n. 120). *See also* Boulder Dam
Colorado River Aqueduct, 210 (n. 31)
Colorado River Commission, 123–24, 135, 144. *See also* Colorado River Compact
Colorado River Compact, 123–25, 133–35, 138, 141, 142, 219 (n. 1), 228 (n. 121)
Columbia River, 158–59, 160–61, 232 (n. 49)
Columbia Valley Authority, 160–61
Competition: between communities or regions, 83, 94–95, 98–101, 108–9, 111–12, 120, 122–25, 133–36, 140–44, 150, 155, 166–67, 170–71 (*see also* Economic decentralization); between government agencies, 150–51, 152–55, 158–59, 160, 164, 167–69, 178–79; within industry, 22, 24, 25, 28–29, 154–55, 175, 176, 181; between interest groups, 10–11, 58–62, 78–82, 85–87, 94–95, 103–5, 106–7, 109, 111–12, 113–14, 161–65, 179–84; between old and new businesses, 32–33, 83, 98, 101
Comprehensive plans: and beach acquisition, 19, 40, 43–46, 49; and

flood control, 11, 85, 87–92, 96, 97; and water resources, 12, 50, 143, 146–47, 148, 151, 157, 171–74, 175, 203 (n. 17). *See also* Multiple-purpose dams; River basin planning
Compton, Calif., 104, 200 (n. 52), 218 (n. 138)
Coney Island, N.Y., 193 (n. 65)
Congress. *See* U.S. Congress
Congress of Industrial Organizations (CIO), 160–62, 164, 196 (n. 2)
Conservation, 127, 156, 160–65, 169. *See also* Oil conservation; Water conservation
Cooke, Morris, 156–58, 162, 171, 174, 175. *See also* President's Water Resources Policy Commission
Coolidge, Calvin, 133–34, 138, 140, 141, 144, 146, 223 (n. 36), 224 (n. 56), 227 (n. 104)
Cooperation: business-government, 11–12, 14, 19, 34–35, 49, 64–66, 77–78, 80–82, 120, 144–47, 150, 171–74, 183; intergovernmental, 5, 6–7, 8, 19, 43–46
Corruption, 24, 73, 76, 88, 101, 103, 128–30, 131–32, 134, 146, 213–14 (n. 77)
Cost-benefit analysis, 11, 108–9, 113, 151, 157, 167–68; and nonreimbursable benefits, 157, 167–71, 175; variations between agencies, 157, 168–69
Costs (monetary): in decision making, 87, 91, 101, 104, 108, 113, 131, 145; of public works, 32, 46, 68, 91, 108, 121, 153–54. *See also* Cost-benefit analysis; Irrigation subsidy
Crawford, Roscoe C., 105
Cyanamid, 128–29, 200 (n. 53), 223 (n. 36)

Daugherty, Robert L., 69–70
Davis, Arthur Powell, 121, 158

Deaths: caused by air pollution, 68, 74, 197 (n. 6); caused by flooding, 91, 220 (n. 7)
Debris basins. *See* Flood control structures
Democracy: functioning of, 9, 49–50, 80–82, 87, 175, 177, 179, 182–83; guaranteeing/protecting, 4, 13, 45, 151, 175, 177, 182; images of, 1, 162, 175, 177; threats to, 1, 13, 45, 127, 150, 162, 174–77. *See also* Private enterprise
Deverell, William, 6
Dewey, Bradley, 57
Dickey, Randall F., 71–78, 106, 203 (n. 85). *See also* California Legislature: Assembly Interim Committee on Water and Air Pollution
Donora, Penn., 68, 197 (n. 6)
Downey, Calif., 109
Duarte, Calif., 83, 213 (n. 62)

Earthquakes, 39, 111, 218 (n. 131)
East Bay Municipal Utility District, 230 (n. 17)
Eaton, Charles A., 137, 139
Eaton, Eugene C., 84–90, 92, 210 (n. 31), 217 (n. 115)
Eckman, Arthur W., 48
Economic decentralization, 155, 176, 220 (n. 39). *See also* Competition: between communities or regions
Economic development, 6–7, 29, 30, 32. *See also* Federal government: projects for local development
Efficiency and inefficiency in government, 150–55, 159, 164, 169–71, 174–79
Eisenhower, Dwight D., 29
Electricity. *See* Power
El Monte, Calif., 85, 94, 96–112, 113–16, 179, 184, 200 (n. 52), 207 (n. 1), 212 (n. 57), 213–14 (n. 77), 219–20 (n. 139); area school districts, 94,

102, 104, 107, 212 (n. 57); city officials, 94, 213–14 (n. 77)
El Monte Chamber of Commerce, 94, 102–4, 105, 115. *See also* Anti-Whittier Narrows Dam Association
El Monte Citizens Flood Control Committee, 13, 85, 94–102, 105, 115
Emergency Recovery Act, 93, 210 (n. 37)
Engineering, 38, 88, 97–98, 108, 111, 113–14, 139, 141–42, 161, 211–12 (n. 53), 220 (n. 2)
Engineers, 38, 63, 70, 87, 91, 108, 117, 226 (n. 88); city or county, 62, 81, 87–90, 92, 94, 100, 104–5, 108, 199 (n. 47), 208 (n. 7), 213 (n. 62), 217 (nn. 115, 125) (*see also* Los Angeles County, Calif.—Flood Control District); consulting, 87, 90, 96–98 (*see also* Bell, John A.; Reagan, James W.; Safley, F. J.); organizations of, 90–92, 125, 139, 162, 163, 176, 197 (n. 6), 209 (n. 25), 229 (n. 131), 232–33 (n. 50). *See also* Technical expertise; U.S. Army Corps of Engineers
Engineers Joint Council, 162, 163, 232–33 (n. 50)
Environmental movement, 13–14, 160–61, 164–65, 188 (n. 21)
Environmental problems and public demand for government action, 20–28, 32–33, 37–40, 52, 55–57, 79–80, 87, 91, 121, 128–29, 138, 153

Fairbanks, Douglas, estate of, 194 (n. 79)
Fall, Albert B., 32
Farmers, 1, 62, 64, 83, 86, 115, 121, 129, 134, 153, 158, 165, 167–68, 170–71, 173, 223 (n. 36)
Farming and farms. *See* Agriculture
Federal agencies, 2, 5, 160–65; criticism of, 85, 96–97, 129, 131–32, 152, 153–55, 160–62, 169; expansion of, 10, 28–29, 150–51, 152–53. *See also* U.S. Army Corps of Engineers; U.S. Bureau of Reclamation
Federal government: and local politics, 2, 11, 85–87, 97–98, 100–102, 113–16, 179–80; and local priorities, 2, 4, 6–7, 11, 12–13, 86–87, 90–92, 151, 179–80, 207 (n. 4), 217 (n. 115); projects for local development, 2, 4, 6–7, 8, 11–12, 39, 87–88, 90–92, 96, 120–22, 124–25, 143, 145, 150, 170–77, 182–83, 188 (n. 1), 207 (n. 1), 215 (n. 93); reinforcing local power structures, 4, 5, 9, 11, 13, 64, 85–87, 101–2, 106–9, 113–16, 151, 179–80; retrenchment of, 5, 12–13, 42, 115–16, 148–51, 237 (n. 7)
Federal Inter-Agency River Basin Committee, 153
Federal power: expansion of, 28–28, 86, 114–15, 119, 120, 127–28, 133, 136, 146–47, 159–60; opposition to, 4, 10, 12–13, 14–15, 20, 87, 113–16, 127, 128–33, 134, 136–38, 142, 146–47, 148–51, 159–60, 162–63, 171–77, 178, 211 (n. 47), 237 (n. 7); and power balance between government and business, 4, 5, 14, 20, 146–47, 148, 152, 159, 171–74, 178–89. *See also* Political rhetoric
Federal Power Commission, 130, 132, 156
Federal Subsistence Homesteads Corporation, 218–19 (n. 139)
Federal Trade Commission, 24, 132
Filibusters. *See* Boulder Canyon Dam Act: Senate filibusters of
Flamming, Douglas, 6, 195 (n. 101)
Flood control, 6, 11, 12, 13, 20, 38, 39, 50, 51, 117, 125, 133, 137, 138, 141, 145, 148, 151, 152–55, 168. *See also* Los Angeles County, Calif.—Flood Control District; Whittier Narrows Dam
Flood Control Act of 1936, 86, 88, 93, 168
Flood control basins. *See* Flood control structures

Flood control structures, 38, 83, 88, 104–5, 110, 208 (n. 7); check dams, mountain dams, and debris basins, 38, 87, 88, 90–91, 94, 104–5, 110, 208 (nn. 5, 7); design debates about, 11, 85, 87–88, 90, 92, 93, 96–97, 100–101, 104–5, 106–9, 153–54, 207 (n. 1), 208 (n. 7), 211 (nn. 47, 53); flood control basins and spreading grounds, 38, 83, 85, 87, 89–90, 93–94, 97–98, 103–5, 108, 110–15, 208 (n. 7), 210 (n. 37), 213 (n. 62); relative costs of, 87, 96, 101, 103–4, 108, 113–14; river channelization and levees, 6, 8, 38, 85, 86, 87–88, 91–94, 96–97, 101, 104, 105, 107–9, 111–12, 113, 116, 153, 207 (n. 1), 208 (nn. 5, 7), 211 (nn. 47, 53), 215 (n. 93)

Floods, 86, 91, 94, 117, 121, 138, 153, 226 (n. 88); effects of urban development on, 8, 88, 97

Fogelson, Robert, 6, 188 (n. 1)

Foothill Cities Smog Abatement Committee, 67

Ford, Henry, 129, 223 (n. 36)

Ford, John Anson, 28, 69

Galambos, Louis, 5, 186 (n. 6)

Garvey, Richard, 213 (n. 76)

Garvey Acres, Calif., 101, 105, 110, 111–12, 115–16, 213 (n. 76)

General Chemical Company, 200 (n. 53)

Geologists, 67, 90. *See also* Engineers

Geology and hydrology: of beaches, 38, 193 (n. 65); of Whittier Narrows and Los Angeles basin, 83, 88

Gila River, 143

Glen Canyon, 125, 130, 222 (n. 27)

Glendale, 66, 89 (ill.), 200 (n. 52)

Grand Coulee Dam, 165

Graves, Sidney, 88

Great Depression, 4, 5, 8, 29, 42–43, 90, 92, 174, 218–19 (n. 139). *See also* New Deal

Groundwater, 8, 83, 104, 123, 166; recharge of, 87, 89–90, 93. *See also* Water conservation

Haagen-Smit, A. J., 74, 204 (n. 94), 205 (n. 109)

Hahn, Kenneth, 75

Hansen Flood Control Basin, 93, 210 (n. 37)

Harding, Warren G., 123, 146

Hawthorne, Calif., 104, 200 (n. 52)

Hayden, Carl, 136–37, 140–43, 222 (n. 27), 228 (n. 121), 233–34 (n. 68)

Haynes, John, R., 7, 122, 139, 145

Hearst, William Randolph, 139

Hedger, Harold E., 100, 108, 217 (n. 125)

Hermosa Beach, Calif., 28, 31, 34, 41, 42, 45, 213–14 (n. 77); City Council 34, 213–14 (n. 77)

Hermosa Beach Junior Chamber of Commerce, 34, 191 (n. 42)

Hetch Hetchy, 230 (n. 17)

Hichborn, Franklin, 132, 224 (n. 52)

Hise, Greg, 6, 187 (n. 11)

Hjelte, George, 42

Homeowners. *See* Property owners

Home rule, 12, 46, 114. *See also* Local control and autonomy

Hoover, Herbert, 123, 133, 138, 142, 144–45, 146, 219 (n. 1), 223 (n. 36)

Hoover Dam. *See* Boulder Dam

Hoult, Lois C., 109

Hoult, Thomas F., 109, 207 (n. 1), 212 (n. 57)

Huntington Beach, Calif., 21–22, 24, 26, 31, 48–49, 189 (nn. 13, 16), 190 (n. 35)

Hydroelectric power. *See* Boulder Dam: and hydroelectric power; Power

Hyperion Point, 26, 28, 39–40, 47–48, 193 (n. 68)

INDEX 257

Ickes, Harold L., 10, 29, 189 (n. 20), 219 (n. 1)
Imperial Irrigation District, 117, 121–22, 136, 144, 145, 148, 221 (n. 11)
Imperial Valley, Calif., 11, 117, 120–23, 135, 138, 140, 141, 144, 220 (n. 3), 226 (n. 85)
Incinerators. *See* Air pollution
Indian reservations. *See* Native Americans
Industry, growth of, 2–4, 8, 17, 19–21, 55–56, 165–67. *See also* Booms; Economic development
Inkwell Beach (Santa Monica, Calif.), 47
Interest groups, 1–4, 10–11, 13–14, 17, 18, 30–31, 41–43, 45, 47, 58–64, 67, 70, 76–77, 79–80, 81, 85–86, 94–105, 107, 109–11, 115–16, 124, 139, 161–64, 169, 179–80, 191 (n. 49), 200 (n. 52), 201 (n. 58), 206 (n. 127), 209 (nn. 17, 29), 214 (n. 79), 216 (n. 99), 217 (n. 115); balancing power of business, 1–5, 14, 113, 114, 160–65; late entry into policy debates, 2–3, 13, 54, 80–81, 187 (n. 7). *See also* Agenda setting; Business groups; Competition: between interest groups; Unions
Interstate Commission on the Delaware River Basin, 169–70
Irrigation, 11, 120–22, 123, 125, 183. *See also* Colorado River: and irrigation; President's Water Resources Policy Commission: and irrigation
Irrigation companies: and Colorado River, 117, 120–22; in Los Angeles area, 83, 88–89, 101–2, 103–4, 110
Irrigation subsidy, 11–12, 117, 121, 127–28, 145, 158, 165–67, 168–69, 170–71, 173
Isaak Walton League, 160–62, 164, 169

Jeffers, William M., 67, 70, 79, 205 (n. 109)

Jim Crow, 46–47. *See also* Segregation
Johnson, Hiram, 121–22, 126 (ill.), 129, 133, 135, 138–43, 145. *See also* Boulder Canyon Dam Act
Jones, Lewis Webster, 156–57
Jones State Beach, N.Y., 35, 192 (n. 58)

Kennedy, Harold W., 67, 205 (n. 109)
King, William H., 133–34, 141
Knowland, William, 110
Koppes, Clayton, 5, 236–37 (n. 5)
Korean War, 174

LAACC. *See* Los Angeles Chamber of Commerce
Labor, 7, 9, 58, 60, 62, 68, 91, 107, 130, 147, 156, 160–61, 164, 171, 186 (nn. 5, 6), 196 (n. 2), 197 (n. 5), 198 (n. 27), 210 (n. 37), 218–19 (n. 139), 232 (n. 41). *See also* Unions
La Cañada, Calif., 91, 209 (n. 24)
LACFCD. *See* Los Angeles County, Calif.—Flood Control District
LACSFC. *See* Los Angeles County, Calif.: Smoke and Fumes Commission
La Follette, Robert M., 24
Land grants, Spanish and Mexican, 17, 32
Larson, Gordon, 71, 73, 74–77, 204 (n. 94)
League of California Cities, 67, 77, 81
Leatherwood, Elmer O., 124, 137, 138, 139
Legitimacy, political. *See* Political legitimacy
Levees. *See* Flood control structures
Local control and autonomy, 4, 8, 12, 14–15, 44, 45–46, 72, 77–78, 114–15, 162–64, 171–77, 178, 180, 184
Local interests. *See* U.S. Army Corps of Engineers

Local politics influencing federal
  policy, 1–2, 4, 5, 6, 9, 11–14, 15, 85–87,
  113–16, 151
Lockheed Aircraft Company, 76, 206
  (n. 129)
Long Beach, Calif., 11, 21, 31, 33–34, 43,
  83, 85, 87–90, 92, 94, 98, 99–100, 101,
  104–9, 111–12, 113, 119, 140, 180, 209
  (n. 17), 215 (n. 93), 216 (n. 106), 218
  (n. 139), 221 (n. 11); Board of Water
  Commissioners, 90, 99–100; Harbor
  Commission, 104, 218 (n. 138)
Long Beach Chamber of Commerce,
  94, 100, 101, 107, 180
Lopez Flood Control Basin, 210 (n. 37)
Los Angeles, Calif. (city): Board of
  Public Service Commissioners, 122;
  City Council, 2, 10, 21, 26, 37, 42,
  43, 56–58, 70, 75, 76, 197 (n. 11), 201
  (n. 58), 220–21 (n. 8); Department
  of Playgrounds and Recreation,
  17, 40, 42, 191 (n. 44); Department
  of Public Works, 39, 193 (n. 68);
  Department of Water and Power, 9,
  122, 145, 156, 220–21 (n. 8); Health
  Department, 56, 75, 197 (n. 9), 198
  (n. 18); Planning Commission, 44;
  Playgrounds and Recreation Commission, 33, 35, 42, 191 (n. 44)
Los Angeles County, Calif.: Board of
  Supervisors, 28, 35, 42, 43, 45, 57–59,
  61–62, 63–65, 67, 69, 71, 75, 77–81, 87,
  88, 90–92, 96–98, 100–103, 108, 111,
  201 (n. 58), 203 (n. 85), 209 (n. 19),
  214 (nn. 79, 80); Department of
  Parks and Recreation, 191 (n. 44);
  Grand Jury, 62, 80–81, 88, 198 (n. 15),
  208 (n. 9); Health Department, 59,
  65, 79, 196 (n. 1) (see also Swartout,
  H. O.); Regional Planning Commission, 44, 45; Smoke and Fumes
  Commission (LACSFC), 58, 61–65
—Air Pollution Control District
  (APCD), 66–78, 87, 100, 180, 184;
  Citizens Smog Advisory Committee, 67, 70, 79, 205 (n. 109); criticism
  of, 68–78; groups in opposition to,
  10–11, 13, 18, 54, 55, 58–64, 67, 78–82,
  110, 205 (n. 116), 206 (n. 127); industrial permits, 69–71, 75–76, 77, 82
—Flood Control District (LACFCD),
  87–88, 90–92, 97, 107, 109, 111; criticism of, 87–88, 96. See also Comprehensive plans; U.S. Army Corps of
  Engineers; Whittier Narrows Dam
Los Angeles Airport, 103
Los Angeles Area Chamber of Commerce. See Los Angeles Chamber
  of Commerce
Los Angeles Athletic Club, 30–31, 42,
  191 (n. 49)
Los Angeles Chamber of Commerce,
  17, 47, 85, 175–76; and Air Pollution
  Control Committee, 77–78, 205
  (n. 116) (see also Beckman, Arnold
  O.); challenges to power of, 58–59,
  61, 70, 75, 78–80; drafting legislation, 2, 10, 52, 63–64, 78, 110, 180;
  Flood Control Committee, 108,
  207 (n. 1), 211 (n. 47); influence in
  local politics, 10–11, 52–53, 60–61,
  70–71, 80–82, 119; providing research
  reports and studies, 2, 10, 52, 60–61,
  78, 80; setting local priorities, 2, 10,
  59, 80; Smoke and Fumes Committee, 60–61, 64–66, 205 (n. 116)
  (see also Pendleton, Morris B.); as
  "special interest," 70–71, 75; supporting local officials, 10, 52, 54, 65–66,
  77–78, 80–83; as voice of the public,
  2–4, 6, 10–11, 52–53, 60–62, 63–66,
  77–78, 80–82
Los Angeles Engineering Council,
  90–92, 209 (n. 25)
Los Angeles General Hospital, 56, 197
  (n. 11)

INDEX   259

Los Angeles Harbor. *See* Port of Los Angeles
Los Angeles Realty Board, 10, 17, 181
Los Angeles River, 8, 85, 88, 89 (ill.), 93–94, 95 (ill.), 103, 104, 207 (n. 1), 211–12 (n. 53)
Los Angeles Taxpayers Association, 124
Los Angeles Times (newspaper), 6, 7, 29–30, 37, 45, 48, 50, 64, 69–70, 73, 74, 75, 81, 99–100, 102, 124, 126, 135, 138, 140, 183, 202 (n. 75), 203 (n. 82), 213 (n. 68), 214 (n. 86), 218–19 (n. 139), 225 (n. 65). *See also* Newspapers and periodicals
Louisiana, 29

Manhattan Beach, Calif., 28, 45, 47, 49, 58, 200 (nn. 52, 53)
Marshall, Robert Bradford, 230 (n. 17)
Mayer, Louis B., 42, 194 (n. 79)
McCabe, Louis, 67–72, 205 (n. 109)
Media and media coverage. *See* Newspapers and periodicals
Medical and doctors' groups, 74, 76, 80
Mellon, Andrew W., 128, 134, 223 (n. 36), 225 (n. 62)
Metropolitan Water District of Southern California, 92, 144
Mexico, 32, 121, 136, 141–42, 219 (n. 1), 220 (n. 4). *See also* Land grants
Minorities. *See* African Americans; Asian Americans; Native Americans; Race
Mississippi River, 86, 138, 226 (n. 88)
Missouri River, 152–54, 160, 232 (n. 49). *See also* Pick-Sloan Plan
Missouri Valley Authority, 154
Montebello, Calif., 109
Monterey Park, Calif., 80, 213 (n. 76)
Morris, Samuel B., 156–58, 166–67, 170, 175, 232 (n. 49), 234 (n. 71)

Mountain dams. *See* Flood control structures
Multiple-purpose dams, 10, 100, 117, 120–22, 127, 144–46, 152–55, 159, 165, 172. *See also* River basin planning
Muscle Shoals, Ala., 128–31, 138, 140, 142, 147, 182, 223 (nn. 36, 37)

National Defense Act of 1916, 128–29. *See also* Muscle Shoals, Ala.
National Electric Light Association, 182
National Industrial Recovery Act, 179
National Reclamation Association, 162, 164
National Resources Committee, 148 (ill.), 156, 158
National Resources Planning Board, 153, 156, 158, 160
National Smoke Abatement Week, 73
National Youth Administration, 42
Native Americans, 161–62, 232 (n. 49)
Navigable waterways and federal authority over rivers, 24, 86, 127
Needles, Calif., 131
Nevada, 11, 117, 120, 123, 133, 135–36, 140, 141–44, 166
New Deal, 8, 12, 13, 19, 39, 82, 90–93, 147, 150, 155–57, 160, 174, 179, 183, 210 (n. 37), 218 (n. 139), 236–37 (n. 5)
New Mexico, 123, 125, 143, 170–71, 173; Economic Development Commission, 170–71, 173
Newport Beach, Calif., 45, 48, 215 (n. 93)
New residents: interests vs. old residents' interests, 3, 8, 9, 20, 33; need for infrastructure and public works for, 8, 39, 88, 102, 150. *See also* Booms
New Right, 8, 14, 20
Newspapers and periodicals, 156, 171; lack of reporting by/unreported by, 25–26, 43–44, 45, 50, 56, 73, 99, 174; participation in policy debates

and editorializing by, 6, 7, 28, 29–30, 32–34, 43–44, 45, 49, 59, 62, 64, 65, 75–76, 81, 94, 102, 124, 126, 130, 139–40, 141, 148, 162, 164, 172, 173–74, 178, 183, 194 (n. 79), 206 (n. 129), 214 (n. 86), 216 (n. 111), 218–19 (n. 139), 223 (n. 38), 225 (n. 65); reporting by, 25–26, 36, 37, 48, 50, 52, 55–56, 58, 69–70, 72, 73, 74, 75–76, 80, 81, 82, 97, 99–100, 105, 109, 128, 134, 135, 138, 173–74, 176, 178, 192 (n. 60), 203 (n. 82). See also *Los Angeles Times*; *New York Times*

New York Times, 141–42, 148. See also Newspapers and periodicals

Niagara Falls, 128–30, 134, 225 (n. 62)

Nicolaides, Becky, 5

Nixon, Richard M., 107, 110, 111, 216 (n. 111)

Norris, George, 129, 132, 138

North Dakota, 153, 154

Norwalk, Calif., 99–100

Nye, Gerald P., 29

Oakland, Calif., 32, 230 (n. 17)

Oil, 2, 7–10, 12, 17–30, 37, 49, 55, 83, 103–4, 110, 146, 151, 180–81, 183–84; Tidelands oil controversy, 28–29, 190 (n. 35). See also Air pollution; Booms

Oil companies, 67, 69–70, 81, 103, 105, 111, 113, 183–84; drafting legislation, 24–26, 28; Independents, 25, 28–29, 70, 184; Majors, 24–26, 29–30, 184, 189 (n. 20), 190 (n. 35)

Oil conservation, 21, 25

Oil drilling: dangers and nuisances from, 8, 9–10, 21, 22–25, 28; economics of, 21–25; effects on beach recreation, 9–10, 17, 24–30, 40–41, 54, 180–81, 184; leases, 9, 22, 24–25; and natural gas pressure, 21, 22, 25; offshore and pier, 9–10, 17, 24–30, 181;

in residential neighborhoods, 9–10, 12, 21–24, 27 (ill.), 28, 189 (n. 13); slant and whipstocking, 26–28

—regulation of: federal, 10, 29; local, 9, 17–19, 20, 21, 26, 28, 180, 184, 190 (n. 30); state, 24–28, 30, 184

Oil fields, 20–22, 24–26, 28–29, 103, 110–11, 146, 184, 189 (n. 13)

Olds, Leland, 156–57, 171. See also Red-baiting

Olmsted Brothers and Bartholomew and Associates, 35

Omnibus Flood Control and Navigation Authorization Act of 1950, 155

O'Neill, Thomas P., Jr. (Tip), 15

Opposition groups. See Interest groups

Orange County, Calif., 21, 31, 32, 45, 48, 221 (n. 11)

Owens Valley, Calif., 122, 220 (n. 8), 230 (n. 17)

Pacific Beach Club, 48

Pacific Coast Club, 33–34, 42, 191 (n. 44)

Pacific Northwest Development Association, 163, 164

Palos Verdes, Calif., 26, 28, 41, 44, 45, 107, 200 (n. 52), 216 (n. 106)

Parks, 5, 28, 32, 34, 35, 36, 37–38, 43, 44, 48, 83, 111, 161, 192 (n. 59), 195 (n. 104)

Pasadena, Calif., 56, 67, 79, 80, 81, 110, 140, 200 (n. 52), 205 (n. 116), 221 (n. 11)

Pendleton, Morris B., 60–61, 63–65. See also Los Angeles Chamber of Commerce: Smoke and Fumes Committee

Percolation. See Groundwater; Water conservation

Phipps, Lawrence C., 139, 141

Pick, Lewis, 153. See also Pick-Sloan Plan

Pickford, Mary, 42, 194 (n. 79)

INDEX **261**

Pick-Sloan Plan, 152–55, 158, 160
Pico, Calif., 109
Pinchot, Gifford, 129
Pittman, Key, 141–42
Pittsburgh, Penn., 54
Playa del Rey, Calif., 21, 26, 28
Political legitimacy, 1–4, 12–14, 51, 52, 64–65, 78–82, 85–86, 95–96, 104, 111, 113–16, 119–20, 160–65, 180–83. *See also* Public opinion—voice or representative of
Political rhetoric: anti-government, 8, 14–15, 49, 87, 115–16, 120, 124–25, 131–33, 136, 171–74; anti-industry, 2, 24, 28–29, 49, 54, 86, 94–95, 101, 103, 105, 111, 113, 115, 127, 128–30, 160, 184; big vs. small, 2, 13, 25, 28, 30, 70, 85, 95, 101, 103, 105, 108–9, 111–12, 114–15, 130, 171, 180, 183–84; and power balance between government and business, 11–13, 15, 115–16, 120, 130, 133, 136, 142, 147, 162–63, 171–74, 175, 178–84 (*see also* Federal power). *See also* Democracy; Red-baiting
Pony Express, 213 (n. 76)
Populists, 127
Port of Los Angeles, 6, 8, 31 (ill.), 83, 86, 88, 104–5, 175, 207 (n. 1), 209 (n. 19), 215 (n. 93)
Power (electric), 8, 55, 116, 117, 120–22, 130–33, 154, 156; contracts, and Boulder Dam, 122, 141, 144–45, 147, 228 (n. 121); development, 11, 12, 117–47, 152, 155, 158, 162, 163, 165, 171–73, 182, 183; federal jurisdiction over, 127–28, 136–43; rates, 11, 156, 165–67, 171–72; subsidy, 11–12, 128, 158, 165–67, 170, 173, 176; supplies, 8, 121–22, 117–19, 124–25, 155, 163; users, 165–66. *See also* Boulder Dam: and hydroelectric power; Irrigation subsidy
Power Trust, 126 (ill.), 132, 138, 145, 226 (n. 87)

Preservation, 160–62, 169
President's Committee on Water Flow, 158
President's Water Resources Policy Commission (PWRPC), 12, 148–77, 178, 179; founding and mission of, 151–52, 155–57, 177; goals of, 162, 165–67, 170–71, 173; influences on, 12, 155–57; and irrigation, 151, 152–55, 158, 165–67, 168, 170, 173, 174, 175; reactions to, 162–65, 169–77, 178, 179; survey by, 157–59, 166. *See also* River basin planning; *Water Policy for the American People, A*
Private enterprise: as defense of democracy, 4, 8, 12, 13, 15, 20, 129–30, 146–47, 148–51, 174–77, 182–83; vs. government enterprise, 32, 129–30, 131–33, 136, 138, 142, 144–46, 148, 174–77. *See also* Democracy
Private utilities, 8, 11–12, 113, 116, 148, 150, 156, 165, 182, 223 (n. 36); and Boulder Dam, 11–12, 123–24, 126–28, 130–34, 138–39, 144–47, 182–84, 222 (n. 24); and Muscle Shoals, 128–30, 182, 223 (n. 36); and public power movement, 11–12, 120, 126–33, 224 (n. 52); and river basin planning, 158, 165, 171–75. *See also* Public relations and propaganda campaigns by business groups; Southern California Edison; Southern Sierras Power Company
Progressives and Progressive Era, 4–5, 7, 14–15, 20, 30, 120, 127, 155, 174, 182, 183, 186 (n. 6), 223 (n. 38), 230 (n. 17), 236–37 (n. 5)
Property, condemning of, 47–48, 101, 195 (n. 104), 216 (n. 107), 217 (n. 119), 220–21 (n. 8)
Property owners, 4–5, 9, 13, 19, 22, 27 (ill.), 34, 42–43, 45, 47, 49, 58–64, 79, 86, 94, 104, 171, 189 (n. 13), 191

(n. 44), 195 (nn. 98, 104), 218–19 (n. 139); displaced by public works projects, 11, 94, 108–11, 112 (ill.), 114–15, 215 (n. 89)
Property Owners League of California, 209–10 (n. 29), 214 (n. 79)
Property rights and beaches, 25, 45
Property values: and beaches, 35, 37–38, 40, 42, 45, 48, 181; and oil, 10, 21, 189 (n. 13); and Whittier Narrows Dam, 88, 94–95, 101, 105, 108–9, 111–14, 115, 216 (n. 107)
Public health, 10, 19, 39–40, 52, 54, 56, 58, 59, 65, 69, 71–77, 79–80, 169, 196 (nn. 1, 3), 197 (n. 11), 204 (n. 94)
Public hearings, 13–14, 45, 67, 71–78, 106–10, 113, 157–58, 172, 174, 176, 202 (n. 77), 203 (nn. 84, 85), 208 (n. 5), 232 (n. 41); Army Corps of Engineers avoidance of, 87, 98–99, 102, 105–6, 113
Public interest, 1–15, 25, 28, 30, 34, 47, 49, 51–52, 70, 103, 119, 146–47, 160–65, 176–77, 180–81
Public opinion, 1, 56, 71, 75, 154, 178, 237 (n. 7)
—voice or representative of, 1, 4, 6, 10, 11, 12–14, 47, 51, 65, 70, 77, 81, 116, 162, 178, 180–82; business groups as, 2, 4, 6, 10, 12–14, 30, 34, 49–51, 52, 54–55, 65, 78, 81, 85–86, 119, 162, 174, 180–82; interest groups as, 2, 4, 13–14, 54, 85–86, 94–95, 116, 162, 182
Public ownership, 10, 19, 30, 32, 34, 40, 42–43, 46, 48–49, 50, 121–22, 126–30, 132, 134, 136–43, 146–47, 150, 174, 195 (n. 99), 223 (n. 38). *See also* Beaches; Public utilities
Public power movement, 11–12, 119–20, 126–33, 142–46, 147, 156, 172, 182, 223 (n. 38); public opinions regarding, 134, 146–47, 237 (n. 7)

Public-private cooperation, 5, 11–12, 14, 34–35, 49, 82, 120, 147, 150, 182–83, 192 (n. 58)
Public protest, 10, 33, 54, 58, 65, 67, 68, 79 (ill.), 80, 94, 101, 102–3, 108, 111, 191 (n. 44)
Public relations and/or propaganda campaigns: by business groups, 57, 116, 120, 132, 138–39, 145, 146, 182, 183, 224 (n. 52); by government agencies, 76–77
Public rights, 17–20, 25, 30, 130–37, 146–47, 181–82, 186 (n. 3)
Public services, 2, 4, 5, 13, 20, 32–34, 45, 46, 114, 126–27, 132, 147
Public utilities, 8, 11–12, 116, 120–21, 126–30, 137, 143, 156, 171–74, 220 (nn. 7, 8)
Public works, priorities for, 160–65, 180–83. *See also* Property owners: displaced by public works projects
Public Works Administration (PWA), 90–92, 179; California State Advisory Board of, 90–91
Pure Air Committee, 80, 206 (n. 127)
PWA. *See* Public Works Administration
PWRPC. *See* President's Water Resources Policy Commission

Race, 5–6, 13, 46–48. *See also* African Americans; Native Americans; Segregation
Reagan, James W., 87–88, 96–98, 100, 113, 208 (n. 7), 212 (n. 57)
Reah, Glanton, 41, 190 (n. 29)
Realty boards, 1, 10, 17, 31, 41, 50, 140, 181
Reclamation Act of 1902, 127, 167
Reclamation Project Act of 1939, 168
Reclamation Service. *See* U.S. Bureau of Reclamation
Recreation, 2, 10, 17, 19–20, 21, 24–37, 39–40, 44, 46–48, 83, 160–64, 169, 179, 180, 181. *See also* Parks

Red-baiting, 45, 49, 107, 129, 137, 142, 156, 161, 162, 171, 172–74, 176, 178, 183
Redondo Beach, Calif., 28, 38, 41, 195 (n. 100), 200 (n. 52)
Regulation of business and industry, 5, 52, 57–58, 182–84; business cooperation with, 7, 10, 24–26, 28, 29, 55, 69, 78–82; voluntary, 7, 52, 59, 60–61, 180. *See also* Air pollution regulation
Reid, F. A., 136
Renne, Roland, 156–57, 163, 166–67, 170
Reports and studies: on air pollution, 10, 52, 56, 58, 59, 60–63, 69, 74, 75, 78, 80, 82, 180, 200 (n. 53), 206 (n. 127); on beach acquisition, 38, 41, 44, 50; on Colorado River, 137, 141, 142, 226 (n. 88); by federal government, 24, 92, 93, 97, 105–6, 132, 137, 141, 142, 146, 158, 226 (n. 88); on flood control, 89–90, 92, 93, 96–99, 105–6, 208 (n. 7); by local government, 56, 58, 59, 60–63, 75, 89–90, 99, 200 (n. 53), 208 (n. 7); from Los Angeles Chamber of Commerce, 2, 10, 52, 61, 78, 82, 180; from other interest groups, 69, 80, 96–98, 206 (n. 127); from Shoreline Planning Association, 38, 41, 44, 50; by state government, 74; on water resources, 151, 155, 157–59, 163, 169, 172–73, 175, 176. See also *Water Policy for the American People, A*
Reservoirs, 83, 88, 94, 97, 103, 104, 108, 109, 121, 154, 170, 215 (n. 93), 203 (n. 17)
Retaining basin. *See* Flood control structures
Richardson, Friend, 134–35
Ringelmann Smoke Chart, 199 (n. 47)
Rio Hondo, 83, 101, 103, 105, 211–12 (n. 53), 215 (n. 87)
Rivera, Calif., 109
River basin planning, 154, 158–60, 162–63, 165, 174–75, 230 (n. 7).

See also President's Water Resources Policy Commission
River basins, 90, 91, 96, 106, 158–60, 170, 210 (n. 37), 231 (n. 31)
River channelization. *See* Flood control structures
Rivers and Harbors Improvement Act of 1934, 91–92, 179
Riverside, Calif., 122, 140, 221 (n. 11)
Rockwood, Charles R., 120–21, 123
Roosevelt, Franklin D., 93, 153, 154
Roosevelt, Theodore, 127
Rubber Reserve Corporation, 56–57
Runoff, 8, 88, 99, 208 (n. 7), 226 (n. 85). *See also* Floods: effects of urban development on
Rural and semi-rural interests, 1, 95, 98, 103, 109; vs. industrial interests, 94–96, 101, 105; vs. urban interests, 1, 5, 101–2, 104, 108, 111, 115, 117, 155, 156–57, 160–62, 165. *See also* Irrigation subsidy

Safley, F. J., 96–98, 100–101, 107, 113, 211–12 (n. 53), 212 (n. 57)
Saint Francis Dam, 88, 146, 183, 220 (n. 7)
St. Louis, Mo., 54–55
Salton Sink, 121
Salt River Project, 103, 233–34 (n. 68)
San Diego, Calif., 32, 140, 163, 215 (n. 93), 221 (n. 11)
San Francisco, Calif., 7, 73, 186 (n. 5), 187 (n. 13), 203 (n. 84), 215 (n. 93), 230 (n. 17)
San Gabriel, Calif., 200 (n. 52), 221 (n. 11)
San Gabriel Mountains, 83, 88, 209 (n. 24)
San Gabriel River, 11, 13, 83, 85, 87–88, 90–91, 92, 93–96, 102–11, 113, 116, 208 (n. 5), 211–12 (n. 53), 213 (n. 62)
San Gabriel River Conservancy, 110–11

San Gabriel Valley, 11, 57–58, 59, 60, 83, 102, 105, 106
San Gabriel Valley Protective Association, 101–2, 209 (n. 17)
San Joaquin Valley, 21, 215 (n. 93)
San Pedro, Calif., 8, 193 (n. 67), 203 (n. 92). *See also* Port of Los Angeles
Santa Barbara County, Calif., 21, 42
Santa Fe Flood Control Basin, 94, 104, 110, 213 (n. 62)
Santa Fe Springs, Calif., 22
Santa Monica, Calif., 28, 30, 31, 40, 41, 42, 47, 173, 221 (n. 11)
Santa Monica Bay, 19, 26, 34, 37, 39–40, 179
Santa Monica Bay Protective League, 47
Santa Monica Mountains, 103
Save the Beach League, 41
Segregation, 6, 10, 19–20, 46–49, 195 (nn. 101, 104)
Sepulveda Flood Control Basin, 93, 210 (n. 37)
Sewage, 19, 26, 37, 39–40, 42, 47, 50, 94, 101, 115, 179, 193 (nn. 67, 68). *See also* Hyperion Point
Shaw, Frank, 213–14 (n. 77)
Shoreline Planning Association (SPA), 10, 19, 29–30, 37–42, 44, 49, 54, 55, 180–81; drafting plans and legislation, 38, 41, 43, 50, 55, 180–81; economic interests of, 20, 33, 36, 37, 41, 50; lack of opposition to, 29–30, 50–51; membership of, 41; as voice of the public, 20, 29–30, 40–41, 43, 49–51, 180–81
Sides, Josh, 6
Signal Hill, Calif., 22, 200 (n. 52), 220–21 (n. 8)
Smith, William, 108, 214 (n. 80)
Smog. *See* Air pollution
Smoot, Reed, 134
Socialism. *See* Red-baiting

South Coast Club, 49
South Dakota, 153–54
Southern California Automobile Club. *See* Automobile Club of Southern California
Southern California Edison, 121–22, 145; and Boulder Dam, 12, 119, 120, 145, 147, 150; and Colorado River hydroelectric permits, 123, 125, 130–32, 144–46
Southern California Gas Company, 50–57, 62
Southern Sierras Power Company, 122, 131, 132, 139, 220 (n. 8)
South Pasadena, Calif., 66, 200 (n. 52), 213–14 (n. 77)
SPA. *See* Shoreline Planning Association
Special interests, 1–15, 24, 25, 28, 30, 74, 75–76, 103–4, 110–12, 115, 160–61, 163, 177; as threat to democracy, 1, 103, 160–61. *See also* Business groups; Interest groups
Spreading grounds. *See* Flood control structures
Standard Oil Company, 21, 28, 58, 76, 198 (n. 18), 200 (nn. 52, 53)
Stanford University, 69, 151
States rights, 29, 136, 137, 143, 147, 163. *See also* Local control and autonomy
Stewart, A. I., 67, 73
Submerged Land Leasing Act of 1921, 25–26
Surf and Sand Club, 33–34, 42, 191 (n. 49)
Swartout, H. O., 65–66, 196 (n. 1), 200 (n. 53)
Swing, Philip, 121–22, 126–27, 129, 132, 133, 135, 138, 142, 144, 145, 182, 224 (n. 56), 226 (n. 88). *See also* Boulder Canyon Dam Act
Swing-Johnson bill. *See* Boulder Canyon Dam Act

Teapot Dome, 24, 129–30, 146
Technical expertise, 63, 86, 91, 96–98, 100, 117–19, 155, 166, 169. *See also* Engineering; Engineers
Temple City, Calif., 200 (n. 52)
Temple School District, El Monte, 94, 110, 111, 212 (n. 57)
Tennessee River, 127
Tennessee Valley Authority (TVA), 130, 147, 154, 158, 160
Texas, 29
Thurber, F. M., 103
Torrance, Calif., 31, 67, 200 (n. 52)
Tourism, 7, 10, 17, 19, 20, 24, 28, 32–37, 40, 41, 45–46, 50, 56, 60, 192 (nn. 59, 60)
Trask, F. E., 91
Truman, Bess, 111
Truman, Harry, 12, 103, 109, 111, 151–52, 155, 157, 159, 174–75, 177, 186 (n. 6)
TVA. *See* Tennessee Valley Authority
Two Forks Dam, 88, 90, 91, 92, 96

Union Oil Company, 67, 70, 76
Union Pacific Railroad, 67, 79, 103
Unions, 6, 7, 9, 56, 107, 160–61, 164–65, 179, 186 (n. 6), 198 (n. 27), 232 (n. 41); disagreements between, 161. *See also* American Federation of Labor; Congress of Industrial Organizations
U.S. Army, Chemical Warfare Division, 200 (n. 53)
U.S. Army Corps of Engineers, 6–7, 8, 11, 38, 93–98, 127, 150–55, 158–59, 160–62, 164, 167–69, 178, 179, 208 (n. 5); criticism of, 85, 96–97, 152, 154–55, 160–62, 169; and "interested parties" and local interests, 85–87, 99–102, 104–6, 116; and Los Angeles County Flood Control District, 11, 85, 87–88, 93–94, 100, 102; political engineering by, 11, 85–87, 93–104, 106–7, 109, 111, 113–14, 115–16, 179. *See also* Federal agencies
U.S. Bureau of Reclamation, 7, 11–13, 103, 117, 120, 127–28, 130, 136, 144–45, 147, 152–55, 158–59, 165–67, 178, 210 (n. 31); criticism of, 153–55, 160–62, 169
U.S. Chamber of Commerce, Natural Resources Committee, 229 (n. 131), 229 (n. 132), 232–33 (n. 50)
U.S. Coast Guard, 42
U.S. Congress, 1, 11–12, 29, 86, 88, 91–95, 97, 98–102, 104–6, 110–11, 116, 120–25, 127–30, 132, 133–46, 148, 150–53, 155, 160, 162, 165, 166–69, 170, 175, 178–79, 182–83
—House of Representatives, 98, 101, 107, 124, 137, 138, 140, 142; House Irrigation Committee, 135–37, 140, 221 (n. 11); House Rules Committee, 138
—Senate, 24, 29, 110, 121, 124, 129, 132, 133, 138, 140–44, 148, 156; Senate Irrigation Committee, 139, 140–41
U.S. Court of Appeals, 122, 220–21 (n. 8)
U.S. Department of Agriculture, 160–61
U.S. Department of the Interior, 10, 127, 132, 137, 142, 144, 145, 159, 219 (n. 1)
U.S. Forest Service, 91, 127, 186 (n. 7), 209 (n. 19)
U.S. Health Service, 58
U.S. Navy, 7, 110; facilities of, 110
U.S. Supreme Court, 86
Upper Colorado River Commission, 161–62
Utah, 120, 123, 125, 133, 134, 135, 137, 138, 140–41, 143, 166

Venice Beach, Calif., 21, 26, 28, 31, 33, 34, 37, 38, 40, 41, 42, 43
Ventura County, Calif., 21, 24, 45, 220 (n. 7). *See also* Saint Francis Dam

Vernon, Calif., 67, 198 (n. 18), 200 (n. 52)
Veterans, 44, 109, 198–99 (n. 27)
Voice of the public. *See* Public opinion—voice or representative of
Voorhis, Jerry, 94, 98–99, 101–7, 108, 179, 216 (n. 111)

Warde, Earnest C., 221 (n. 13)
War production, 5, 7, 8, 9, 128–29, 174, 175, 187 (n. 12), 214 (n. 79); and air pollution, 56–57, 61, 62, 183; and oil, 28; preventing regulation of industry, 38–40, 56–57, 61, 65, 66, 183, 200 (n. 53)
Warren, Earl, 67
Water conservation, 11, 88–89, 90, 99, 100, 127, 151, 152, 163, 175, 210 (n. 31), 211 (n. 47), 216 (n. 106)
Water policy, 12, 127, 148–77
Water Policy for the American People, A, 12, 148, 159, 165, 171–76, 178
Water Power Act of 1920, 11, 126, 129, 147, 182, 224 (n. 52). *See also* Boulder Dam; Muscle Shoals, Ala.
Water rights, 21, 88–89, 109, 121–25, 135–37, 140–41, 143, 163, 174, 228 (n. 120), 230 (n. 17); new, 90, 209 (n. 17)
Water supply, 6, 8, 83, 88, 127, 186 (n. 2), 230 (n. 17); and Whittier Narrows Dam, 83–84, 92. *See also* Colorado River
Weaver, Sylvester, 47
Western Oil and Gas Association, 69, 206 (n. 129)
Westport Beach Club, 33
White, Gilbert F., 156–57
Whittier, Calif., 83, 85, 94, 109, 110, 112, 113, 217 (n. 125), 218 (n. 131)
Whittier Narrows, 83, 85, 88, 90, 209 (n. 17)
Whittier Narrows Dam, 11, 54, 83–116, 117, 119, 179, 184; Congressional appropriations for, 101–2, 104–6, 110–11; downstream communities, 11, 83, 85, 90, 93, 96, 99–102, 105–8, 109, 111, 113–14, 116, 184 (*see also* Long Beach, Calif.; Whittier, Calif.); flood control design debates, 96–98, 102–9, 211 (n. 53); and Long Beach water supply, 83, 92; opponents, 94–98, 98–99, 100, 101–7, 108, 109, 110–11, 115, 209 (n. 17); public hearing on, 102, 105–9; supporters, 84–86, 94, 99–100, 104, 106–7, 108; upstream communities, 11, 85, 100, 213 (n. 62) (*see also* Azusa, Calif.; Duarte, Calif.; El Monte, Calif.; Garvey Acres, Calif.). *See also* U.S. Army Corps of Engineers
Whittington, William M., 137, 215 (nn. 89, 91)
Wilbur, Ray Lyman, 144–45, 219 (n. 1)
Wild, H. Mark, 5
Wilson, Woodrow, 127, 129
Wilson Dam. *See* Muscle Shoals, Ala.
Women and women's clubs and organizations, 44, 76, 79 (ill.), 196–97 (n. 3), 198–99 (n. 27), 202 (n. 77), 205 (n. 116)
Work, Hubert, 132–33, 142
Workers, 9, 62–63, 83, 91, 156, 171, 196 (n. 2), 197 (n. 5), 218–19 (n. 139). *See also* Labor
World War I, 128–29. *See also* War production
World War II, 9, 37, 39–40, 42, 44, 58, 60, 82, 102, 116, 150, 175, 183, 214 (n. 79), 236–37 (n. 5); population growth, 3, 9, 55, 60, 160. *See also* Booms; War production
Wyoming, 123, 125, 134. *See also* Colorado River: Upper Basin

Young, C. C., 25

www.ingramcontent.com/pod-product-compliance
Lightning Source LLC
Chambersburg PA
CBHW030109010526
44116CB00005B/159